Going Public in Good Times and Bad

A Legal and Business Guide

Robert G. Heim, Esq.

Cover Design: *Michael Ng*

Interior Page Design & Production: *Amparo Graf*

Library of Congress Cataloging-in-Publication Data

Heim, Robert G., 1968-
   Going Public in Good Times and Bad : a legal and business guide / by
   Robert G. Heim.
      p. cm.
   ISBN 0-9705970-6-1

   1. Going public (Securities)—Law and Legislation—United States—
Popular works. 2. Incorporation—United States—Popular works. 3. Internet
service providers—Legal status, laws, etc.—United States—Popular works.
4. Going public (Securities)—United States—Popular works. 5. Internet
service providers—United States—Popular works. I. Title.

KF1440 .H45 2001
346.73'06622—dc21   2001053565

ACKNOWLEDGMENTS

I'd like to thank my law partner Howard S. Meyers for his suggestions and thoughtful comments on the book. I'd also like to thank my family for their support, particularly my parents Robert George Heim and Eileen Heim, as well as my sister Roseann DiBona. Finally, I'd like to thank Maria Lamothe for her help with the book.

Contents

CHAPTER 1

Introduction 1

CHAPTER 2

Is an IPO Right for Your Company? 11

The Most Important Reason to Conduct an IPO 14

*The Capital Raised in an IPO Can Make the
Company a Better Competitor in the
Marketplace* 15

*An IPO Creates a Market for the Company's
Securities* 18

*An IPO Can Make It Easier for the Company
to Arrange Future Rounds of Funding* 20

*Public Companies Can Raise Capital
at a Lower Cost* 23

*Public Companies Gain Increased Prestige and
Name Recognition* 24

*A Publicly Traded Company Can Use Its Own Stock
to Acquire Other Companies* 24

CHAPTER 2   (Continued)

Publicly Traded Companies Can More Easily
Share the Wealth with Employees   26

Publicly Traded Stock Presents Fewer Estate
Tax Problems   27

Disadvantages of Going Public   28

An IPO Is Expensive   28

Disruption Caused by the Due Diligence
Investigation   30

A Public Company Must Make Detailed Public
Disclosures   31

Publicly Traded Companies Have Enormous Pressure
to Maintain Stock Price Appreciation   32

Loss of Control of the Company   33

Shareholder Lawsuits   34

CHAPTER 3

Pre-IPO Financing **35**

Securities Law Concerns   40

Regulation D   42

State Securities Laws   45

Practice Pointers for Securities Attorneys   47

Preparing a Business Plan Is Critical to Securing
Financing   50

Drafting the Business Plan   52

The Elements of a Business Plan   54

The Private Placement Memorandum   60

Successfully Approaching Potential Investors   66

The Stages of a New Company's Growth and
Development   67

*Finding and Persuading Angel Investors and Venture
  Capital Funds to Invest in Your Company*   68

Negotiating and Structuring the Investment   70

Private Placements by Broker-Dealers   75

Pre-IPO Financing in Bad Economic Times   75

Appendix 3A   79

Appendix 3B   90

Appendix 3C   98

Appendix 3D   101

Appendix 3E   108

Appendix 3F   112

Appendix 3G   117

Appendix 3H   134

Appendix 3I   142

Appendix 3J   153

Chapter 4

Selecting and Operating the Board of Directors . . . 155

The Duty of Care   160

*The Importance of Proper Decision Making
  Procedures*   163

Limiting the Exposure of Directors   166

The Duty of Loyalty   167

The Business Judgment Rule   172

Appendix 4   178

CHAPTER **5**

Selecting an Underwriter and Understanding
the Underwriting Process **181**

Selecting an Appropriate Underwriter 184

Responsibilities of the Underwriter 192

Costs 194

The Letter of Intent 195

Appendix 5A 196

Appendix 5B 206

Appendix 5C 208

CHAPTER **6**

Due Diligence and the Preparation of the
Registration Statement **211**

The Securities Act 214

The Prefiling Period 216

Gun Jumping 218

The Registration Statement 221

The SEC Review Process 226

The Waiting Period 228

Post-Effective Period 231

CHAPTER **7**

Marketing and Communications for Companies
that Want to Go Public **233**

Marketing and Communications for a Start-Up
Company 236

The Keys to Effective Marketing for a Start-Up
Company 241

*Special Marketing Concerns Relating to Venture
  Capital Investors* 245

*What to Do if Your Company Has Been Unsuccessful
  At Raising Money* 247

*Marketing Considerations for a Company Preparing
  for an IPO* 251

*Marketing Considerations for a Publicly Traded
  Company* 252

*Working with Professional Financial Public
  Relations Firms* 252

*The Use of the Internet for Marketing and
  Communications* 258

Conclusion 259

Appendix 7 260

CHAPTER 8

Being Public—Post IPO Responsibilities 267

*Reporting and Disclosure Obligations
  of the Company* 271

*Rules Related to Corporate Governance Promulgated
  by the Stock Exchanges and Nasdaq* 288

*Choosing Where to Trade and the Applicable
  Standards* 296

Auditor Independence Standards 303

*Special Issues Public Companies Face in Bad
  Economic Times* 306

Appendix 8A 309

Appendix 8B 324

Appendix 8C 335

Appendix 8D 345

Appendix 8E 355

CHAPTER 8 (Continued)

Appendix 8F 366

Appendix 8G 378

Appendix 8H 382

CHAPTER 9

Alternative Methods of Going Public—Direct Public Offerings and Reverse Mergers 393

Direct Public Offerings Over the Internet 395

The Reverse Merger 399

CHAPTER 1

INTRODUCTION

Almost every entrepreneur dreams of taking his company public one day. The rewards of going public are well known—increased prestige for the company, a liquid market for the company's stock and, hopefully, a handsome profit for those who founded the company. Many entrepreneurs, however, never realize this goal and it is not because of a lack of dedication or a lack of hard work. Rather, the primary reason is that many entrepreneurs lack the knowledge of what is required to prepare for and conduct an Initial Public Offering ("IPO") of stock. Executives and their attorneys must have a detailed knowledge of law, accounting and finance to successfully take a company public.

Market conditions can also have a dramatic impact on an entrepreneur's chances of successfully completing an IPO. Investors' interest in purchasing stock in new offerings can vary widely from year to year and from industry to industry. For example, in the late 1990s almost any company that had ".com" after its name could successfully complete an IPO. However, in the latter part of 2000 and all of 2001 the IPO market was much more challenging, both for technology-oriented companies as well as for companies in more traditional industries. This book will provide entrepreneurs with strategies for preparing to go public, even in challenging market conditions.

This book also provides entrepreneurs and their attorneys with the practical knowledge required to successfully start a new media company and take it public. The strategies explained throughout the book apply to companies in a broad range of industries, including technology, new media and biotechnology. The book is essentially a road map that shows growing companies how to conduct their business to maximize the chances of a successful IPO. Throughout the book, the author provides practical real world advice based on his extensive experience working with public and private technology and new media companies. Numerous legal forms with commentary have also been included. Each stage of a company's development is covered—from the earliest stages after the corporate formation to post-IPO operations. Throughout the book emphasis is placed on the specific steps that a company can take at each stage of its development to advance towards the goal of an IPO as quickly and as effectively as possible.

Initially, it is important to define what "going public" means. A public company is one with shares that have been sold to members of the general public through a registered offering. There are several important differences between public companies and private companies which have not offered their stock for sale to the public. When a company is first incorporated, it is a private entity and generally its founders are the only shareholders. The investors are usually the founders and their family and friends. Often, those who invest in a private company are very familiar with the business of the company and personally know the founders and managers. Private companies generally have a very small number of shareholders and conduct small businesses. A successful private company can grow into a business with substantial revenue and many employees but it still will have only a small number of shareholders.

In contrast, a public company generally has a large number of shareholders—anywhere from 500 to over 1 million. By law, before any company can publicly offer its stock for sale it must register that offering with the U.S. Securities and Exchange Commission ("SEC"). The registration process is an elaborate one. It involves preparation and filing of a lengthy disclosure document with the SEC providing detailed information to investors about the company's business and management. The process of preparing a registration statement is discussed in detail in Chapter 5.

A company's sale of its shares in a registered public offering for the first time is called an initial public offering, or an IPO. The investors who buy stock in a company's IPO become shareholders of the company and the stock can be freely traded by investors on a securities exchange. Essentially, a public company is a company that has chosen to raise capital from outside investors by selling shares of stock to the investing public. By choosing to go public, a company becomes subject to a wide variety of rules and regulations designed primarily to protect investors and ensure that the company makes ongoing disclosure of important business events. At the federal level, the SEC is the agency that is primarily responsible for regulating publicly traded companies.

In recent years, there has been an explosion in the number of companies going public, many of which are technology and new media companies. In 1999, a total of 492 companies went public, raising an average of $130 million in each offering. The total amount of money raised through IPOs in 1999 was $63 billion. In the year 2000, 422 companies went public and raised an average of $422 million in each offering. The total amount of money raised through IPOs in 2000 was $97 billion.[1] Because many investors in technology and new media IPOs earned large profits there is a great deal of interest from investors in the new media sector. Investors' interest in participating in IPOs has also had the effect of stimulating a strong interest in financing companies prior to their IPOs. Generally speaking, pre-IPO financing is obtained from sophisticated investors and venture capitalists in nonpublic sales of

---

[1] Hoovers Online *www.Hoovers.com* (http://www.hoovers.com/ipo/statistics/0,1334,183,00.html).

stock. Pre-IPO financing is extremely important for new media companies because it allows them to develop their business to the point that an IPO is feasible. Because of the importance of pre-IPO financing to new media companies, all of Chapter 3 is devoted to this subject. That chapter contains a number of hard-to-find forms to which new media executives and their lawyers can refer when structuring their company's pre-IPO financing.

A recurring theme throughout this book is that it is never too early for a company to begin preparing for an IPO. A company that hopes to go public and raise millions of dollars in financing will have to be structured and operated differently than a company that is merely conducting a small business. It is much easier to start the company off with good accounting, legal and financial practices than to have to go back later and fix things when the company is ready to seek financing. Implementing good practices is particularly important for newly formed companies because in the rush to develop and grow the company's business it is easy to overlook important legal and accounting issues.

Early preparation is important because the vast majority of new companies require a significant amount of capital from investors before an IPO is feasible. However, prior to making an investment in a new media company, sophisticated investors will perform an extensive due diligence investigation to ensure that the company is in compliance with all legal regulations and that strong financial controls are in place. Sophisticated investors will also check to make sure that the company has put all important contracts in writing and has complied with all corporate formalities. In addition, they will want to know that all of the company's intellectual property has been properly acquired and is protected with patents and copyrights. Investors are likely to pass on any company where proper legal, accounting and financial practices have not been put into place. Therefore, a company that desires to go public should ensure that it complies with good legal and accounting practices from day one. This will increase the company's chances of obtaining funding when it needs it. Chapter 3 discusses in detail how a company can implement good legal and accounting practices at an early stage.

As a company develops and approaches the time when an IPO is a realistic possibility, the company's executives and its lawyers must become familiar with the process of selecting an underwriter and registering an offering of securities with the SEC. By becoming aware of how the IPO process works, new media executives will be in a better position to budget for an IPO and successfully complete it. The entire process of selecting an underwriter and offering securities to the public is discussed in Chapters 4 through 6. In addition, once a company is public it becomes subject to important ongoing regulation both by the SEC and the exchange on which its stock trades. Chapter 8 describes in detail the post-IPO regulations that apply to public companies.

The advent of new technology, and in particular the Internet, has led to exciting new opportunities for companies to raise capital from investors in public offerings. These new opportunities are particularly effective when market conditions for an IPO are challenging and an underwriter may be hard to locate. Because of the popularity of the Internet, many investors have become comfortable trading for themselves through online accounts. Moreover, the popularity of IPO investments in the 1990s has opened the door to participation in this market to many retail investors who had not previously invested in IPOs. The large number of interested investors allows companies to go directly to the public with an IPO without the necessity of hiring an underwriter or other middleman. Many investors are experienced and confident enough to analyze a new IPO on their own and make an independent decision about whether to invest in the company. Accordingly, companies may still successfully complete an IPO—even in challenging economic times—by directly approaching investors in a registered public offering undertaken by the company itself.

A growing number of companies are using the Internet to reach millions of investors through Direct Public Offerings ("DPO"). The SEC has enacted special rules to allow companies to use the Internet to raise capital directly from investors without using an underwriter or stock brokerage firms. DPOs can be extremely cost-effective because companies can deliver lengthy disclosure information to investors in electronic rather than paper form. In addition, the use of e-mail and Web sites makes it very easy for the company to market the DPO and attract potential investors. A company that successfully conducts a DPO over the Internet also saves the significant amount of money that it would otherwise have to spend on underwriters' fees and stockbrokers' commissions. The Internet DPO, the special rules involved and other alternative methods of going public are discussed in Chapter 9.

The advent of the Internet has also given investors the ability to easily and quickly receive the most up-to-date information released by publicly traded companies. Pre-Internet, only professional investors could afford to have "real time" information electronically delivered to their computer terminals. Now such corporate information is readily available to anyone who has an Internet connection. Because average investors can now receive corporate information as quickly as professional investors, new rules have been implemented by the SEC to ensure that companies do not selectively disclose information to favored analysts or institutional investors. The new rules, which are contained in SEC Regulation FD,[2] are designed to ensure fair disclosure to all investors of important corporate information. They are rather controversial and public companies are still adjusting to them. However, all companies contemplating going public must be aware of the new disclosure rules, which are discussed in detail in Chapter 8.

---

[2] 17 C.F.R. Parts 210, 240.

In addition to the rules relating to fair disclosure, the SEC recently promulgated rules relating to auditor independence. The SEC, in adopting the new auditor independence rules, addressed the concerns that many investors had regarding whether auditors were truly independent of the companies they audited. Questions relating to auditor independence had been growing because auditing firms were providing their clients with significant amounts of non-audit consulting services. In many cases, the fees received by an auditing firm for non-audit work are many times greater than the fees received for an audit. Therefore, the SEC was concerned that auditors may not give a company's financial statements the scrutiny they deserve for fear of jeopardizing the fees for non-audit work. Accordingly, the new auditor independence rules prohibit auditing firms from providing certain non-audit services to public companies and also require disclosure of the fees received for non-audit work. These rules are designed to prevent not only actual conflicts of interest between the auditor and its client, but also the appearance of conflicts of interest. The SEC's auditor independence rules are discussed in Chapter 8.

Effective marketing and communications strategies can make all the difference for a new media company. These strategies are important no matter what stage of development the company may be in. Chapter 7 provides valuable guidance for companies that do their own marketing as well as advice about when professional public relations firms should be used. The chapter also discusses important concerns that a new media company should consider when working with firms that specialize in "finding" investors. A sample contract between a new media company and a finder is included in the appendix to Chapter 7.[3]

---

[3] See Appendix 7 in Chapter 7 *infra*.

Taking a company public is a complex and expensive process that can easily be derailed if the company is not properly prepared. However, entrepreneurs and new media executives can greatly increase the chances of successfully bringing their companies public if they are familiar with how the IPO process works and what specific steps should be taken early on in the company's development to implement good legal and accounting practices. This book contains concrete and practical guidance for new media executives and their lawyers relating to all facets of a company's journey from a private business to a public company.

IS AN IPO RIGHT FOR YOUR COMPANY?

Conducting an IPO is the dream of almost every entrepreneur. In fact, many companies start out with the goal of becoming a publicly traded company as quickly as possible. An IPO is certainly a major milestone for any company that reaches that point in its growth and development. However, prior to embarking on the expensive and time-consuming process of preparing for an IPO, careful consideration must be given to the advantages and disadvantages of going public and operating as a publicly traded company. Consideration must also be given to the possibility that market conditions for an IPO may change significantly from the time a company decides to begin preparing for an IPO to the time it actually conducts the IPO. Investment bankers refer to a "window" of opportunity that opens and closes for new companies to go public. Once a company becomes publicly traded, a whole new set of laws and regulations apply to its operations as well as to the individual officers, directors and shareholders. As a result, significant new responsibilities arise—as well as new pitfalls that the company must avoid. Therefore, it is critical that a realistic appraisal of the advantages and disadvantages of an IPO be made to ensure that the company will make a successful transition from privately held to publicly traded. If this type of appraisal is not made, a great deal of time and money can be wasted preparing for an IPO that may never come to fruition.

As if these considerations were not enough, the company's management and financial advisors must also consider the current financing climate to ensure—to the extent possible—that there will be interested investors who will purchase the company's securities when the time of the public offering arrives. Because the financial markets are so volatile, especially with respect to Internet and technology companies, there is always a great deal of speculation about whether the financing window will be open for a particular company when it is ready to conduct its IPO. Although nobody can control the future financing climate, management and its advisors should be prepared for a variety of scenarios.

THE MOST IMPORTANT REASON TO CONDUCT AN IPO

While there are numerous benefits associated with conducting an IPO, the most important reason for any company to go public is that it needs capital to fund the future growth of its business. Simply stated, the need for growth capital should be the primary driving force behind any IPO. Every company contemplating an IPO must have a specific plan that addresses how it will use the capital received in the IPO to build the business and increase its earnings. The company's growth prospects will certainly be the reason why investors desire to purchase the company's shares. To successfully sell its shares to the investing public, a new company must have an exciting "story" to tell investors about why they should turn over their money to the company. The story must include information about how the proceeds will be used to build the company and generate profits for investors. With this bedrock principal in mind we can more effectively assess the advantages and disadvantages of becoming a publicly traded company.

First, let's examine the advantages of being a publicly traded company.

THE CAPITAL RAISED IN AN IPO CAN MAKE THE COMPANY A BETTER COMPETITOR IN THE MARKETPLACE

A major benefit of conducting an IPO is that the capital raised can be used by the company to gain significant advantages over less well-financed competitors. With the new capital, extensive advertising and marketing can be undertaken to increase awareness about the company and its products and, hopefully, generate significantly more sales. Often, the capital raised in an IPO is also used to hire additional employees so that the company can grow smoothly and handle greater numbers of sales. Internet companies frequently use the capital from an IPO to acquire new and more efficient technology and computer hardware. Many Internet and technology companies simply require large amounts of capital to successfully operate their businesses. This is particularly true of those companies that provide hardware and other materials needed to build the infrastructure of the Internet. Raising capital through an IPO can provide this much-needed capital.

On a more intangible level, conducting an IPO often significantly boosts employee morale and gives a company's business model a sense of validation. A company that has a workforce filled with employees with high morale and enthusiasm will be in a very strong competitive position. Moreover, the capital acquired in an IPO can give a company a sense of stability, at least for the short term, so that management can focus on building the business and not merely surviving day to day. While intangible, the benefits associated with high morale, enthusiasm and a sense of stability should not be underestimated. High employee morale is particularly important with Internet companies because dissatisfied employees can easily leave and find jobs with other Internet and technology companies. The many costs associated with high employee turnover—including lost productivity due to having constantly to train new employees—should be avoided whenever possible.

One of the great competitive advantages that any Internet or technology company can have is known as the "first mover advantage." The theory behind the first mover advantage is that when a new market niche develops in the Internet arena, the company that is first to exploit that market and become a dominant player will have an incredibly strong competitive edge. Many Internet executives believe that gaining a first mover advantage is critical to the success of a company and will make the difference between dominating the market and being a distant second.

First mover advantage is particularly important to companies that operate in a networked business environment. The networked business environment concept involves bringing increasingly large numbers of paying customers into the network that a company is offering. The best way to illustrate the first mover advantage and a networked business environment is with an example. America Online was the first company successfully to offer instant messaging to large numbers of customers who subscribed to its service. An instant message allows America Online's customers to send real time messages to other America Online customers who are online at that time. Consequently, the more people who use America Online's network, the more valuable the instant messaging service becomes to each individual customer. If only a small number of people are using America Online, the instant messaging service's utility is severely limited. However, if millions of people are using America Online and its instant message service the utility increases dramatically.

One of the key concepts of a networked business model is that the network's value is directly tied to the number of customers using the network. Another key concept is that once a particular network has achieved critical mass and has acquired a large number of customers, additional customers who enter the marketplace will be most likely to sign up with the leading network. A competing company offering a similar network with a smaller number of participating customers will have a hard time attracting new customers because of the limited value that a smaller network, by definition, has. Therefore, unless the smaller network is offering significantly more features or significantly more value than the larger network, the larger network will be likely to obtain virtually all of the new customers that come into the marketplace. That's the value of having the first mover advantage—the company that is first to establish itself as the dominant player in a particular market will be the most likely candidate to sustain future growth while its competitors fall farther and farther behind. Once an Internet company becomes known as the dominant player in a particular market niche, even one that does not involve a networked business model, it is very hard for competitors to gain a market share.

The capital that an IPO brings into a new company can be extremely valuable, especially if the company operates in a market that does not yet have a dominant player. The new capital can be used for a variety of marketing purposes—both online and off-line—to help ensure that customers see the company as the dominant player in the marketplace. Very often, the company that obtains the first mover advantage and acquires a significant percentage of market share can expect to grow rapidly because customers will be naturally attracted to the value inherent in that company's products and services.

The importance of having the first mover advantage is what accounts for the often frantic pace of business in the Internet and technology world and the strong emphasis on market share acquisition. The difference between first place and second place is often the difference between fortune and bankruptcy for many Internet and technology companies. A successful IPO can give a company the capital it needs to achieve first place.

The new capital raised in an IPO can also allow a company to put into place the infrastructure it will need to provide its services to

17

large numbers of customers. A hallmark of the new economy is that companies must often spend large sums of money to establish their technological infrastructure before a single customer can sign up and use the services offered. However, once the infrastructure is operational, the cost of adding each new customer is very small. An IPO can be the ideal method for financing this type of business model.

An IPO Creates a Market for the Company's Securities

One important reason that companies go public is that the IPO provides a mechanism for the founders of the company and its early stage shareholders to profitably sell some or all of their shares to other investors, namely the investing public. These sales can occur either in the IPO itself or in the aftermarket that develops after the IPO. While founders and other early stage shareholders can make money in a number of other ways, such as arranging for a buyout of the company by another firm, conducting an IPO has been a very popular and profitable option.

It is important to understand the mechanics of an IPO to appreciate fully how founders and early stage investors can benefit from taking their company public. In a typical IPO, a company is selling newly issued shares indirectly to the investing public. For example, the company and its financial advisors may decide that the market will permit it to sell 2 million shares at $10 per share in its IPO. It is the company that sells the stock and it is the company that receives the proceeds from the sale of the stock, minus the underwriter's fee and other professional fees. While it is a great event for the company, in this example, to acquire almost $20 million for its capital needs, the question arises: how do the founders and early stage investors benefit from the IPO?

The first way that the founders and early stage investors benefit is that a company's underwriters often permit some of them to include a portion of their own shares in the IPO. However, the number of shares that the founders and other early stage investors are permitted to sell in the IPO will be strictly limited by the underwriter. The underwriter limits the number of such shares in order to prevent the appearance that the insiders are bailing out and unloading their shares on the investing public. Presumably, if the company has great prospects, the founders and early shareholders—who frequently have the most information about the company's growth potential—would want to keep their shares and watch them continue to increase in value. Nevertheless, underwriters will often permit founders and early stage investors to include a small percentage of their shares in the IPO. When that happens, the money that is raised from the sale of those shares will go to the individual owners of the shares and not to the company. If the founders or early stage investors are selling some of their shares at the time of the IPO, that fact is always spelled out clearly in the company's prospectus.

The second way that founders and other early stage investors benefit from an IPO is through the development of a liquid aftermarket in a company's stock. During the process of preparing for the IPO, a company's underwriter will usually arrange for the company's stock to trade on one of the exchanges or on the Nasdaq. If investors are bullish on the company, the price of the stock can increase significantly from the IPO price. Stock that was originally offered at $10 per share can quickly climb to $40 or $50 per share or more. In the aftermarket, investors purchase and sell a company's stock among themselves and the company does not receive the sales proceeds from any of these aftermarket sales.

The development of an active and liquid market in a company's securities can be very beneficial to the founders and early stage investors because it provides a ready market in which to sell their

19

securities. In contrast, it is notoriously difficult for shareholders of privately held companies to find buyers for their shares. Even the shareholders of valuable and profitable privately held businesses often cannot sell their shares when they decide to do so. By creating a public trading market for their shares, founders of Internet companies can unlock the value of their stock. When that happens, the founders and other early investors may decide to sell some or all of their stock holdings in the market—often at a significant profit. It is important to keep in mind, however, that there are SEC rules that govern the manner of sale and the number of shares that such individuals can sell at any given time. In addition, underwriters will usually require the founders and early stage shareholders of the company to enter into "lockup agreements" in which the shareholders agree not to sell their shares in the open market for a minimum period of time, typically 180 days, although the trend has been towards significantly shorter lockup periods.

Even with the restrictions on sale contained in SEC rules and the lockup agreement, founders and early stage shareholders often sell their shares in the market over time at substantial profits. The ability to sell large numbers of shares at very profitable prices is a significant benefit of conducting an IPO.

AN IPO CAN MAKE IT EASIER FOR THE COMPANY TO ARRANGE FUTURE ROUNDS OF FUNDING

Becoming a publicly traded company can pave the way for future financing. Every public company has to go through an exhaustive process of due diligence and have its business plan thoroughly vetted. The company's accounting records have to be audited, often by a prestigious public accounting firm. In addition, the company must file detailed reports with the SEC concerning its business, management and outlook. Independent analysts may write about the company's operating results and prospects. Perhaps most importantly, numerous individual and institutional investors will have shown their belief in the future success of the company by purchasing its stock. These facts can provide a great deal of comfort to people or institutions that are considering providing future debt or equity financing to the company. A publicly traded company also has established relationships in the investment banking community. These relationships can lead to financing sources and strategies that would not be available to a privately held company. Also, Internet companies that are perceived to have good future growth potential often are able to return to the capital markets for substantial amounts of new equity financing from public investors, even if the company has not achieved profitability and is operating at a significant loss.

The advantages of having easier access to the capital markets should not be underestimated. Many entrepreneurs can tell war stories about the stresses involved with wondering whether the next round of financing will come in or whether the company will be forced to shut down. Internet and technology companies that have high burn rates of cash are particularly vulnerable in this area. Capital is the lifeblood of any business, and companies often require substantial infusions of capital over time before they can achieve profitability. While being a publicly traded company does not eliminate all of the difficulty with raising new financing, it does make it easier to do so. As a result, managers of publicly traded companies can concentrate on running the business, as opposed to running around looking for capital. It must be remembered, however, that merely because a company is publicly traded will not guarantee access to future financing. A financially troubled public company may have just as much difficulty raising money as it would if it were a private company.

The ability to raise capital quickly can also be very beneficial to a public company in bad economic times. When the economy is poor, venture capital investors for private companies are extremely hard to locate. Likewise, bank loans for new businesses are also difficult to arrange when economic conditions are tough. Even when equity or debt financing can be arranged under such conditions the terms of the financing can be onerous. Equity investors will demand low valuations for the company's stock, which will allow them to purchase more stock with less money. Interest rates on loans can also be prohibitively high. However, a company that is publicly traded will often be able to arrange financing on significantly better terms than a nonpublicly traded company. The market price of the company's stock will provide an excellent benchmark in valuing any shares that may be issued for new funding. In addition, there are many potential funding options open to a publicly traded company when economic times are tough. In addition to banks and venture capitalists, publicly traded companies can turn to registered broker-dealers and other financial institutions more readily than a private company could. Public investors may also see the bad economic times as an opportunity to buy into a company at a far better price than if the shares received their full valuations.

One of the most overlooked advantages to being a publicly traded company is that banks and other lenders will no longer require personal guarantees for loans and other debt financing. There are numerous examples of executives of new enterprises who have mortgaged their homes or relied on personal credit cards to fund their businesses. Unfortunately, there are also numerous instances where these executives have lost their homes and other personal assets when the business did not work out. Personal guarantees are also often required by landlords when office space is rented to privately held companies. The ability to obtain financing without any personal guarantees from those affiliated with the company is certainly an added advantage of going public—especially if the company is growing and desires a significant amount of debt financing.

PUBLIC COMPANIES CAN RAISE CAPITAL AT A LOWER COST

Not only does being a publicly traded company make it easier to raise capital, it also provides the capital, whether it be debt or equity, at a lower cost. The costs are lower because there are simply more available financing sources and options available—all of these sources are competing to provide the company with the needed capital. This competition provides significant benefits to the company. There is an old saying—the fastest way to get a lending proposal from one bank is to get a lending proposal from another bank. When financing sources are competing to provide capital, the cost of that capital goes down. When the financing is debt, this competition translates into lower interest rates for the company and more favorable terms for the loan. When the financing is equity, competition among investors means that the company can sell fewer shares for a higher price per share, thereby preserving as much value as possible for the existing shareholders. In contrast to this, when privately held companies seek equity capital, the share price that potential investors are willing to pay to acquire the shares is subject to a substantial "illiquidity discount" because it may be virtually impossible for the investor to resell the shares of the private company. Moreover, minority shareholders of publicly held companies have much more protection than minority shareholders of private companies. This is due to the many protections that have been put into place by the SEC, the stock exchanges and the Nasdaq relating to board composition, shareholder voting, accounting policies and public disclosure requirements. Therefore, investors are much more willing to take a minority interest in a publicly traded corporation than they are in a privately held corporation.

Acquiring capital at a lower cost can translate directly into either lower prices for a company's products or services or a greater profit margin. In the highly competitive business world, a lower cost of capital can give a company a strong advantage over its competitors, not to mention more profits for the shareholders.

Public Companies Gain Increased Prestige and Name Recognition

When a company goes public and its shares begin to trade on an exchange or on the Nasdaq system, analysts begin to follow the company, the financial press may write stories about the company, and individual investors may take an active interest in the stock, especially if it shows strong growth potential. Internet and technology companies have been of particular interest to individual investors. Web sites such as Silicon Investor, Raging Bull, Motley Fool and the message boards on Yahoo are filled with information and posts about new and established Internet and technology companies. All the publicity can add up to greater name recognition than if the company were privately held. And this can easily transition into greater awareness of a company's products and services and, as a result, more sales.

A Publicly Traded Company Can Use Its Own Stock to Acquire Other Companies

An important, but sometimes overlooked, benefit of being publicly traded is that the company can use its publicly traded shares to acquire other companies. As mentioned above, growth and the acquisition of market share often drive the business strategies of Internet companies. The desire to achieve first mover advantage is primary for many Internet companies. Therefore, Internet companies may not have the time or the expertise that is needed to start a business in a particular market from scratch. Even if a company did have the time and expertise to start a new business in a particular market, the business would be new and untested and, more likely than not, subject to tough competition.

One way that a company can avoid some of these risks and still achieve rapid market share growth is to acquire another company that is already operating successfully in the particular market. Acquiring another company, as opposed to starting and building a new one, can save a company years of research and development time. Acquisitions of other companies have been a central feature of many successful technology companies such as Cisco Systems Inc., the well-known computer networking company. Shareholders of target companies obviously have to be compensated for the shares that they are relinquishing. One way publicly traded companies can do this is by giving its own shares to the shareholders of the target company. Acquiring other companies with stock often means that the acquiring company does not have to put up any cash or arrange financing for the acquisition. In a way, a company's ability to issue shares that can then be used for valuable acquisitions is akin to the ability to print money. In good economic times, the market can place high valuations on shares of public companies that are perceived to have strong growth prospects. Such high value shares can be used to acquire other companies in all-stock transactions.

Of course, the value of the shares used as currency for acquisitions is only as good as the company that is issuing the stock. No shareholders in strong target companies would relinquish their shares for publicly traded shares in a financially troubled company. The ability to rapidly acquire other companies in exchange for stock is unique to publicly traded companies—shareholders of strong target corporations are just not interested in receiving stock in private companies that have no plans or prospects for an IPO.

In contrast to the benefits that a successful acquisition can produce, certain legal and business commentators have pointed out a dark side to the use of stock to acquire other companies. When one company in a particular market begins to acquire other companies in that same market, competition is reduced. Likewise, a company that enters a new market by acquiring another company, as opposed to starting a brand-new business, has avoided increasing the amount of competition in a given market. Reduced competition can lead to increased prices and less innovation—two substantial drawbacks for consumers. Acquisitions in the Internet and technology arena are increasingly drawing the attention of antitrust regulators, both in the United States and Europe. Therefore, publicly traded companies, especially larger ones, must be prepared to demonstrate that any significant acquisition would not have a detrimental impact on competition in a particular market. In addition, the United States' 1998 antitrust case against Microsoft demonstrates that regulators can and will examine a company's competitive conduct in the marketplace if that conduct is perceived to stifle fair competition.[1]

PUBLICLY TRADED COMPANIES CAN MORE EASILY SHARE THE WEALTH WITH EMPLOYEES

Once a company is publicly traded, its stock can easily be used to provide employees with incentive-based compensation. By adopting a stock option plan, or an employee stock ownership plan, employers can provide employees with unique financial incentives. Employee ownership and stock options give everyone a personal stake in the company and thus a strong incentive to make the company as valuable and successful as possible. In addition, accounting and tax rules in the United States allow companies to treat stock options and stock grants quite favorably on their balance

---

[1] United States v. Microsoft Corp., Civil Action No. 98-1232 (D.D.C. May 18, 1998) (appeal pending/ settlement proposed).

sheets, especially when compared with cash compensation. The SEC has also established regulations that make it easy for employees to sell stock that they have acquired from their employers in the marketplace. The ease with which employees may sell shares of publicly traded stock makes stock grants by publicly traded companies much more valuable than stock grants by privately held companies. Of course, compensating employees in stock can also provide a significant financial upside to these individuals should the company's share price increase.

By compensating employees with stock, publicly traded companies, or private companies that are planning an IPO, can attract talented executives and employees that they may not otherwise have been able to retain. Issuing stock to employees avoids pulling much-needed cash out of a company's bank account and, as previously noted, makes employees stakeholders in the success of the company.

PUBLICLY TRADED STOCK PRESENTS FEWER ESTATE TAX PROBLEMS

A final advantage of becoming a publicly traded company is that often it reduces the detrimental effects of the estate tax on the founders of the company. Once a business owner dies, his estate will have to pay an estate tax that will depend in large part on the value of the business. If the business is successful, the estate tax can be quite significant. However, the estate may not have the funds to pay the tax because, while the business may be worth a great deal of money, much of the value is held in the form of private stock. This can present quite a dilemma for the heirs. The business may not be readily salable and there will be difficulty in selling the privately held stock. In addition, issues often arise over how to calculate the correct valuation of a business because no public, liquid market exists for the owner's shares. As a result, complex financial planning will be needed to ensure that adequate funds are on hand at the time of the business owner's death.

For the business owner who took his company public, however, the difficulties with estate taxes are greatly reduced. The value of stock in a publicly traded company can be readily calculated and the proper amount of stock may be sold by the heirs, if necessary, to pay the estate tax.

DISADVANTAGES OF GOING PUBLIC

As the foregoing discussion illustrates, there are many advantages in conducting an IPO and becoming a publicly traded company. But before management embarks on this course of action, the costs and disadvantages of going public must be given serious consideration. The following discussion focuses on these costs and disadvantages.

AN IPO IS EXPENSIVE

While a company can raise a significant amount of capital through an IPO, it must be prepared to foot a fairly large bill for the professional services that are required for the IPO. Attorneys' fees, accounting fees and other expenses can easily add up to $400,000 to $500,000 for a typical IPO. One cost associated with going public that can easily be overlooked is the underwriting fee. Typically in an IPO the underwriter will receive a fee equal to 7% of the offering. Companies contemplating going public sometimes do not focus enough attention on this fee because it is money that the company never receives—the underwriter buys the company's stock at a discount and then resells the stock to investors at full price. Because the underwriting fee is not an out-of-pocket expense, it can be easy for management to overlook this cost. While it is difficult to negotiate a smaller underwriting fee, management should at least realize that the company is paying such a fee and plan accordingly. When times are bad, the out-of-pocket fees for an underwriting must be budgeted well in advance so as to ensure that the process, once under way, can be completed.

Another cost that should not be overlooked is the significant amount of time that management will have to spend working with the attorneys and investment bankers in preparing the registration statement and other materials needed for the IPO. Company executives have to locate and make available large numbers of documents and this can require a substantial time commitment not only from senior management but also from the support staff. In addition, executives will have to sit down with the lawyers and investment bankers for detailed discussions about all of the company's operations. These interviews are extremely important because they help ensure that all of the information placed in the company's registration statement and prospectus is completely accurate. Finally, management will have to read and reread the lengthy registration statement and prospectus to ensure that no material misrepresentations or omissions are contained in them. Each hour that the management and employees of a company spend in providing information to the lawyers and investment bankers is an hour that is lost in running the operations of the company. Preparing for an IPO requires substantial time commitments from numerous employees, and productivity can easily decline if management does not adequately prepare for the process.

In addition to the initial costs of the IPO, there are ongoing costs associated with being a publicly traded company. Quarterly and annual reports must be filed with the SEC and the annual report must also be printed and mailed to the shareholders. In addition, the SEC has promulgated regulations governing other aspects of the publicly traded company's operations, including rules governing proxy solicitation and short swing trading profits. The costs associated with operating as a publicly traded company can run between $20,000 and $100,000 per year for a newly public company, not an insignificant amount.

DISRUPTION CAUSED BY THE DUE DILIGENCE INVESTIGATION

The one cost that companies underestimate the most is the disruption that occurs in a company's business during the time leading up to the IPO. Once a company decides to go public a detailed registration statement must be prepared for filing with the SEC. The registration statement will set forth all material aspects of the company's business and operations. If any false statements are included in the registration statement, or if any material information is omitted, the company, its officers and its underwriter can face substantial legal liability. As a result, the underwriter and its attorneys will make a detailed review of all areas of a company's business. All material contracts will be reviewed. Key executives will be interviewed. Past business transactions will be scrutinized. Intellectual property rights, including patents, copyrights and trademarks will be reviewed. This detailed analysis of a company's business and operations is known in industry jargon as "due diligence." The disruptive effects of the due diligence review process are enormous and management of the company is often not adequately prepared. The managers fail to anticipate the level of disruption. It is important for management to stay focused on the business of running the company throughout the process of preparing for an IPO.

Perhaps the worst part of the due diligence process is that in almost every instance the review will turn up some problem or issue that appears to be an emergency that could sink the IPO. Perhaps the minutes of an important board meeting can't be located. Or a review of the company's contracts with key customers reveals some troubling clause. Or issues arise regarding a company's intellectual property rights in an important asset. Usually all of these issues can be addressed and corrected in a short period of time. However, when a company's managers hear about one of these issues for the first time they will inevitably conclude that the company's chances for an IPO are irrevocably destroyed. It is during these times that a company's attorneys and financial advisors should prevail with cool heads and work through whatever issues have come up. In the vast majority of cases, appropriate corrective action or disclosures can easily address the problem.

A PUBLIC COMPANY MUST MAKE DETAILED PUBLIC DISCLOSURES

A company that is publicly traded lives life in a fish bowl. All of the material operations and functions of the company must be disclosed to the public through the filing of annual, quarterly and, if necessary, special interim reports with the SEC. In addition, detailed financial statements must be included with the SEC filings. In contrast, privately held companies often guard their operational details and financial statements from disclosure lest a competitor gleam some advantage from the information. Adjusting to a life of full disclosure can be difficult, especially in the beginning, as the company and its advisors wrestle over questions about what information is material—and is therefore required to be disclosed—and what information is not material.

The company must also be prepared to answer inquiries from the financial press, analysts and shareholders. Often investor relations departments are established to handle these inquiries. As a publicly traded company, management's actions are often questioned by third parties such as the media or other shareholders, and senior executives may be called upon to explain their decisions and actions.

Corporate management must also be made aware that it is not just the company that is subject to the SEC's public disclosure requirements. Individual officers, directors and significant shareholders of the corporation must report their trading activity in the company's securities through certain SEC filings known as Forms 3, 4 and 5.[2] Shareholders that own over 5% of a corporation's securities must also file reports of their trading activities known as 13Ds. Investors often analyze the trading of a company's officers, directors and significant shareholders to determine whether they should buy or sell the corporation's stock. This can lead to a reluctance on the part of officers, directors and significant shareholders to sell significant portions of their stock holdings at any given time because the market may interpret their actions as a sign to bail out of the company's stock.

The members of the management team of a publicly traded corporation must also be prepared to have their salaries and stock compensation packages scrutinized by investors and financial analysts. The financial press regularly prints stories concerning the pay packages of managers of publicly traded companies. Questions can be raised about corporate managers if their salaries and stock option grants seem too high in light of the company's performance. Management of publicly traded companies, therefore, must be prepared to accept the public disclosure of personal financial details that would not otherwise be required if the company were privately held.

PUBLICLY TRADED COMPANIES HAVE ENORMOUS PRESSURE TO MAINTAIN STOCK PRICE APPRECIATION

Shareholders of publicly traded companies will expect to profit from their investment through an increase in the stock's price and, in some

---

[2] Forms 3, 4 and 5 are contained in Appendices 8D, 8E, and 8F, respectively, in Chapter 8 *infra*.

cases, through dividend payments. Shareholders who invest in Internet and technology companies are often seeking quick increases in the price of a company's stock and they are not at all concerned about dividends, especially since many Internet and technology companies are several years away from profitability. Many investors in the technology sector have abandoned the buy and hold philosophy of investing and, instead, are expecting significant increases in the short-term prices of the stocks they buy. This philosophy has led investors to engage in a great deal of short-term trading of stocks, hoping to make fast profits.

The active trading style of investors, especially in the Internet sector, has led to a great deal of volatility in the stock prices of technology companies. The end result is that a lot of pressure is placed on executives of Internet companies to increase the share price of their companies' stock. Often, increasing the share price will require a company's management to take an aggressive approach to the company's short-term growth. Management must be sure to balance the short-term goal of share price appreciation with the company's long-term business objectives. This balancing act becomes more difficult in publicly traded companies because of the huge amount of pressure by investors to maintain the company's stock price appreciation.

LOSS OF CONTROL OF THE COMPANY

When a company goes public it sells a significant portion of its outstanding common stock to numerous investors. As a result, the founders of a company and its management can lose control of the company should the public shareholders band together and seek substantial changes in the corporation. Proxy fights can be waged and directors can be appointed who have a very different view on how to run the company than the founders or current managers. While there are certain steps a company can take to limit these dangers—such as issuing shares with limited voting rights—these types of management protections can make the stock considerably less valuable, and an underwriter may even be unwilling to sell anything other than stock with full voting rights.

SHAREHOLDER LAWSUITS

A fact of life for today's publicly traded companies is that they face a high risk of being sued by their shareholders for securities law violations. Shareholder suits often take the form of class actions and can seek substantial damages from not only the company, but also from the individual officers and directors. Frequently these suits allege that the company and its management made material misrepresentations or omissions in their SEC filings or in communications with the investing public through press releases or media interviews. Having an appropriate officers' and directors' insurance policy is absolutely essential for any publicly traded company. In fact, most directors will not even consider sitting on the board of a publicly traded corporation unless an adequate insurance policy is in place that will protect them. The costs of these policies are usually paid by the company and can be quite expensive. Congress attempted to curb some of the more aggressive class action suits by passing the Private Securities Litigation Reform Act of 1995.[3] However, whether this statute ultimately accomplishes its goals of reducing frivolous class actions has yet to be conclusively determined.

---

[3] Pub. L. No. 104-67, 109 Stat. 737 (codified in scattered sections between 15 U.S.C. §§ 77 and 79).

PRE-IPO FINANCING

G oing from a newly incorporated company to a publicly traded company will require capital—often substantial amounts—along the way. Companies usually need capital to hire additional employees, create advertising and marketing campaigns and complete product development. If a company is Internet-based, computer programmers are often needed to complete the development of a Web site or to implement large-scale advertising campaigns that can promote awareness of the company and its Web site. Creating a sophisticated e-commerce Web site can easily cost hundreds of thousands of dollars. In the vast majority of cases, the amount of capital needed to build and develop a company is far beyond the means of the individual founders. Therefore, outside financing will be needed to help the company to grow as quickly as possible. Outside financing is particularly important for those companies that want to obtain a first mover advantage and put their products or services in the market as quickly as possible. A new company must grow to the point where an IPO is a realistic possibility. This chapter discusses the various forms of pre-IPO financing that are available to entrepreneurs and provides practical strategies for obtaining the needed capital.

Initial start-up financing for companies typically comes from the founders. In exchange for their infusion of capital, founders are issued shares in the company. The number of shares issued to each of the founders is subject to negotiation, but usually the amount of money and personal time that is devoted to the business are the decisive factors. The amount of financing that the founders are able to provide varies from company to company and is dependant on the financial resources of the founders as well as their desire to invest in a new venture. The need for additional financing can quickly become apparent as a company begins to grow and develop its business. For instance, additional programmers may be required to complete development of a software program or expensive computer equipment must be purchased.

There are several sources that a company can turn to for the financing that it needs. Common sources of funding are wealthy individuals known as "angel investors," venture capital funds and private placements by a broker-dealer. Some companies also retain individuals or entities that act as "finders" of capital, usually for a stock and/or cash commission based on the amount of money raised. Each of these options has advantages and disadvantages and it is important for entrepreneurs to be aware of them.

Because of the high risk involved in providing capital to a new enterprise almost all outside financing sources will seek an equity interest in the company as opposed to structuring the financing arrangements strictly as debt. Outside financing sources will generally not be willing to lend money to a new company because the company is unlikely to have the cash flow necessary to make interest payments on the loan. In addition, the holders of debt cannot expect large returns on their investment. The maximum gain that a debt holder can receive is the interest on the loan—no matter how well a company performs over the years. Investors will generally not be willing to risk their funds in a new venture unless there is the possibility of substantial gains if the company does well. Of course, investors will be aware that whenever the possibility of significant gains is present there will also be the possibility that the entire investment could be lost. Therefore, it is especially important for entrepreneurs to anticipate an investor's concerns about the riskiness of the investment and make a persuasive presentation about the potential success of the company.

For similar reasons, bank loans will not be available to new companies, particularly Internet or technology companies, which typically do not have valuable hard assets to secure loans. Banks prefer to lend money to companies that have been in business for at least three years and have established cash flow from which interest payments can be made. Banks are much more comfortable making loans to traditional companies that will use the money to invest in plants, machinery, equipment or warehouses. That is because if the company defaults on the loan payments, the hard assets and equipment can be sold and the proceeds used to pay off the bank's debt. In contrast, an Internet or technology company's most valuable assets are its intellectual property, such as its Web site, computer codes and software technology. These are not the types of assets that can be readily sold in the event a company defaults on its loan payments. Therefore, the founders of a company must be prepared to give up some of the equity in their corporation to obtain financing in the early stages of a company's development. The number of shares that must be issued by the company and the amount of money that it receives are subjects of intense negotiations and will be treated in detail later in this chapter.

No matter what sources of funding are pursued, the founders of a new company must always evaluate a potential investor not just with respect to the amount of money that the investor brings to the table. The founders must also factor in other extremely important intangibles such as professional contacts, industry experience and business acumen. Early stage investors can add tremendous value and bring a great deal of resources to a new company, especially if the company's management is relatively young and inexperienced. The early investors can help the company establish and refine its business goals and act as a sounding board for new ideas. Well-connected early stage investors can also help recruit experienced management for key positions and provide important introductions to suppliers, vendors and consultants. Experienced early stage investors can also be helpful in arranging later rounds of financing for the company.

SECURITIES LAW CONCERNS

Prior to going out and raising capital, entrepreneurs must have a solid understanding about the laws that govern the capital raising process. Any sale of stock constitutes the sale of a security, and federal and state securities laws heavily regulate the offer and sale of a corporation's securities to investors. The primary federal laws are the Securities Act of 1933[1] (the "Securities Act") and the Securities Exchange Act of 1934.[2] These laws were enacted by Congress shortly after the great stock market crash of 1929. The Securities Act is designed to provide full disclosure to investors about the business that they intend to invest in and to prevent fraud in the sale of securities. Section 5 of the Securities Act governs the public offering of securities and requires detailed disclosure documents to be filed with the U.S. Securities and Exchange Commission and provided to all potential investors. Compliance with Section 5 is extremely time-consuming and expensive and is required only when the company conducts its IPO. Prior to conducting a public offering of securities, a company may sell securities in nonpublic, private offerings to a limited number of investors. Section 4(2) of the Securities Act provides an exemption from the registration requirements of Section 5 for "transactions by an issuer not involving any public offering."[3] The exemption contained in Section 4(2) of the Securities Act

---

[1] 15 U.S.C. §§ 77a *et seq.*

[2] 15 U.S.C. §§ 78(a) *et seq.*

[3] 15 U.S.C. § 77(d)(2).

exempts from the registration requirements the types of private transactions that are discussed in this chapter, namely those involving angel investors, venture capital funds and private placements by broker-dealers. These nonpublic offerings are also known as "private placements" and extreme caution must be taken to ensure that a private placement does not inadvertently result in a public offering. If a company conducts a public offering of its securities without registering the offering under Section 5, the SEC can impose significant penalties upon it, including substantial fines and civil penalties. In addition, if a company improperly raises capital in its early stages, it will have a great deal of difficulty raising capital in later rounds of financing from sophisticated investors who will undoubtedly uncover the problem during the due diligence investigation of the company.

The Securities Act does not set out a bright line test for determining what constitutes a private offering and what constitutes a public offering of securities. Until the SEC issued a series of rules known as Regulation D,[4] there was a good deal of debate over when an offering of securities would be considered a public offering instead of a private offering. In the landmark case *SEC v. Ralston Purina Company,*[5] the Supreme Court held that the number of offerees, their level of sophistication and their access to company information would be important factors in determining whether an offering was public or private. The Supreme Court, however, did not adopt a bright line test and uncertainty remained. In order to give issuers more assurances that their offerings would not be deemed public offerings, in April 1982 the SEC adopted Regulation D setting out a number of conditions that, if complied with, will ensure that an issuer's offering is deemed to be nonpublic.[6]

---

[4] 17 C.F.R. §§ 230.501 et seq.

[5] SEC v. Ralston Purina Company, 346 U.S. 119, 73 S.Ct. 981, 97 L.Ed. 1494 (1953).

[6] See 17 C.F.R. §§ 230.501 *et seq.*

Regulation D

The SEC has promulgated various rules, which are known collectively as Regulation D,[7] that help provide guidance on when an offering will be considered a private offering. Included within Regulation D are three rules—Rules 504, 505 and 506[8]—that govern the private placement of securities. Rule 504 concerns sales of securities up to $1 million, Rule 505 concerns the sale of securities up to $5 million and Rule 506 relates to the sale of securities without regard to any dollar limitations. Essentially, to avoid having to provide investors with detailed information relating to the company's business and finances, all early stage investors in a company, regardless of the dollar amount of their investment, should be "accredited investors" as that term is defined in Regulation D. An individual qualifies as an accredited investor if (1) the person is worth over $1 million or (2) if the person had an income in excess of $200,000 in each of the two most recent years or (3) joint income with that person's spouse in excess of $300,000 in each of those years *and* (4) has a reasonable expectation of reaching the same income level in the current year. Properly structured venture capital funds will also be considered accredited investors because all of their individual members will themselves be accredited investors. Since venture capitalists are often reluctant to invest in companies that have shareholders that are not accredited investors, by limiting a company's outside shareholders to accredited investors, the company will make future rounds of financing easier.

When conducting a private placement, a company must be aware of the restrictions that federal securities laws impose on such offerings. The following restrictions are the most important ones to heed.

---

[7] 17 C.F.R. §§ 230.501 to 230.508.

[8] 17 C.F.R. §§ 230.504, 230.505 and 230.506, respectively.

1. ***No General Solicitations.*** When conducting a private placement of securities, companies are prohibited from engaging in a general solicitation of investors. This prohibition is in place to ensure that the offering remains private and nonpublic. Accordingly, cold calls, mass mailings or e-mails and public solicitations on the Internet are not permissible means of attracting investors to a company's offering. Likewise, public meetings and seminars are also prohibited. Therefore, the best course of action is for the founders of the company to personally approach a limited number of individuals with whom they have a preexisting relationship. The SEC, however, does recognize that there are other ways to show the absence of a general solicitation.[9] In order to demonstrate compliance with the prohibitions on general solicitation, the issuer should keep a log that contains the name and address of each person who was provided with information relating to the offering. Such controls demonstrate the issuer's commitment to complying with the prohibitions against general solicitations.

2. ***Limitations on Resale.*** Investors who purchase stock from a company in a private, nonregistered offering must be made aware that their securities will have restrictions on their resale. Generally, such securities will be difficult to sell to other investors because there will not yet be any public market for the securities. Even if an investor can locate another investor willing to purchase the company's securities, the company will require that an opinion of counsel be obtained to ensure that the sale is in compliance with all applicable securities laws. In fact, the company has an independent legal obligation to make sure that any securities sold in a private placement are not indiscriminately resold by the original investors. A company should take all necessary steps to ensure that its securities are

---

[9] SEC Rel. No. 33-6825 (effective April 19, 1989).

not indiscriminately resold, including: (a) undertaking reasonable inquiry to determine if the purchaser is acquiring the securities for himself or for other persons; (b) providing written disclosure to each purchaser prior to sale that the securities have not been registered and, therefore, cannot be resold unless they are registered or unless an exemption from registration is available; and (c) placing a legend on the certificates stating that the securities have not been registered under the Securities Act and setting forth or referring to the restrictions on transferability and sale of the securities.

3. *State Securities Laws Must Be Followed.* Preliminary note 2 to Regulation D makes clear that nothing in Regulation D obviates the need to comply with any applicable state law relating to the offer and sale of securities. Accordingly, any issuer that intends to sell securities must check the laws of the state where it is located, as well as the laws of the state where the potential investor is located, to ensure that all state law requirements are met.

4. *Notice of the Private Placement Must Be Filed with the SEC.* While companies do not have to file a registration statement in connection with a nonpublic sale of securities, there is a requirement that a notice of the sale be filed with the SEC. Specifically, five copies of a Form D notice must be filed with the SEC no later than fifteen days after the first sale of securities. The Form D can be obtained by calling the SEC's headquarters in Washington, D.C. A sample is included as Appendix 3I below.

5. *Informational Requirements.* If an issuer accepts money from investors who do not meet the definition of an "accredited investor" as set forth in Regulation D, then the company is obligated to provide detailed written information regarding its operations and financial status. However, because

of the extensive disclosure requirements that come into play when nonaccredited investors are allowed to participate in the offering, issuers will generally limit their nonpublic offerings to accredited investors only.

6. ***Antifraud Laws Still Apply.*** Regulation D reminds issuers that nonpublic offerings of securities must comply with the antifraud provisions of the securities laws, and refrain from making misrepresentations or omissions in connection with the offer and sale of its securities. It is the responsibility of the issuer to make a reasonable determination that all of its investors are accredited. This can be done by having each proposed investor complete a suitability questionnaire. A sample suitability questionnaire is included as Appendix 3F. By limiting a company's outside shareholders to accredited investors, the company will make future rounds of financing easier because venture capitalists are often reluctant to invest in companies that have shareholders that are not accredited investors.

STATE SECURITIES LAWS

In addition to the federal laws that govern the offer and sale of securities, each state has its own securities laws that apply in this area. State securities laws are often known as "blue sky" laws and have been in place going back to 1911. Companies that are raising capital must be aware of the restrictions imposed by state laws as well as federal law because a violation of state securities laws can have significant consequences for the company, including fines and even criminal liability. Unlike the uniform body of federal law that exists, state law is fragmented among the fifty states and varies significantly from state to state. An issuer and its counsel must determine whether a particular state's law applies and, if so, how the laws will impact on a proposed offering. Fortunately, great efforts have been made at the state level to implement procedures that simplify the capital raising process for new and growing companies and reduce the costs of compliance with various state laws. The work of the state securities regulators has been coordinated by the North American Securities Administrators Association ("NASAA"), and their efforts have led to the promulgation of the Uniform Securities Act and the Uniform Limited Offering Exemption. While such uniform laws exist in many states, a company and its counsel must still check the laws of the state where a prospective investor is located because several states, notably New York, California and Texas, have special provisions.

Although a small offering exemption has been adopted in many states, it is important to check each applicable state's laws because the states often change the specific language of the model act when enacting the legislation.

When considering state law issues, one of the most important things for an issuer to be mindful of is whether a particular state requires any filings prior to the time that an investor is solicited. For example, in New York a filing must be made with the Attorney General, and a filing fee must be paid, prior to the time that any investors are solicited to invest in securities. By this filing the issuer either registers as a dealer or applies for and obtains an exemption prior to offering its securities to investors. In contrast, most states do not require a formal filing and the payment of a filing fee until after the investor is solicited and agrees to invest in the company.

Issuers of securities must keep in mind that all states have restrictions on the manner of offering securities that are similar to the restrictions contained in Regulation D. Therefore, issuers must be extremely careful and take steps to ensure that their offering will not be construed as a public offering of securities. A large number of states, however, relax the solicitation requirements so long as the solicitations are only sent to institutional investors or accredited investors.

Compliance with state securities law issues can be extremely challenging for both an issuer and its counsel. States are frequently changing and updating their blue sky laws and it can be difficult to keep up with the changes in each of the fifty states. As a result, special blue sky counsel is sometimes engaged, particularly when the size of the private placement warrants the retention of additional attorneys. To keep costs down, new companies are well advised to limit the number of states in which they will approach investors with their private placement. By doing so, issuers can ascertain the state law requirements in a limited number of states in a cost-effective manner.

PRACTICE POINTERS FOR SECURITIES ATTORNEYS

Attorneys who represent companies that are seeking capital can take several important steps to ensure that private placements of securities are not deemed to violate any of the registration or antifraud provisions of the federal securities laws. First, the officers of the company should be clearly instructed that a public offering of securities is not allowed in a private placement. Therefore, the offering cannot be advertised and investors cannot be solicited with random e-mails. Posting information about the offering on a Web site that is accessible to the general public will also constitute a public offering and must be avoided. It is a good practice for the company's officers to solicit only a limited number of investors with whom they have a preexisting relationship. If written information about the offering is sent out to potential investors, such as a business plan or a stock subscription agreement, a written log should be kept reflecting who the information was sent to. By keeping a log, the company can prove that it only approached a limited number of people and, therefore, no public offering of securities was made.

Attorneys should always advise companies that are seeking capital to prepare a written disclosure document that describes the business of the company and the securities being offered. The level of detail in the written material will vary from offering to offering. However, in all cases the attorney should make sure that the company's written material presents a complete picture of the new venture, including any material adverse information. Providing investors with false information will expose the company to legal liability for securities fraud. The written disclosure materials should also contain a detailed discussion about the risk factors associated with the investment. The discussion of risk factors must be tailored as much as possible to the individual company, and boilerplate disclosures should be avoided.

Potential investors should also be informed in writing that they have the opportunity to ask the company's officers any questions that they may have regarding the new venture. Including such written disclosures in the business plan will protect entrepreneurs against accusations by investors that they were unaware of the risky nature of their investment. Towards that end, companies should also obtain written representations from potential investors that they are sophisticated and that they meet the definition of an accredited investor under Regulation D. Such representations are typically contained in the stock subscription agreement.

In order for an offering of securities to fall within Section 4(2)'s exemption from registration, the purchaser must buy the securities for investment only and not for resale. Therefore, investors must be told that they may not purchase the company's securities with a view towards distribution. Subsequent resales of the securities acquired in a private placement can result in the entire offering being deemed a public offering. Therefore, the investor should represent in the stock subscription agreement that he is acquiring the securities for his own account for investment and not with a view to reselling the securities. To further protect the company, the attorney should ensure that all stock certificates that are issued in a private placement contain an appropriate legend stating that the securities have not been registered and that they may not be resold without the benefit of registration or an exemption therefrom. The following is an example of an appropriate certificate legend:

> "THE SECURITIES REPRESENTED BY THIS CERTIFICATE WERE ACQUIRED FOR INVESTMENT ONLY AND NOT FOR RESALE. THEY HAVE NOT BEEN REGISTERED UNDER THE SECURITIES ACT OF 1933, AS AMENDED, OR ANY STATE SECURITIES LAW. THESE SECURITIES MAY NOT BE SOLD, TRANSFERRED, PLEDGED, HYPOTHECATED OR OTHERWISE DISPOSED OF UNLESS FIRST REGISTERED UNDER SUCH LAWS, OR UNLESS THE COMPANY HAS RECEIVED EVIDENCE REASONABLY SATISFACTORY TO IT, OR AN OPINION OF COUNSEL ACCEPTABLE TO THE COMPANY, THAT REGISTRATION UNDER SUCH LAWS IS NOT REQUIRED."

Because of the limitations on resale, securities that are acquired in a private placement transaction are deemed to be "restricted securities." Any time an investor wishes to resell shares acquired directly from the company in a private transaction, an opinion of counsel should be obtained by the investor and provided to the company stating that the proposed sale is in compliance with all federal and state securities laws. The sale of restricted securities should be done in compliance with Rule 144[10] promulgated by the SEC under the Securities Act. Rule 144 sets forth certain conditions that must be met for the sale of restricted securities, including holding periods, limitations on the number of securities that may be sold and notification requirements.

Finally, attorneys for companies that are raising capital should ensure that the transactions are properly documented through the execution of a stock subscription agreement by each investor. Also,

---

[10] 17 C.F.R. § 230.144.

an investor questionnaire should be filled out by each investor prior to the time the company accepts the investor's money so that the company has a good faith basis in concluding that the investor is an accredited investor suitable to invest in the company's securities. A sample subscription agreement and investor questionnaire are included at the end of this chapter as Appendices 3B and 3C, respectively.

At the time each investor is given a subscription agreement and questionnaire the investor should also be given a business plan that describes the company and its management team. The next section discusses the importance of having a business plan and how to draft one properly.

PREPARING A BUSINESS PLAN IS CRITICAL TO SECURING FINANCING

A well-thought-out business plan is a critical element of the capital raising process for a new company. Many angel investors and most venture capital funds will not consider meeting with an entrepreneur without first receiving and reviewing its business plan. A new company that has prepared a business plan has taken the first step in convincing potential investors that the business idea has been thought through and researched and that the affairs of the corporation are being handled in a professional manner by the company's founders. A well-written business plan will succinctly present the company's business idea in an exciting manner. It will describe the industry in which the company operates, its competition and why its Web site, product or service is commercially viable. One important benefit of preparing a business plan that is often overlooked is that it requires the entrepreneur to make a detailed analysis of the market in which his company will operate. The business plan also forces the entrepreneur to define exactly how the business idea will be successfully developed. It is not uncommon for entrepreneurs to learn new and valuable information about the markets in which they will operate and about their target customers while preparing the business plan. On occasion, significant parts of the company's marketing strategy may be revamped based on the information uncovered during the preparation of the plan. Preparing the business plan will also give the entrepreneur and investors written benchmarks and goals for the business. This can be invaluable because it will help the entrepreneur track whether the business is on course to meet its goals.

To attract any significant amounts of financing for a new company, the business plan must convincingly demonstrate that the company can be a major player in a large market. As a rule of thumb, venture capitalists will invest only in companies that operate in markets with a current or anticipated valuation of $1 billion or more. In addition, venture capital funds will expect the business plan to show how the company can reach a value of at least $100 million within three to five years. Sales and market forecasts for your company, as well as the industry that it operates in, are critical components of a business plan. Remember that the sales and market forecasts contained in a business plan must be based on properly conducted market research. Anybody can create a business plan that contains extremely optimistic sales and revenue forecasts. However, in today's environment, many investors will expect that a company will conduct market research to back up its sales and market forecasts. The market research will confirm that there is a demand for the company's products and services among its target customers. It should also demonstrate that the company's anticipated pricing policies will be commercially viable. While this kind of market research has not always been required by investors, those who conduct this research will have a distinct advantage in persuading investors to invest in their company.

DRAFTING THE BUSINESS PLAN

The company's business plan must balance several considerations. First and foremost it must present the company's business idea in an exciting manner designed to persuade investors to invest in the company. An important role of the business plan is to sell your idea to outsiders. Throughout the entire drafting process it will be extremely helpful if the entrepreneur places himself in the shoes of the potential investors who will be reading the business plan. Think about what information you would expect to have if you were making an investment. The business plan must convey what makes the company unique and why the company has a competitive advantage in the marketplace.

While the business plan must sell potential investors on the company and the investment opportunity, at the same time it must also be completely truthful and accurate. If there is a particularly strong competitor in the market that your company operates in, that fact must be discussed. If your company has experienced setbacks in the past, those setbacks must be discussed and the company must explain what steps it has taken to prevent their recurrence. Business plans that are overly rosy may be considered too good to be true by investors, who will then pass on the investment opportunity.

An effective business plan is one that is inviting and easy to read. Accordingly, the business plan should be laid out in an attractive and easy to read manner. Don't crowd the pages with a great deal of small type. Instead, use headings to break up the discussion and use readable type. Bullet points, tables and charts can be used to present data in a clear, effective manner. Also the judicious use of color in charts and other places can make for a memorable business plan. The appropriate length for the business plan will vary for each business. However, most plans are between twenty and forty pages. Once the initial draft of the business plan is completed, it is wise to get feedback from people who are not involved with the company to ensure that the plan is understandable and persuasive.

A common error that is made in many business plans for Internet and other new economy companies is to delve into too much technical detail about a product, service or computer program. This is particularly true if the company's business plan involves deploying new technology to solve a problem or provide a service to customers. Internet companies are often founded by individuals with a great deal of knowledge about technology or software programs and they naturally write about technology at an advanced level. A business plan should only present the company's technology at a basic level. It should not overwhelm the reader with technical jargon or acronyms. The expertise of investors is finance, not technology, and an overly technical discussion can easily turn off a potential investor. Sophisticated investors will hire experts anyway to evaluate the technology before investing. Therefore, instead of describing the technology in detail, the business plan should clearly explain in basic terms what the technology does, why there is a need for the technology and who will use and benefit from the technology. Do not assume that the readers of the business plan are familiar with the basic problems that your technology is trying to solve. Entrepreneurs with a technical background who have never raised capital are often stunned when potential investors ask why there is a need for the new technology that they have developed. Therefore, it is important to anticipate and answer even the most basic questions about your technology in your business plan.

Entrepreneurs should be aware that the trend over the last few years has been for business plans for Internet and technology companies to be prepared relatively quickly so that the company can launch its product or services as fast as possible. Investors in today's Internet and technology companies will not expect to see the lengthy and very detailed business plans that were common in the 1980s and early 1990s. Instead, investors would much rather see the company focusing on getting its technology to the market and letting the market validate the concept. Therefore, entrepreneurs should not spend an excessive amount of time preparing the business plan or providing overly detailed discussions and models in the business plan.

THE ELEMENTS OF A BUSINESS PLAN

While every business plan is unique, there are areas that every plan will be expected to address. The following discussion provides an overview of the elements of a business plan and the subjects that should be covered in each segment.

Executive Summary. Every business plan should start with an Executive Summary, providing an overview of the venture and introducing the management team. It is also important for the Executive Summary briefly to describe the market that the company will operate in and why the company has a competitive advantage. The overriding goal of the Executive Summary is to describe why the business presents a good investment opportunity. Most potential investors will want to read this section first to determine whether this is the type of venture in which they will be interested. Although the Executive Summary only provides a short introduction to the business, it may be the deciding factor in whether the potential investor will read on or dismiss the investment opportunity. Professional investors receive hundreds of business plans a year and do not have time to read each one in its entirety. Therefore, potential investors attempt to sift quickly through the large number of business plans and select the most promising ones for detailed review. The Executive Summary is one of the most important parts of the business plan because it will determine whether the potential investor goes on to read the entire plan or summarily dismisses the investment opportunity.

Accordingly, the Executive Summary must make a convincing case that your business is worthy of investment.

The Executive Summary should grab the reader's attention from the start and succinctly state why the business presents a good investment opportunity. Remember that the investor's primary goal will be to generate a significant return on capital. Accordingly, it is important to state right up front the current or anticipated market size in which the company operates and what gives the company a competitive advantage in that market. The Executive Summary must make a convincing case that the company can grow to be a significant player in the target market.

The Executive Summary should also briefly discuss the company and its origins, the stage of development the company and its projects are in, the amount of money sought and how the investor's money will be used to grow the company. It is a good practice to write the Executive Summary after the business plan is completed because the summary will act as an introduction to the entire business plan.

Industry Analysis. After the Executive Summary, the business plan should provide a detailed Industry Analysis. The Industry Analysis section will describe the market in which the company operates and the potential customers for its products or services. The discussion of the company's market and target customers is an extremely important part of the business plan. To attract significant amounts of capital the company must demonstrate that it is operating in a market that either is large or is anticipated to be large. It is even better if the market is growing and does not have well-established competitors. The Industry Analysis section should also discuss the current industry participants.

It must also discuss any studies that have been conducted by the company or by third parties that validate the company's discussion of market size and growth. Frequently, industry groups and investment firms publish detailed studies of particular markets. Such studies can be cited in the business plan along with any studies that were commissioned by the company itself. A good source of background information can be found in the SEC filings of publicly traded companies that operate in your industry. These filings can be accessed on the SEC's Web site at *www.SEC.gov.* The Industry Analysis section should also describe the company's target customers in detail. This discussion should include pertinent demographic or geographic information relating to the target customers. This section is also the place to discuss any major social, technological or economic trends that may impact on the company's business.

The goal of the Industry Analysis section is to provide the potential investor with the information needed to understand the company's products or services. It gives the potential investor the necessary background information to recognize the market opportunity that the company is attempting to take advantage of. The Industry Analysis section should also contain a discussion about the global market in which the company operates as well as the global competition that the company will face. In today's international economy, it is a mistake for any business that plans to be a significant player in a large market to focus exclusively on U.S.-based markets and competitors. Failing to focus on such global issues could signal to potential investors that the company's management has not carefully thought through its business and its competitors.

Description of Business. The Description of Business section of the business plan contains a detailed description of the company's products, services or technology. This section describes exactly what the company does. Diagrams and charts can be included if they will be helpful. The Description of Business section should also discuss any legal protections that the company has in place for its intellectual property, including patents, copyrights or trademarks. Potential investors will want to ensure that the company has done all it can do to protect its intellectual property. Proper intellectual property protection will ensure that the company can commercially exploit its new technology or business idea without a competitor using the same technology in its business. Patents and other types of intellectual property protection can provide very effective barriers to competition and, consequently, they can significantly enhance the attractiveness of a company for investment. Therefore, if the company has any patents or other protections in place on key technology, it is very important to state clearly that fact in the business plan. The Description of Business section is also the place to discuss any setbacks that the company has experienced in the past and the steps that the company has taken to prevent such setbacks from occurring in the future.

The Description of Business section should also clearly state what stage the company's business is in and what significant steps, if any, must be completed prior to commercial launch. If the company has an estimated timetable for the development and launch of its products or services, that should also be included.

Operations. The Operations section of the business plan discusses the company's facilities, space, location, capital equipment and labor needs. If the company will continue to design software or develop new technology, this section should discuss the processes that will be put in place to facilitate such design and development. Also, this section should discuss whether the company will rely on independent contractors or part-time or full-time employees in carrying out its business plan.

Competition. The Competition section of the business plan will discuss who the company's competitors are—and every company has competitors. If an entrepreneur believes that there are no competitors for his company, then he has not done his homework and will appear extremely naïve to potential investors. The Competition section is the place to compare the strengths and weaknesses of your products, services or technology with those of your competitors. Also, the size and market share of each significant competitor should be discussed. If the company plans to take market share away from existing competitors, this section should include a discussion of how that will be accomplished.

Marketing and Sales Strategy. The Marketing and Sales Strategy section of the business plan discusses which customers the company will target and why. The company should discuss in detail its competitive advantages in the marketplace and why customers will chose its products, services or technologies over those of its competitors. The Marketing and Sales Strategy section should also describe how the company intends to implement its various strategies in the marketplace. One element that should be discussed that is often overlooked is the company's pricing strategy and how it was arrived at. Appropriate pricing is critical to the success of any company, and it is also the basis on which sales and revenues forecasts are made. The company should explain why it thinks its potential customers will pay the prices that the company has set. A market or pricing study done by a reputable market research firm can help confirm that the company's pricing strategy and sales forecasts are accurate. In this part of the business plan, the company should also compare its prices with the prices of its competitors.

The Marketing and Sales Strategy section should also describe how the company will promote awareness of its Web site or other technologies. Potential subjects for discussion are what kinds of advertising will be undertaken, whether Internet banner ads will be used and whether any special promotions or celebrity endorsements will be considered.

Management Team. This part of the business plan is critical because potential investors will look closely at the management team of a new company to determine the company's likelihood of success. The management of a new venture is one of the most important considerations that an outside investor will have. In fact, there is a saying in the venture capital community that "money follows management." This is particularly true with a brand-new enterprise because there is no operating history on which to base an investment decision. Investors will greatly prefer investing in a company with an excellent management team and an average product over a company with an average management team and an excellent product. Therefore, this part of the business plan should emphasize the background and achievements of the company's management team. If the management team has experience in the company's industry or has successfully started or run other companies, that should also be emphasized.

It is important to note that investors will look for a true management team where the skills of the individual members complement one another. Therefore, detailed background information on the management of the company should be provided so that investors understand what qualities the team members are bringing to the venture. Towards that end, this section should discuss any specialized skills or expertise that a member of the company's management team possesses. It is not critical that every management position be filled for early rounds of financing, but the founders of the company should have a vision of what management positions will need to be created and filled in the future. This part of the business plan should also discuss the management team's compensation. High salaries for management will be a red flag for potential investor, who will expect management to align their interests with shareholders by taking lower salaries and equity positions and/or options in the company. Typically, management's equity and options will vest over a number of years. Management's compensation should be structured so that the managers have a strong financial incentive in making the company a success. This section of the business plan should also discuss who is on the board of directors and any specialized skills or contacts that the board members bring to their positions.

Financial Statements. The final part of the business plan should be the financial statements of the company, including an income statement, a balance sheet and a statement of cash flow. The company should also provide three years of projected financial statements that are consistent with the company's sales, revenue and costs forecasts. If any assumptions were made in preparing the financial statements, they should be discussed in this section.

THE PRIVATE PLACEMENT MEMORANDUM

Instead of a business plan, companies will often use a private placement memorandum as the basic document that communicates the business of the company to investors. A private placement memorandum contains a detailed discussion about the company, its operations and its management, just as in a business plan. However, a private placement memorandum is more formal than a business plan and is generally used when a company has already decided upon the type and number of securities it is offering to investors. The private placement memorandum will also contain a much more detailed discussion about the risks involved with making an investment with the company. One of the purposes of the private placement memorandum is to provide investors with a written disclosure document that lists the primary risks of investing in the business. By providing detailed risk disclosures, companies hope to limit their liability in the event that they are accused of making misrepresentations or failing to disclose material information. A private placement memorandum is generally used with more established companies and is prepared by a securities attorney.

A private placement memorandum for a new company generally contains the following sections:

1. **Cover Page.** The cover page identifies the name of the company, the number of shares that are being sold and the price for each share. It also lists the name of the person to whom the memorandum is given. Tracking the names of the offerees will document the number of offers that the issuer has made so that the issuer can establish the nonpublic nature of its solicitations. The cover page should also state that the offering memorandum is confidential and is intended only for the person to whom it is addressed.

2. **The Warning Page.** The warning page informs the investors that the securities being offered are highly risky and that only investors who can afford to lose their entire investment should consider purchasing the company's securities. The warning page also states that neither the Securities and Exchange Commission nor any state regulator has approved or disapproved of the securities being offered. It is also good practice to inform potential investors that the securities being sold by the company will be "restricted" and, therefore, the investors will not be able to resell the securities that they acquire without first obtaining a written opinion of counsel stating that such resales are permitted under federal and state securities laws. By placing the risk disclosures and other warnings in a prominent place at the beginning of the private placement memorandum, the issuer will be protecting itself from later claims by investors that they were unaware that the securities were risky or that the securities could not be immediately resold. The warning page should also refer the investor to the detailed risk disclosure section that is contained in the body of the memorandum.

3. **Summary.** The summary section of the memorandum is extremely important because it gives the company the opportunity to present the investment opportunity in a succinct and persuasive manner. Many potential investors will read the

summary section in its entirety and then skim the remaining sections of the memorandum. Therefore, all key points that the company wishes to convey in the memorandum should be briefly stated in the summary section. The nature of the company's business and the background and experience of the company's management team should be given particular emphasis in the summary section. It is a good practice to state at the beginning of the summary section that all of the information presented in the summary is qualified by the more detailed discussion that takes place later in the memorandum.

4. **The Offering.** This section provides details to the investors about the securities being offered. For instance, the company discusses how many shares are being offered, the price per share and whether any brokers are being used to assist in distributing and selling the securities.

5. **Risk Factors.** The risk factors section is used to convey to potential investors the potential risks that go along with an investment in the company's securities. This section will be extremely important if an investor later claims that he was misled into investing in the company by overly optimistic statements in other parts of the memorandum. Courts will generally read the memorandum as a whole document and the risk factors section will demonstrate that the company did provide adequate warnings about the potential risks associated with the investment. It is important to tailor the risk disclosures to the company and its particular business and not use boilerplate disclosures. Some of the common risks that are discussed in the risk disclosure section are: the company is a start-up without a history of operations, the company's market is new and untested, the fact that the company relies on certain key employees, the importance of a certain small number of customers to the company's success, the continued control of the company by the founders after the offering is

completed, the absence of a public market for the company's securities, the highly competitive market in which the company operates, the fact that the offering price for the securities was arbitrarily determined and that the company does not pay dividends. The foregoing list is not meant to be exhaustive; however, it does provide a good starting point for some of the risks that the company should discuss in this section of the memorandum.

6. ***Use of Proceeds.*** The use of proceeds section will describe how the investors' money will be used. A general breakdown of anticipated expenditures should be provided. However, the company should draft this section to allow itself the flexibility it will need to adjust its spending as the business environment changes. Therefore, it is advisable to allocate a significant percentage of the money raised to "working capital," as this will allow the company a great deal of discretion to use the money appropriately as business conditions change. It is important to note that investors will be concerned if a significant portion of the money raised will be used to pay the founders' salaries because investors prefer to see the financial success of the founders tied to the company's performance.

7. ***Capitalization.*** The capitalization section discusses how many shares of stock the company has outstanding, whether there is more than one class of stock and whether any stock has special rights, such as preferential voting rights. This section also discusses how many shares of stock will be controlled by the founders and how many shares will be controlled by the new investors.

8. ***Business of the Company.*** This section of the memorandum is generally longer than the other sections because it contains detailed information about the company's business, the markets it operates in and the company's competitors. Typically,

in this section the company provides information about the size of the market in which it operates and how the company intends to market and sell its products or services. After reading this section, a potential investor should be convinced that the company will operate in a market that is large enough to support rapid growth and that the company will have a competitive advantage over its competitors. In addition, if the company has conducted any marketing research to support the claim that there is a demand for its products or services, that research should be discussed in this section.

9. **Management of the Company.** In this section, the company should list the names of its executive officers, the titles of each person, their ages and a brief description of their responsibilities. It is important to include a paragraph or two of biographical information for each officer. The biographical information should include the schools attended, the degrees obtained and any relevant managerial work experience. If any of the officers of the company have been involved with other successful start-up companies, that fact should be highlighted. This section should also discuss the compensation of the officers and any stock option plan that is in effect. The company should also disclose if any officer of the company has been convicted of a crime, has been the subject of an enforcement action by any securities regulator or has filed for bankruptcy.

10. **Directors of the Company.** This section is similar to the management section and should list the names of each director, their ages and a paragraph or two of biographical information for each individual. Investors generally prefer to see a board comprised of members with a range of expertise. For instance, the board of a new media company may consist of a director who has technical expertise in the company's business, a director who has significant experience growing

other start-up companies and a director who has good contacts in the world of venture capital and capital raising. By bringing together individuals who have different talents and experience, the board can create synergy and help the company successfully carry out its business plan. The company should also disclose if any director of the company has been convicted of a crime, has been the subject of an enforcement action by any securities regulator or has filed for bankruptcy.

11. ***Certain Transactions.*** This section of the private placement memorandum should describe any transactions between the company and any party that is related to or affiliated with the company or any of its officers, directors or shareholders. Examples of items that are discussed in this section include any loans made by the company to its officers or directors, any contracts between the company and a business owned by an officer or director and whether the company is renting office space from an officer or director. Related party transactions are generally considered to be material and should be disclosed in the offering memorandum. The memorandum should also discuss whether or not the company is receiving fair value for any related party transactions.

In addition to the typical sections of the private placement memorandum set forth above, the company should also include other sections that are pertinent to its individual business. The goals of the private placement memorandum are to include all material facts about the company and to provide adequate warnings to potential investors. It is always a good idea to include a paragraph at the end of the memorandum stating that potential investors should feel free to contact the company should they have any questions or require additional information. The name and telephone number of a contact person at the company should be provided for this purpose.

SUCCESSFULLY APPROACHING POTENTIAL INVESTORS

Once a company has completed its business plan it can begin seriously approaching potential investors. Before going public, a company is likely to have several "rounds" of private financing as it progresses from one stage of its development to the next. Investors prefer to finance a company in stages because it allows the company to have a fairly well-defined path of growth. Also, investors may not be willing to commit a large amount of money to a brand new company at the outset; rather, they would prefer to invest more limited amounts of money over time as the company progresses with its development and growth.

In attempting to raise money for a new enterprise, the founders of the company must take care to avoid making a public offering of their company's securities. Federal and state securities laws require that the sale of securities be registered with the SEC, and appropriate state agencies, unless there is an available exemption from registration. As is discussed in more detail below, an exemption from registration is available so long as no public offering of the company's securities is made. Indiscriminate solicitations to numerous potential investors would likely be deemed an illegal public offering and should be avoided at all costs. Entrepreneurs, therefore, should not send unsolicited e-mails to strangers soliciting investments, they should not post their business plan on an Internet site for all to see and they should not give out their business plan to large numbers of strangers. Instead, entrepreneurs should only approach those people with whom they have a preexisting relationship or those who are professional investors, such as venture capitalists or angel investors. Not only is an unregistered public offering of securities illegal, but it will also raise significant problems for a company when it attempts to raise future rounds of financing from investors who would then be concerned about the company's latent legal liabilities. The rules that govern whether an offering of securities is public or private are complex and a competent securities attorney should be consulted if the company has any questions in this area.

THE STAGES OF A NEW COMPANY'S GROWTH AND DEVELOPMENT

A new company that is ready for its first round of outside financing will often approach wealthy individuals, known as angel investors, to provide seed financing. In the 1980s and early 1990s angel investors were concentrated in areas with a great deal of entrepreneurial activity such as Silicon Valley in California. Since then, however, angel investors can be found in almost every region of the United States. Seed capital is a relatively small amount of capital—anywhere from $50,000 to $500,000—provided to a business to prove a concept and to qualify for future start-up capital, perhaps from a venture capital fund. Often seed capital is used to develop a preliminary version of the company's products or Internet site. Seed capital can also be used to begin development of software that is believed to be commercially viable. In addition, seed capital is often used to conduct market research in an attempt to define the target customers and their willingness to purchase the company's technology, services or products. When considering whether to accept money from a particular angel investor, the company should also consider whether the angel investor is willing and able to bring other resources to the company such as professional contacts and business advice. Experienced angel investors often have contacts at venture capital firms who can provide larger amounts of capital when the company is ready for additional investment.

After the infusion of seed capital, if the company's business idea continues to be promising, the company may attract start-up financing from a venture capital fund. A venture capital fund is a private entity that manages a portfolio of private equity investments. Typically, a venture capital fund will be an active investor and will seek to assist the company with refining its business plan, attracting talented management and helping in the development and marketing of the company's technology, products or services. Venture capital funding often is used by a company to complete development of its Web site or complete the preparation of software programs or other technology. Internet companies receiving start-up financing are typically in business for less than a year and have not yet made their products or services available commercially. At this stage in the company's growth, the company will make more detailed marketing studies, assemble key management and generally prepare to do business.

If the company's business idea continues to appear viable and it has spent most of its start-up financing, the company may attract first-stage financing. Money raised in first-stage financing can be used to bring the company to the point where it can launch its Web site and also purchase the necessary advertising and marketing. Once the company begins commercial operations, it may engage in second- and third-round financing to expand its business and continue to grow. The number of private financings that a company will require prior to going public varies greatly and is dependent on the needs of the particular company and the IPO market in general. In each round of financing, new investors may be brought into the picture or earlier investors may completely provide for the company's new capital needs.

FINDING AND PERSUADING ANGEL INVESTORS AND VENTURE CAPITAL FUNDS TO INVEST IN YOUR COMPANY

Finding angel investors and venture capitalists to invest in a first time entrepreneur's company can be a daunting task. Traditional methods of meeting angel investors and venture capitalists include introductions by lawyers, accountants or other professionals who work with start-up companies. In addition, today there are other resources, such as the Internet and various industry organizations, that entrepreneurs can use to find potential investors. Some of these resources can be found listed at the end of this chapter. When a first-time entrepreneur is seeking financing from a venture capital firm, researching the investment preferences of the various firms can pay great dividends. All venture capital firms have preferences for the types of investments that they are interested in making. Some venture capital firms specialize in certain subsections of the Internet and high-tech industries. Therefore, if your company is creating an e-commerce Internet site it is not productive to send your business plan to a venture capital firm interested in investing only in computer chip or software companies. In addition, many venture capital firms have minimum and maximum levels of investments that they will consider. Some firms will only invest in later rounds of financing while some firms prefer investing in the start-up stage. Also, focusing your attention on firms that are located in the geographical location of the business and its management is productive because most venture capitalists prefer to be close to the companies they invest in so that they can participate effectively in the company's growth and development. Finally, certain venture capital firms are lead firms, and they prefer to be the first investors in a particular deal. Other venture capital firms are not lead firms, and will only invest if another venture capital firm takes the initiative and decides to make an investment. Obviously, a new company that has not yet received any money from venture capitalists will be much better off pursuing lead venture capitalists. Information about the preferences of various venture capital funds can be found in publicly available directories and through venture capital industry associations. By focusing your efforts on meeting appropriate venture capitalists, you can significantly reduce the time and effort it takes to raise capital.

If an angel investor or venture capitalist has reviewed your business plan and likes the idea, he will ask for a meeting to discuss your business in more depth. This first meeting is critical for the entrepreneur because it will be an important opportunity to demonstrate to a potential investor that you and your management team are ready for the challenges of successfully growing the company. Preparation for this meeting is essential. You must be prepared to discuss the details of your company's business, marketing strategy and competitors. It can be highly effective if you bring a demonstration model of your Internet site or your software so that the potential investor knows exactly what you are trying to do in your business. Also, charts, diagrams and slides can be very helpful. You must be prepared for the potential investor to challenge your assumptions and ask detailed questions. It is advisable that the entrepreneur rehearse for this meeting with somebody else.

When meeting with potential investors, be sure to include in your presentation a discussion about the company's exit strategy for investors. This may include an IPO or a merger or a buyout by another company. The investors will be concerned about your planned exit strategy because that is how they profit from their investment.

If after the meeting the potential investor is still interested in making an investment, he will begin conducting due diligence on the company and begin negotiating the terms of his potential investment. The due diligence review is designed to confirm that the corporation has been properly formed, that it owns the technology that it says it owns, and that all of the necessary contracts and agreements have been entered into.

NEGOTIATING AND STRUCTURING THE INVESTMENT

In each round of financing between the company and its potential investors, the parties will engage in intense negotiations over many topics, including the valuation placed upon the company, the number of shares to be issued by the company, benchmarks for future performance and who will retain corporate control. Obviously, it is in the interest of the founders of the company to sell as little equity as possible in their new venture for as much money as possible. Investors, however, will want as big a percentage of ownership as their investment dollars will buy.

Generally speaking, structuring an investment by an angel investor will be less complex than structuring an investment by a venture capital firm. Angel investors often will accept common stock in exchange for their investment. The common stock will give the angel investor the same rights as the founders, proportional to their share ownership. Keeping the number of angel investors as low as possible will benefit the company because it ensures greater flexibility and makes it easier for the company to work with all of its shareholders.

Structuring an investment by a venture capital firm, however, will be a great deal more complicated. As with angel investors, there will be intense negotiations over the valuation of the company and the percentage of ownership that the venture capitalist will acquire in return for the investment. However, with venture capitalists there are numerous other complex points that must be negotiated. For instance, venture capitalists often will seek convertible preferred stock, rather than common stock, in exchange for their investment. The holders of preferred stock have superior rights over the holders of the common stock. In the event of a liquidation of the company, the preferred stock holders will be paid in full before any of the common stock holders receive any money. In addition, the preferred stock sought by venture capitalists will often contain an accruing dividend of 8%-10% per year. This dividend is not payable unless the company is liquidated or sold or if the preferred stock is redeemed. The accruing dividend is designed to provide the venture capitalists with a minimum level of return on their investment. The dividend is usually waived at the time of the company's IPO and, in the event of an IPO, the preferred stock will be converted into common stock at a predetermined exchange rate.

Venture capitalists will also seek dilution protection. Dilution occurs when stock is sold later at a lower price than the earlier investors paid. While various types of anti-dilution protections are available, they are all designed to insure protection for the venture capitalist's investment in case the company's valuation falls for purposes of future stock sales. Venture capitalists are also likely to seek a seat on the company's board to ensure a basic level of oversight and control of the corporation.

Other protections that will be sought by venture capitalists include restrictions on the payment of dividends and a ban on undisclosed dealings with entities affiliated with the founders. In addition, in exchange for an investment by a venture capitalist, the company will likely have to agree not to incur debt over a certain amount and not to change the size of the board of directors. Finally, it is common for the company also to agree to provide venture capitalists with periodic financial statements and company budgets for review and comment.

If the negotiations proceed and preliminary agreement is reached on the terms of the investment, the venture capitalist will prepare a term sheet and submit it to the company along with a letter of intent. Most of the provisions of the term sheet are intended to be nonbinding, and more formal contracts will be prepared. However, term sheets often contain an exclusivity provision that is intended to be binding. An exclusivity provision requires the company to negotiate exclusively with that particular venture capitalist for a defined period of time, usually thirty to sixty days. The management of the company must ensure that it is beneficial for the company to give up the right to negotiate with other potential investors for that period of time. Typically, time is of the essence in the Internet economy, and any substantial delay in obtaining financing can be detrimental. The company should attempt to limit the exclusivity provision to as short a time period as possible. In addition, the company should bargain for a clause that states that if the venture capitalist breaks off the negotiations, the exclusivity clause will no longer be effective. The management of the company must carefully review the entire term sheet to make sure that it accurately reflects the discussions held. Corporate counsel should also be consulted to ensure that the terms are fair and consistent with industry standards.

If the term sheet is acceptable to the company, legal agreements will then be prepared to facilitate the transaction. Typical documentation for a venture capital investment will include:

> Subscription Agreements, which are also known as Securities Purchase Agreements. The subscription agreements set out the terms of the securities purchase and the rights of the new securities holder. The subscription agreements also contain representations and warranties from the investor and from the company.

> A Voting Agreement that spells out how the founders and the venture capitalist will vote their shares.

> A Registration Rights Agreement, which, in the event of an IPO, will require the company to register with the SEC and the state securities regulators the sale of the investor's shares along with the sale of the shares of the company.

> A Stockholder Agreement that may contain restrictions on transfer of the investor's securities, rights of first refusal, and the right of the investor to participate in future rounds of financing.

> Employee Agreements that set out the duties of the company's managers along with their compensation, bonuses and incentive options. Typically, the employment agreements allow the company to terminate managers on

short notice without cause but subject to certain severance rights and the buy back of the employee's shares. Employment agreements also contain vesting schedules for management's stock and options.

➤ Noncompete and Confidentiality Agreements for the company's management team.

➤ Intellectual Property Assignments documenting that the founders have turned over to the company all of their rights to the relevant intellectual property, which may include patents, copyrights or other valuable trade secrets.

Examples of a stock purchase agreement and a voting agreement are set forth in Appendices 3G and 3H, respectively.

Venture capitalists typically negotiate the right to purchase additional shares of the company in the event that certain milestones are reached or future financing is required. Also, venture capitalists that acquire a majority position in the company frequently will negotiate the right to take control of the board of directors if the company's performance milestones are not met. This allows the venture capitalist to bring in new management if the company fails to grow and develop as anticipated. Alternatively, a venture capitalist with a minority stake likely will require the company to repurchase its shares in the event the milestones are not reached. This provision can be of limited protection, however, since state laws generally forbid a company from repurchasing shares from stockholders if such a repurchase would render the company insolvent.

The terms and contracts involved when a venture capitalist invests can be complex and unfamiliar to new entrepreneurs. It is always wise to have a competent corporate attorney representing the company or its founders in these transactions because terms that are unfamiliar can have significant consequences to the founders' rights in the company. Frequently terms can be negotiated and transactions structured so that the interests of the founders as well as the venture capitalists are protected.

PRIVATE PLACEMENTS BY BROKER-DEALERS

On occasion, a new company that shows growth potential may contract with a registered broker-dealer, who will then conduct a private placement on behalf of the company among several investors. A private placement of securities is a nonpublic offering to a limited number of investors. The terms of a private placement are very similar to the terms of a venture capital investment; however, the shareholders that acquire stock in a private placement sponsored by a broker-dealer generally are not as active as a venture capitalist investor. Rather, the company looks to the broker-dealer itself for business contacts and advice. Typically, the broker-dealer expects to participate in and arrange for future rounds of financing for the company and may also assist in the company's IPO if it is large enough. Companies should always check with the National Association of Securities Dealers, Inc. ("NASD") prior to contracting with any broker-dealer to ensure that there have been no significant regulatory problems with the firm or any of its employees. The NASD's regulation division can be found at www.NASDR.com. This Web site will allow users to make online requests for a firm's disciplinary history. After a request is received, the NASD will provide the requester with a summary of all enforcement actions brought by a federal or state regulator and a description of any customer arbitrations in which the firm has been involved.

PRE-IPO FINANCING IN BAD ECONOMIC TIMES

The ease with which a private company can raise financing depends heavily on the overall condition of the economy as well as the current IPO market. First-time entrepreneurs are often surprised to learn that their ability to raise capital is heavily dependent on the market's current interest in IPOs, even though a private company may be a year or more away from an IPO. When the IPO market is strong, pre-IPO financing is easier to obtain because investors see a clear exit strategy. Sophisticated investors know that the IPO window can close suddenly. This fact will often lead investors to place strong pressure on the company to conduct an IPO as quickly as possible before that window shuts. However, even when the IPO market is active, it is often limited to specific industries. For example, in the late 1990s investors were primarily interested in IPOs of Internet and technology companies. Even established, profitable companies in other industries had a difficult time finding an underwriter for an IPO because of the market's seemingly insatiable demand for Internet and technology stocks.

Because market conditions and industry trends can change quickly, it is important for companies seeking pre-IPO financing to be attuned to current market conditions. Being familiar with the IPO market will provide an advantage to companies in the pre-IPO stage because they can gear their business plan to the interests and requirements of potential investors. A business plan is something that must remain flexible so that it still remains workable, even in tough economic times. For example, it is unrealistic to have a business plan that calls for an IPO within months of obtaining pre-IPO financing if the IPO market is not strong. An investor who sees such a business plan will conclude that the entrepreneurs who put the plan together are not being realistic. Accordingly, a company must ensure that its business plan is viable in the current economy. When economic conditions begin to change from good to bad, companies should plan on raising as much money as possible in each financing round with the understanding that additional rounds of funding may be difficult to close.

If a company is seeking capital in an economy that has been slow for some time, the goal of raising as much capital as possible must be balanced against the likelihood that the company will receive a much lower valuation in bad economic times than in good ones. For practical purposes, a lower valuation will mean the company will have to sell more stock for less money than it would be required to do in good economic times. In fact, bad economic times can affect many of the terms of a venture capital investment. In bad economic times, venture capitalists will push for special rights in exchange for their investment. For example, it is not uncommon for venture capitalists to seek what is called "liquidation preferences" whereby the venture capitalists will get back their entire investment plus unpaid dividends in the event the company goes bankrupt. However, in bad economic times when the likelihood of a bankruptcy is greater, venture capitalists will seek to have liquidation rights that entitle them to receive back two to three times their initial investment in the event the company goes bankrupt. In addition, in bad economic times, a venture capitalist will seek further protection in the event that the company does not meet certain revenue or sales benchmarks. For example, a company that does not meet its benchmark may be required to issue additional shares to the venture capitalist, thereby diluting the founders' shares of the company. Entrepreneurs find these types of special protections to be extremely onerous and unfair because they shift many of the risks away from the venture capitalists and onto the founders. Entrepreneurs believe that venture capitalists are trying to obtain all of the upside potential inherent in being a shareholder of the company without being willing to take the risks associated with a new business.

Entrepreneurs trying to raise money in bad economic times must be aware of these types of provisions. Typically, they are included in the term sheet that the venture capitalist will provide to the company. These special rights will also be contained in the stock purchase agreement and the other legal contracts that are part of a venture capital transaction. Venture capitalists often will be willing to negotiate the terms that were provided in the first term sheet. An entrepreneur and his attorney should feel free to discuss these rights and the applicable provisions at an early stage.

APPENDIX 3A

Internet Co., Inc.
Term Sheet
Series A Round of Preferred Stock

This appendix presents a typical term sheet that a new media company would receive from a venture capital firm. The term sheet serves to memorialize the principal terms of the agreement reached between the new media company and the venture capitalist firm. However, a term sheet is not intended to be binding on either party. The parties will only become bound once the stock purchase agreement is signed. Commentary is provided throughout.

Amount Invested: $10,000,000

> **COMMENTARY:** *This line sets forth the total amount of money that the venture capitalist will be investing in the new media company.*

Investor: RH Venture Capital, L.P.

> **COMMENTARY:** *This line sets forth the full legal name of the entity that will invest in the company.*

Type of Security: Series B Convertible Preferred Stock.

COMMENTARY: *This line describes the securities that will be issued in exchange for the money invested. Typically, a venture capitalist will insist on receiving preferred stock instead of common stock so that in the event the company is liquidated the venture capitalist will receive a return of its capital before any of the common stock holders. It is also common for venture capitalists to negotiate a deal that involves both preferred stock and convertible debt. In a convertible debt deal, the company would be required to pay interest on the debt until such time as the investor converts the debt into stock. A convertible debt deal gives the venture capitalist more protection against a full loss of the investment while preserving the opportunity to convert its investment into equity. When preferred stock has been previously issued to investors, the next round of financing is called Series B, with the first round being Series A.*

Pre-Money Valuation: $10,000,000

COMMENTARY: *The company's pre-money valuation is the value placed upon the company by the venture capitalist prior to its investment in the company. In contrast, the post-money valuation is the value of the company after the venture capitalist invests. The post-money valuation is calculated by adding the pre-money valuation and the amount of the venture capitalist's investment. In this example, the post-money valuation would be $20,000,000. The post-money valuation is also* *used to calculate the percentage of ownership that the venture capitalist will have after making its investment. The ownership interest is calculated by dividing the venture capitalist's investment by the post-money valuation of the company. In this example, the venture capitalist's ownership interest in the company will be 50%.*

Capital Structure Following Series A Round:
Existing holders of Common Stock   40%
Option Pool   10%

COMMENTARY: *The option pool is the amount of stock that must be set aside to fulfill any exercise of outstanding stock options. Options primarily will be granted to employees of the company as a way of attracting talented individuals without having to lay out large amounts of cash. Options also provide employees with an incentive to make the company as successful as possible because as the value of the company increases, so does their stock. The amount of stock that will be required to be set aside will vary depending on how many management-level employees must be hired in the future. A figure of 10% is on the low side of option pools and the option pool can go all the way up to 35%.*

Holders of Series A Preferred Stock   50%
Total   100%

COMMENTARY: *This section summarizes the structure of the company's capitalization after the venture capitalist invests. This is a useful section of the term sheet because it sets forth in a summary manner the different classes of shareholders and any option pool that may be in place. A company's capitalization can be complex and this section ensures that all parties are aware of each class of shareholders.*

Use of Proceeds: The Company shall use the proceeds from this financing to complete development of its Web site, conduct additional marketing research and provide for general working capital purposes, including the payment of salaries and administrative expenses.

COMMENTARY: *The use of proceeds section of a term sheet is a critical section. The venture capitalist will want to know exactly where its money will be spent. Investors will object if an excessive amount of money is going towards executive compensation instead of towards marketing or development of the company's products.*

Anti-Dilution: The terms of the Series A Preferred Stock will contain standard "weighted average" anti-dilution protection with respect to the issuance by the Company of equity securities at a price per share less than the applicable conversion price then in effect. The conversion rate of the Series B Preferred Stock into common stock will be adjusted to take into account any of the following events: stock dividends, stock splits, recapitalizations, mergers and other similar events. Anti-dilution protection shall not be triggered by the issuance of up to 500,000 shares of Common Stock (or options therefor) issued in accordance with the Company's Stock Option Plan.

> **COMMENTARY:** *The concept of dilution is extremely important to understand. Dilution occurs when the company sells stock in the future at prices per share that are lower the earlier investors paid. When that occurs, the earlier investors' shares are considered to be "diluted." In order to protect against dilution, venture capitalists will insist on anti-dilution protection, which will provide for the issuance of additional shares to the venture capitalist in the event that its shares are diluted.*

Shareholder Voting Rights: On any matter submitted for approval by the Company's shareholders, each share of Series B Preferred Stock will be entitled to the number of votes that it would be entitled to if the preferred shares had been converted into shares of Common Stock. Also, without the consent of the holders of the Series B Preferred Stock, the Company is prohibited from engaging in any of the following acts:

a. issuing any series of securities with rights superior to the Series B Preferred Stock.

b. exchanging or reclassifying any stock affecting the Series B Preferred Stock or any recapitalization involving the Company and its subsidiaries taken as a whole.

c. paying any dividends on shares of the Company's stock.

d. redeeming or repurchasing any of the Company's securities, other than from employees of the Company upon termination of their employment pursuant to prior existing agreements validly entered into by the Company.

e. entering into a transaction with management or any member of the board of directors.

f. amending the Company's Certificate of Incorporation or Bylaws in a way or manner that would materially change the rights of the Series B Preferred Stockholders.

g. incurring or guaranteeing any debt or obligation, even if such debt or obligation is within the ordinary course of the Company's business, in excess of $100,000.

h. dissolving, liquidating or filing for Bankruptcy.

i. merging the Company into another corporation or other entity, or selling or otherwise disposing of all or substantially all of the Company's assets.

j. changing the size of the Board of Directors or changing any procedure concerning the designation, nomination or election of the Board of Directors and/or their individual members.

k. changing, amending, or repealing any of the rights, obligations or powers of the Series B Preferred Stock.

l. making an expenditure of more than $100,000 at one time or an aggregate expenditure of $300,000 in any twelve-month period without prior written approval of a majority of the Series B Preferred stockholders.

COMMENTARY: *This section of the term sheet sets forth exactly what voting rights the new investor will acquire. In addition, as a condition of investment, the company often must agree to special restrictions. These restrictions give the venture capitalist veto power over certain corporate actions that would otherwise be within the power of the board of directors or officers of the company.*

Conversion Features: Each share of Series B Preferred Stock shall be convertible, at any time, at the option of the holder, into shares of Common Stock, at a conversion ratio of one share of Common Stock for each share of Series B Preferred Stock. The Series B Preferred Stock is required to be converted to Common Stock upon the date of effectiveness of a registration statement with the SEC regarding an initial public offering of Common Stock of the Company.

COMMENTARY: *When a company issues securities that may be converted into common stock, it is important to define the circumstances under which the conversion may take place and how many shares of common stock will be acquired in the conversion. Often, the conversion ratio is not 1:1.*

Liquidation Preference: The holders of Series B Preferred Stock shall have preference upon liquidation over all holders of Common Stock and over the holders of any other class or series of stock that is junior to the Series A Preferred Stock for an amount equal to the greater of (1) the amount paid for such Series A Preferred Stock plus any declared or accrued but unpaid dividends, and (2) the amount which a holder would have received if the holder's shares of Series B Preferred Stock were converted to Common Stock immediately prior to such liquidation. Thereafter, the holders of Common Stock will be entitled to receive the remaining assets of the Company.

COMMENTARY: *This section of the term sheet details the preferences the holders of preferred stock will receive in the event of a liquidation of the Company. As is set forth in the terms of the paragraph, the holders of the Preferred Stock will be reimbursed in full prior to the time that any money is made available to the common stockholders.*

Board of Directors: The Board of Directors of the Company shall be composed of seven members. Of these seven members, the holders of the Series B Preferred Stock shall have the right to designate two directors and the founders of the Company shall have the right to designate two directors. The remaining directors shall be designated by the four previously designated directors.

COMMENTARY: *When a venture capitalist invests in a company it will often seek representation on the company's board. This will allow the venture capitalist to closely monitor the Company's development and growth. Board representation will also provide the venture capitalist with an early warning of any developing problems in the Company's business.*

Options and Vesting: All stock and options that are owned by the Company's founders, management, and employees will vest over a two-year period. The stock that is currently held by the founders will be considered to be 50% vested as of the closing of this financing, with the balance to vest in equal monthly installments over two years.

> **COMMENTARY:** *Vesting schedules help to ensure that founders, management and employees stay with the company. If an employee leaves prior to the time that his stock is vested, the unvested stock will be given up by the employee and will revert back to the company.*

Registration Rights: At the earlier of five years from the date of the closing of the Series B financing or six months after the Company's initial public offering, the holders of shares of Series A Preferred Stock or shares of Common Stock issued upon conversion thereof shall have the right to demand an "S-1" registration with the SEC with an aggregate offering price in excess of $10,000,000.

The holders of Series A Preferred Stock will also be entitled to "piggyback" registration rights on Company registrations.

The Company will bear all expenses related to all registrations and underwritings.

> **COMMENTARY:** *Because the goal of many companies is to go public, registration rights ensure that the venture capitalist will be able to include its shares in any public offering of securities at the expense of the company. Without registration rights, the company could decide not to include the preferred stock holders in any public offering.*

Covenants: While any Series B Preferred Stock is outstanding, the Company will:

a. maintain adequate property, fire, liability and business insurance;

b. comply with all applicable laws, rules, and regulations;

c. require that all senior employees execute noncompetition and nondisclosure agreements with the Company; and

d. require that agreements concerning the assignment be in place with all senior officers and founders of the Company.

Financial Statements and Other Reports: The Company will provide all budgets, internal management documents, reports of operations, reports of adverse developments, communications with shareholders or directors, press releases and registration statements. In addition, the Company will provide the holders of Series A Preferred Stock with unaudited quarterly and audited yearly financial statements.

Right of First Refusal: Holders of Series B Preferred Stock shall have a *pro rata* right, based on their percentage of fully diluted equity interest in the Company, with an undersubscription right up to the total number of shares being offered, to participate in subsequent stock issuances.

> **COMMENTARY:** *This Paragraph provides that in the event the company engages in future rounds of financing, the investors in the Series B offering of preferred stock shall be permitted to participate in any new rounds of financing on a pro rata basis.*

Payment of Expenses: The Company will reimburse the holders of Series B Preferred Stock for reasonable legal fees in connection with the transaction, payable at closing and only in the event that the transactions contemplated by this term sheet are consummated, up to a limit of $20,000.

> **COMMENTARY:** *Any time the company is agreeing to pay or reimburse expenses it is very important to have an upper limit on such expenses. This will prevent the company from being presented with unexpectedly large bills. A clause requiring the reimbursement of legal expenses is something that the company should try to eliminate from a term sheet. Only an investor with a strong bargaining position can negotiate this type of clause.*

INTERNET CO., INC.   RH Ventures, LP

By: _____   By:_____
          Title   Title

Appendix 3B

Subscription Agreement
for Internet Co., Inc.
Regulation D Offering

Persons interested in purchasing shares of Internet Co., Inc. (the "Company" or "Issuer") must complete and return this Subscription Agreement and associated documents along with their check or money order or wire transfer funds (see Wiring Instructions set forth below) to:

> Internet Co., Inc.
> Attn: John Smith
> 488 Madison Avenue
> New York, NY 10022

Subject only to acceptance hereof by the Issuer in its discretion, the undersigned hereby subscribes for the number of shares at the aggregate subscription price set forth below.

An accepted copy of this Agreement will be returned to the Subscriber as a receipt and the executed stock certificates shall be delivered to each Investor within thirty (30) days of the close of this Offering, The shares being offered hereto are offered in reliance upon an exemption from registration with the Securities and Exchange Commission (SEC). Accordingly, this offer has not been reviewed by the SEC or most State Securities Boards, nor has any such agency made any finding or determination as to the fairness of investments in the Common Shares.

Securities Offered—The Company is offering 500 shares of common stock at $10,000 per share. This Subscription is one of a number of such subscriptions offered to a limited number of sophisticated investors.

Minimum Subscription—In connection with this subscription, the undersigned hereby subscribes to the number of shares shown in the following table.

Number of Shares = _____

Multiply by Price Per Share   X $ 10 Per Share

Aggregate Subscription Price = _____

Payment shall be made by check or money order payable to Internet Co., Inc., or by following the wiring instructions below.

Wiring Instructions:

> Bank Name:
> Main Address:
> Branch Address:
> Transit/Routing Number:
> Account Number:

1. ***Representations and Warranties.*** In connection with this investment in the Company, the Investor represents and warrants as follows:

   a. The Issuer and the other purchasers are relying on the truth and accuracy of the declarations, representations and warranties herein made by the undersigned. Accordingly, the foregoing representations and warranties and undertakings are made by the undersigned with the intent that they may be relied upon in determining his/her suitability as a purchaser. Investor agrees that such representations and warranties shall survive the acceptance of Investor as a purchaser. Investor indemnifies and agrees to hold harmless the Issuer and each other purchaser from and against all damages, claims, expenses, losses or actions resulting if any of the warranties and representations contained in this Subscription Agreement are untrue.

b.   The Investor represents, warrants and covenants that he is a natural person twenty-one (21) years of age or older and that (i) his adjusted gross income was at least $200,000, or joint income with spouse in excess of $300,000, annually for the previous two years, and he reasonably expects to have adjusted gross income of the same level in the current taxable year; or (ii) he has a net worth of at least $1,000,000 (excluding home, furniture and personal automobiles) (if a corporation, on a consolidated basis according to the corporation's most recent audited financial statements); (iii) he is acquiring the common stock for his own account, for investment only, and not with a view toward the resale, transfer or further distribution thereof; (iv) any sale or other disposition of this stock will not be made without registration or other compliance with the requirements of the Securities Act of 1933 and the rules and regulations thereunder, and any applicable state securities or blue sky laws; (v) notwithstanding anything contained herein to the contrary, the Investor will not sell or otherwise dispose of his stock, except by operation of law, after the date on which the Company accepts the Investor's subscription offer; and (vi) by signing this document he acknowledges that he has received, read and understood the memorandum and the exhibits thereto, that he is familiar with their contents and that all questions directed to the Company have been answered to his satisfaction and all requests for information directed to the Company have been fulfilled.

c. Prior to tendering payment for the shares, the Investor received a copy of and read the Company's Confidential Private Offering Memorandum dated October 29, 2001.

d. The Investor acknowledges that the stock certificates to be issued will bear the legend:

"THE SECURITIES REPRESENTED BY THIS CERTIFICATE WERE ACQUIRED FOR INVESTMENT ONLY AND NOT FOR RESALE. THEY HAVE NOT BEEN REGISTERED UNDER THE SECURITIES ACT OF 1933, AS AMENDED, OR ANY STATE SECURITIES LAW. THESE SECURITIES MAY NOT BE SOLD, TRANSFERRED, PLEDGED, HYPOTHECATED OR OTHERWISE DISPOSED OF UNLESS FIRST REGISTERED UNDER SUCH LAWS, OR UNLESS THE COMPANY HAS RECEIVED EVIDENCE REASONABLY SATISFACTORY TO IT, OR AN OPINION OF COUNSEL ACCEPTABLE TO THE COMPANY, INDICATING THAT REGISTRATION UNDER SUCH LAWS IS NOT REQUIRED."

e. The Investor represents that he is acquiring the securities for his own investment and is aware of the applicable restrictions imposed upon the transferability and resale of the securities.

2. **Responsibility.** The Company will exercise its best judgment in the conduct of all matters arising out of or under this Agreement and will not be liable to the Investor for any loss or damage which may occur despite the good faith exercise of its best judgment.

3. **Miscellaneous.**

a. This Subscription Agreement will be governed by and construed in accordance with the Laws of the State of New

York without giving effect to the conflicts of law provisions thereof.

b. This Subscription Agreement contains the entire agreement between the parties. The provisions of this Agreement may not be modified or waived except in writing signed by the parties hereto.

c. The headings of this Agreement are for convenience or reference only and they shall not limit or otherwise affect the interpretation of any term or provision hereof.

d. This Subscription Agreement and the rights, powers and duties set forth herein shall, except as set forth herein, bind and inure to the benefit of the heirs, executors, administrators, legal representatives, successors and assigns of the parties hereto.

e. The Investor may not assign any of his rights or interest in and under this Subscription Agreement without prior written consent of the Company, and any attempted assignment without such consent shall be void and without effect.

f. The Investor and his spouse or co-subscriber, if any, is (are) resident(s) or citizen(s) of the United States for United States federal income tax purposes, or if the Investor or his spouse or co-subscriber, if any, is (are) not resident(s) or citizen(s) of the United States for federal income tax purposes, the Investor will furnish a form W-8 properly filled out and executed.

Please register the share(s) that I am purchasing as follows:

Name: _____ Date: _____

As (check one)

❑ Individual ❑ Tenants by the Entirety (for spouses)
❑ Tenants in Common ❑ Joint Tenants ❑ Existing Partnership
❑ Corporation ❑ Trust
❑ Minor with adult custodian under the Uniform Gift to Minors Act

For the person(s) who will be the registered investor(s):

_____

Signature of Subscriber

_____

Residence Address

_____

Name of Subscriber (Printed)

_____

City or Town

_____

Signature of Co-Subscriber

_____

State Zip Code

_____

Name of Co-Subscriber (Printed)

_____

Telephone Number

_____

Subscriber Tax I.D. or Co-Subscriber Tax I.D. or Social Security Number

_____

E-mail Address, if available

ACKNOWLEDGEMENT FOR
INDIVIDUALS

STATE OF   )

                                         :ss.:

COUNTY OF   )

On _____, before me personally came _____, to me known and known to me to be the individual described herein, and he executed the foregoing Subscription Agreement.

_____
Notary Public

ACKNOWLEDGEMENT FOR
CORPORATIONS

STATE OF   )

                                         :ss.:

COUNTY OF   )

On _____ before me personally came _____ to me known, who, being by me duly sworn, did depose and say that he is a _____ (title) of _____ (Name of Corporation) and that he executed this Subscription Agreement, and that he has full and complete authority to execute this Subscription Agreement in the name of and on behalf of _____. (Name of Corporation)

_____
Notary Public

ACCEPTED BY:

Internet Co., Inc.

By: _____   Date: _____

        Officer

ALL INFORMATION WILL BE TREATED CONFIDENTIALLY

APPENDIX 3C

Investor Qualifications

Investment in the common stock of Internet Co., Inc. involves a high degree of risk and is suitable only for persons of adequate means who have no need for liquidity with respect to this investment and who can afford the risk of a complete loss of their investment.

Subscriptions will be accepted from "Accredited Investors," as the term is defined in Regulation D ("Regulation D") promulgated under the Securities Act of 1933, as amended (the "Act"). Accredited investors are those who, at the time of sale of the shares, fall within certain categories enumerated in Rule 501(a) of Regulation D, including any of the following:

i.   any individual who had an individual income in excess of $200,000 (or joint income with his or her spouse in excess of $300,000) in the last two years and who reasonably expects an individual income in excess of $200,000 (or such joint income in excess of $300,000) in the current year (for purposes of this offering, individual and joint income shall equal adjusted gross income, as reported in the investor's federal tax return (less for individual income only, any income attributed to a spouse or to property owned by a spouse) and increased by the following amounts (but not, for individual income only, any amounts attributed to a spouse or to property owned by a spouse): (1) the amount of any tax-exempt interest received, (2) the amount of losses claimed as a limited partner in a limited partnership, (3) any deduction claimed for depletion, (4) amounts contributed to an IRA or Keogh plan, (5) alimony paid, and (6) any amount by which income from long-term capital gains has been reduced in arriving at adjusted gross income pursuant to the provisions of Section 1202 of the Internal Revenue Code);

ii.   any individual whose individual net worth, or joint net worth with that individual's spouse, exceeds $1,000,000 (including the value of home, home furnishings and automobiles);

iii. any trust, with total assets in excess of $5,000,000, not formed for the specific purpose of acquiring the securities offered, whose purchase is directed by a "sophisticated person" as that term is defined in SEC Rule 506(b)(2)(ii); and

iv.   any entity in which all of the equity owners are accredited investors.

Each investor must also make certain representations to the general effect that such investor:

i.   does not have an overall commitment to investments that are not readily marketable that is disproportionate to his/her net worth, and that his/her investment in the shares will not cause such overall commitment to become excessive;

ii.   has adequate net worth and means of providing for his/her current needs and personal contingencies to sustain a complete loss of his/her investment in the Company at the time of investment, and has no need for liquidity in his/her investment in the shares;

iii. is acquiring shares for his/her own account, for investment only and not with a view toward resale or distribution; and

iv. is aware that he/she will not be able to liquidate his/her investment in the event of an emergency or for any other reason because the transferability of shares will be subject to restrictions in the Subscription Agreement and will be affected by restrictions on resale imposed by the Act and the securities laws of certain states.

In addition, an investment in the shares must not exceed ten percent (10%) of an investor's net worth. The Company reserves the right to accept subscriptions from subscribers who do not meet all of the above suitability standards but who are otherwise qualified to purchase the shares.

I QUALIFY AS AN ACCREDITED INVESTOR UNDER THE ABOVE DEFINITION UNDER REGULATION D, RULE 501 AS DEFINED IN PARAGRAPH _____.

SIGNED BY:_____ Date: _____

APPENDIX 3D

Purchaser Questionnaire

I understand that it is contemplated that the shares to be offered by Internet Co., Inc. (the "Company") will not be registered under the Securities Act of 1933, as amended, (the "Act"). I also understand that in order to assure that the offering will be exempt from registration under the Act, you are required to have reasonable grounds to believe, and must actually believe, prior to making a sale that each prospective investor (1) is able to evaluate the merits and risks of the investment in the corporate Shares, or (2) is represented by a purchaser representative who is able to evaluate the merits and risks of the investment. In order to obtain facts needed to determine that a person is a qualified offeree, it is necessary for me to complete this questionnaire.

I make the following representations with the intent that they may be relied upon by the Company or Placement Agent in determining my suitability as an investor in the Shares:

1. Potential Investor's Name:

   _____

   Age: _____

   Co-Owner's Name, if any: _____

   Age of Co-Owner: _____

2. Residence Address:

   _____

   How long at that address: _____

3. Business Address: _____

   _____

4. Telephone Number: _____

5. Occupation: _____

6. a. Current Employment and Position Held:

   _____

   b. Approximate Annual Income: specify salary(s), investment
      income or other income:

   _____

7. Educational Background:

   _____

   Degree: _____

8. I prefer to have correspondence sent to: _____

   _____

   _____

9. I represent that I, as an individual, fall within one of the
   following classifications (check one):

   ❑ a. My net worth is at least $1,000,000 (excluding home,
        furniture and personal automobiles) (if a corporation, on
        a consolidated basis according to its most recent audited
        financial statements); or

❑ b. My adjusted gross income was at least $200,000, or joint income with my spouse was in excess of $300,000 annually for the previous two years and I had during the most recent tax year, or estimate that I will have during the current tax year, "taxable income" (as defined by Section 63 of the Internal Revenue Code of 1954, as amended) of at least the same amount. (If a partnership, each partner satisfies either classification (a) or (b) above.)

❑ c. If a trust, the TRUST has total assets in excess of $5,000,000; the TRUST was not formed for the specific purpose of acquiring the shares; and the purchase by the TRUST is directed by a person who has such knowledge and experience in financial and business matters that he/she is capable of evaluating the merits and risks of an investment in the shares. The grantor of the TRUST may revoke the TRUST at any time; the grantor retains sole investment control over the assets of the trust and the grantor is a natural person who has initialed (a) or (b) aforesaid of this Section 9 and

A TRUST MUST ATTACH A COPY OF ITS DECLARATION OF TRUST OR OTHER GOVERNING INSTRUMENT, AS AMENDED, AS WELL AS ALL OTHER DOCUMENTS THAT AUTHORIZE THE TRUST TO INVEST IN THE SHARES. ALL DOCUMENTATION MUST BE COMPLETE AND CORRECT.

❑ d. If a partnership, the PARTNERSHIP has total assets in excess of $5,000,000; the PARTNERSHIP was not formed for the specific purpose of acquiring the shares; and the purchase by the PARTNERSHIP is directed by a person who has such knowledge and experience in financial and business matters that he/she is capable of evaluating the merits and risks of an investment in the shares. Each of the partners of the PARTNERSHIP is a natural person who is able to certify that he/she can comply with (a) or (b) aforesaid of this Section 9 and

IF THE PARTNERSHIP CANNOT COMPLY WITH THE REQUIREMENT THAT IT HAS TOTAL ASSETS IN EXCESS OF $5,000,000, YOU MUST PROVIDE A LETTER SIGNED BY A GENERAL PARTNER OF THE UNDERSIGNED PARTNERSHIP LISTING THE NAME OF EACH PARTNER (WHETHER A GENERAL OR LIMITED PARTNER) AND THE REASON SUCH PARTNER QUALIFIES AS AN ACCREDITED INVESTOR (ON THE BASIS OF NET WORTH, INDIVIDUAL INCOME OR JOINT INCOME), OR EACH PARTNER MUST PROVIDE A COMPLETED INDIVIDUAL INVESTOR QUESTIONNAIRE.

❑ e. If a corporation, the CORPORATION has total assets in excess of $5,000,000; the CORPORATION was not formed for the specific purpose of acquiring the shares; and the purchase by the CORPORATION is directed by a person who has such knowledge and experience in financial and business matters that he/she is capable of evaluating the merits and risks of an investment in the shares. Each of the shareholders of the CORPORATION is a natural person who is able to certify that he/she can comply with (a) or (b) aforesaid of this Section 9 and

IF THE CORPORATION CANNOT COMPLY WITH THE REQUIREMENT THAT IT HAS TOTAL ASSETS IN EXCESS OF $5,000,000, YOU MUST PROVIDE A LETTER SIGNED BY A OFFICER OF THE UNDERSIGNED CORPORATION LISTING THE NAME OF EACH SHAREHOLDER AND THE REASON SUCH SHAREHOLDER QUALIFIES AS AN ACCREDITED INVESTOR (ON THE BASIS OF NET WORTH, INDIVIDUAL INCOME OR JOINT INCOME), OR EACH SHAREHOLDER MUST PROVIDE A COMPLETED INDIVIDUAL INVESTOR QUESTIONNAIRE.

❑ f. If a retirement plan, the RETIREMENT PLAN certifies:

❑   (I)   it is an employee benefit plan within the meaning of the Employee Retirement Income Security Act of 1974 (ERISA); or

❑   (II)   The investment decisions are made by a plan fiduciary as defined in Section 3(21) of ERISA and (i) is either a bank, insurance company or registered investment advisor or (ii) is a savings and loan association or (iii) the RETIREMENT PLAN has total assets in excess of $5,000,000; or

❑   (III)   The RETIREMENT PLAN is self-directed, with investment decisions made solely by persons each of whom is a natural person who is able to certify that he/she can comply with (a) or (b) aforesaid of this Section 9 and

IF THE ABOVE (f)(I) OR (f)(II) IS NOT INITIALED, YOU MUST PROVIDE A LETTER SIGNED BY A PERSON DULY AUTHORIZED BY THE RETIREMENT PLAN LISTING, AS APPLICABLE (1) THE NAMES OF THE PERSONS (OR ENTITIES) MAKING THE INVESTMENT DECISIONS, OR (2) THE NAMES OF ALL OF THE PARTICIPANTS IN THE PLAN AND THE REASON OR STATEMENT SUCH PERSON (OR ENTITY) QUALIFIES AS AN ACCREDITED INVESTOR (ON THE BASIS OF NET WORTH, INDIVIDUAL INCOME, JOINT INCOME OR OTHERWISE), OR EACH SUCH PERSON (OR ENTITY) MUST COMPLETE THE APPROPRIATE QUESTIONNAIRE.

ALL DOCUMENTS GOVERNING THE PLAN AS WELL AS ALL OTHER DOCUMENTS AUTHORIZING THE RETIREMENT PLAN TO INVEST IN THE SHARES MUST BE ATTACHED TO THE RETIREMENT PLAN. INCLUDE, AS NECESSARY, DOCUMENTS DEFINING PERMITTED INVESTMENTS BY THE RETIREMENT PLAN AND DOCUMENTS DEMONSTRATING AUTHORITY OF

THE SIGNING INDIVIDUAL TO ACT ON BEHALF OF THE PLAN. ALL DOCUMENTATION MUST BE COMPLETE AND CORRECT.

10. _____ (Please Initial) Considering the foregoing and all other factors in my financial and personal circumstances (including, but not limited to, health problems, unusual family responsibilities, and requirements for current income), I am able to bear the economic risk of an investment in such Shares, including a loss of my entire investment, and have no need in the foreseeable future for liquidity in an investment in such Shares.

11. _____ (Please Initial) If I decide to purchase Shares, I will do so for investment purposes only and with no present intention, agreement, or arrangement for the distribution, transfer, assignment, resale, subdivision, or hypothecation thereof. And I understand that, in any event, such interest will in all likelihood be subject to restrictions against transferability thereof.

12. _____ (Please Initial) I have, either myself or together with my advisor, sufficient knowledge and experience in financial, business and tax matters, to be capable of evaluating the risks and merits of an investment in the business outlined in this Offering Document.

13. Check one of the following:

   ❑ a. I intend to rely solely on my own knowledge and experience in making an investment decision as to whether to invest in any Shares.

   ❑ b. I intend to rely solely on my advisors in reaching such an investment decision.

   ❑ c. I intend to rely on a combination of my own knowledge, judgment and experience and the knowledge, judgment and experience of my advisors.

14. Investment Experience of Purchaser:

Have you ever invested in:

Stocks: ❏ Yes ❏ No Bonds: ❏ Yes ❏ No

Initial Public Offerings: ❏ Yes ❏ No

Private Placements: ❏ Yes ❏ No

The frequency with which you invest in marketable securities is:

❏ often ❏ occasionally ❏ never

The frequency with which you invest in unmarketable securities is:

❏ often ❏ occasionally ❏ never

15. a. You (Check one)

❏ have ❏ have not elected anyone to serve as your Purchaser Representative to assist or advise you in connection with evaluating the risks and merits of a prospective investment.

b. If you have elected a Purchaser Representative, please provide the name, address and qualifications of each person so designated on the Purchaser Representative Statement.

All of the foregoing answers that I have provided to the questions above are true, correct and complete to the best of my knowledge.

_____

Name (Please Print)

_____ Date _____

Signature of Investor

APPENDIX 3E

Purchaser Representative Statement

Offering: Internet Co., Inc.
488 Madison Avenue
New York, N.Y. 10022

Name of Purchaser Being Represented: _____

The undersigned Purchaser Representative hereby acknowledges, represents and warrants to the Company that he has been retained by the above-named Purchaser to act as such person's purchaser representative and that he qualifies as such under Paragraph (h) of Rule 506 under the Securities Act of 1933, as amended (the "Act"). By reason of the knowledge and experience of the undersigned in business and financial matters in general, and investments in the same type of security or issuer as the securities of the Company in particular, the undersigned is capable of evaluating and has, in fact, evaluated an investment in the securities on behalf of the above-named prospective purchaser.

The undersigned further acknowledges that he has received a copy of the Private Placement Memorandum, and all exhibits thereto setting forth information relating to the Company and the Shares, as well as any other information that he deems necessary or appropriate to evaluate the merits and risks of this investment. The undersigned further acknowledges that he has had the opportunity to ask questions of, and to receive answers from, representatives of the Company concerning the terms and conditions of the offering and the information in the Private Placement Memorandum.

The undersigned further acknowledges, represents and warrants that he has disclosed in writing to the above-named offeree, in accordance with the requirements of Rule 506, details regarding material relationships, if any, between him and his affiliates and the Company and its affiliates. A copy of such written disclosure, if any, is attached hereto and incorporated by reference herein.

To the best knowledge of the undersigned, all of the statements made by the above-named offeree in the foregoing Statement of Potential Investor Suitability are true, complete and accurate. The undersigned represents and warrants to the Company that the information contained in this Purchaser Representative Statement is true, complete and correct.

I make the following representations with the intent that they may be relied on by the Offering and its Company in determining my suitability as a Purchaser Representative to any potential investor in an offering of a type similar to this Offering.

1. Name, Address and Occupation of Purchaser Representative:

   _____

   _____

   _____

2. Are you an affiliate, director, officer, employee of the Offering Company or any affiliates thereof?

   _____

   _____

3. If the Answer to No. 2 is yes, what is the relationship?

   _____

4. I have, either myself or together with my client, sufficient knowledge and experience in financial, business, and tax matters to be capable of evaluating the risks and merits of an investment in Private Placements and making an informed investment decision with respect thereto.

5. Current employment and position held:

   _____

6. Educational Background:

   _____

   _____

   Degree(s) (if any): _____

7. Area of experience (e.g., legal matters, tax matters, real estate, research and development, oil and gas or geothermal energy drilling programs, financial or business consultant, etc.):

   _____

   _____

8. Describe any and all material relationships that now exist, which have existed over the past two years or are contemplated in the future between yourself (or your affiliates) and the Offering Company (or its affiliates).

   _____

   _____

If none, so state:

_____

_____

9. The undersigned has received $ _____ from the issuer or its affiliates within the past two (2) years as a result of such relationships.

_____

Name (Please Print)

_____

Signature of Purchase Representative

APPENDIX 3F

Suitability and Representation Letter

Internet Co., Inc.
488 Madison Avenue
New York, NY 10022

TO WHOM IT MAY CONCERN:

The undersigned is furnishing the following information to enable you to determine whether you may make offers and sales to me of shares in Internet Co., Inc. Private Offering dated October 30, 2001 (the "Offering") without registration of the shares under the Securities Act of 1933, as amended (the "Securities Act"). The undersigned understands that his/her questionnaire does not constitute an offer to sell or an offer to purchase the Interests or any other securities.

The undersigned represents that the information set forth in this letter is complete and accurate and that the undersigned will notify you immediately of any change in any of the information occurring prior to the closing of the sale of the shares. The undersigned specifically represents the follows:

1. The undersigned has received and reviewed a copy of the Offering Circular dated October 30, 2001.

❑ Yes   ❑ No

2. The undersigned knows that no federal or state agency has made any findings or determination as to the fairness for public or private investment in the shares nor any recommendation or endorsements of the shares as an investment.

❏ Yes   ❏ No

3. The undersigned has a net worth of at least $1,000,000 and expects to have during the current tax year "gross income," as defined in Section 61 of the Internal Revenue Code of 1986, as amended ("the Code"), of at least three times the amount of the proposed subscription price of the shares, and the proposed subscription price of the shares does not exceed 10% of his/her net worth.

❏ Yes   ❏ No

4. The undersigned recognizes the speculative nature and risks of loss associated with a developmental stage company.

❏ Yes   ❏ No

5. The undersigned's financial situation enables the undersigned to bear the risks of the total loss of said investment and the shares constitute an investment suitable and consistent with the undersigned's investment program.

❏ Yes   ❏ No

6. The undersigned recognizes that no assurance exists that the Congress, the Internal Revenue Service (the "IRS"), or the courts will not change, amend or interpret the Code and the regulations promulgated under the Code to reduce or defer certain tax benefits of investment in the shares.

❏ Yes   ❏ No

7. The undersigned knows that no public market exists for the shares and that the undersigned may not have the ability to liquidate his/her investment readily.

❑ Yes   ❑ No

8. The undersigned, in making the decision to purchase the shares, has relied on an independent investigation made by the undersigned and/or the undersigned's Purchaser Representative and the undersigned (alone or together with the Purchaser Representative) has had the opportunity to examine all documents; to ask all questions and receive answers from the Company; and to obtain any additional information, to the extent the Company possess the information or could acquire it without reasonable effort or expense, necessary to verify the accuracy of the information set forth in the Offering Memorandum.

❑ Yes   ❑ No

9. The undersigned has not received and has not relied upon any representations concerning the Offering, its business or prospects, or any other matters, except as set forth in the Offering Memorandum or given in response to questions raised by the undersigned or undersigned's Purchaser Representative.

❑ Yes   ❑ No

10. The undersigned is acquiring the shares solely for his/her own account for investment purposes only and not with a view towards their distribution within the meaning of the Securities Act. The undersigned has no agreement or other arrangement, formal or informal, with any person to sell, transfer or pledge any part of the shares or which guarantees the undersigned any profit or indemnifies the undersigned for any loss, with

respect to the shares. The undersigned has no plans to enter into any agreement or arrangement of that nature. The undersigned understands that the he/she must bear the economic risk of the investment for an indefinite period of time because the undersigned cannot sell or otherwise transfer the shares in the absence of compliance with the registration provisions of all applicable securities acts. In addition, the undersigned understands that the Company has no obligation to register the shares under the Securities Act of 1933.

❑ Yes   ❑ No

(Please Complete 11 (a) or 11 (b).)

11. (a) The undersigned has not designated a Purchaser Representative. The undersigned has had sufficient opportunity to make inquiries of the Company, and its officers in order to supplement information contained in the Offering Memorandum respecting the offering. The Company has made all information requested available to the undersigned's satisfaction, and the undersigned has had the opportunity to verify the information. The undersigned has knowledge and experience in business and financial matters with respect to investments generally and, in particular, investments generally comparable to the offering enabling the undersigned to utilize the information to evaluate the risks and merits of the investment and to make an informed investment decision.

❑ Yes   ❑ No

11. (b) The undersigned has designated _____
to act as Purchaser Representative for the undersigned in connection with the purchase of the shares. The undersigned has discussed the investment fully and

completely with the Purchaser Representative and has had all inquiries answered to his/her satisfaction.

❑ Yes   ❑ No

(If the undersigned designates a Purchaser Representative, the Purchaser Representative must complete and deliver to the undersigned and to the Company a disclosure and acknowledgment form attached hereto as Exhibit 1.)

The undersigned has read, acknowledged and answered Paragraphs 1-11.

_____   _____

Signed   Date

APPENDIX 3G

Internet Co., Inc.
Preferred Stock Purchase Agreement

(Date)

COMMENTARY: *This agreement will only be used with sophisticated investors who are making a substantial investment in a new media company. It generally will not be used for the initial angel round of financing and it is generally prepared by a venture capital fund. Venture capital funds will often insist on receiving preferred stock instead of common stock in the company. In the event of a liquidation, all of the preferred stockholders of the company would be repaid in full before any of the common stockholders. In addition, the venture capitalist fund may also receive dividend rights that are superior to the common stockholders.*

This Preferred Stock Purchase Agreement (the "Agreement") is made and entered into as of the ___ day of _____, 2001 by and between Internet Co., Inc., a Delaware corporation (the "Company") and the investors listed on the exhibit to this Agreement (each a "Purchaser" and together the "Purchasers").

Recitals

WHEREAS, the Company desires to secure additional working capital in order to enable it to carry out its business plan and develop and expand its facilities; and

WHEREAS, the Purchasers are prepared to furnish the additional working capital upon the terms of this Agreement;

> **COMMENTARY:** *Although recitals are not part of the formal contract, they do orient the reader to the general nature of the terms of the agreement. Recitals should be kept short and simple to avoid the possibility of a contradiction occurring between a recital and a term in the contract.*

NOW, THEREFORE, the parties hereby agree as follows:

1. *Purchase and Sale of Preferred Stock.*

    1.1 *Sale and Issuance of Preferred Stock.* Subject to the terms and conditions of this Agreement, the Purchasers agree to purchase at the Closing, and the Company agrees to sell and issue to each Purchaser at the Closing, that number of shares of Preferred Stock (the "Stock") that is set forth opposite each Purchaser's name on the addendum attached hereto. The purchase price for the Stock is $2.00 per share.

> **COMMENTARY:** *This paragraph is the essence of the agreement—the Company agrees to issue and sell the preferred stock and the purchasers agree to buy the stock*

at an agreed-upon price. The price in a stock purchase agreement should always be given in a per share amount so that the money due from each purchaser can be easily calculated. This will simplify the mathematical calculations at the closing if the purchasers are buying different amounts of preferred stock.

1.2 *Closing; Delivery.*

a. The purchase and sale of the Stock shall take place at the offices of Meyers & Heim LLP, 488 Madison Avenue, New York, New York, at 10:00 A.M., on _____, or at such other time and place as the Company and the Purchasers mutually agree upon (the "Closing"). Prior to the Closing, the stockholders and directors of the Company shall have approved the actions of the Company's board in entering this Agreement and shall have consented to the issuance of the Stock as set forth in this Agreement.

COMMENTARY: *The closing usually takes place at the office of the Company's lawyer, especially when there are a number of purchasers buying stock at once. The closing should be set far enough in advance to allow the purchasers time to make arrangements to have money available to send to the Company.*

b. At the Closing, once the Purchasers have tendered payment for the Stock, the Company shall deliver to each Purchaser a certificate representing the Stock being purchased. The Purchasers must pay for the

Stock either by check payable to the Company or by wire transfer to the Company's bank account.

c. If the full number of authorized shares of the Stock are not sold at the Closing, the Company shall have the right, at any time prior to _____, to sell the remaining authorized but unissued shares of the Stock to one or more additional purchasers as determined by the Board of Directors or to any Purchaser hereunder who wishes to acquire additional shares of Series B Preferred Stock at the price and on the terms set forth herein. Any additional purchaser so acquiring shares of Series B Preferred Stock shall be considered a "Purchaser" for purposes of this Agreement, and any Series B Preferred Stock so acquired by such additional purchaser shall be considered "Stock" for purposes of this Agreement and all other agreements contemplated hereby.

COMMENTARY: *This paragraph confirms that if the Purchasers do not acquire all of the stock being issued by the Company, the Company can locate additional purchasers after the closing and such purchasers will acquire the stock under the terms and conditions set forth in the Agreement.*

2. ***Representations and Warranties of the Company.*** The Company hereby represents and warrants to each Purchaser that:

COMMENTARY: *The representations and warranties contained in a stock purchase agreement are extremely important and they are heavily negotiated between the Company and the Purchasers. As a general matter, the*

> *Company will desire to make as few representations as possible while the Purchasers will want the Company to make numerous broad representations, particularly about its financial condition and potential liabilities. If a representation is false when made, or a contractual warranty is breached, legal liability will result. Therefore, the Company must make certain that every representation is 100% accurate and every warranty can be carried out. In stock purchase agreements, the Company makes far more representations and warranties than the Purchaser does.*

2.1 *Organization, Good Standing and Qualification.* The Company is a corporation duly organized, validly existing and in good standing under the laws of the State of Delaware, and has the corporate power and authority to own its properties and carry on its business as is now conducted or proposed to be conducted. The Company is duly qualified to transact business and is in good standing in each jurisdiction in which the failure to so qualify would have a material adverse effect on its business or properties.

2.2 *Capitalization.* The authorized capital of the Company consists of, or will consist of, immediately prior to the Closing:

a. Five million (5,000,000) shares of Preferred Stock.

b. Twenty-five million (25,000,000) shares of Common Stock, 6,000,000 shares of which are issued and outstanding immediately prior to the Closing.

c. All of the outstanding shares of Common Stock and Preferred Stock have been duly authorized and fully paid, and are nonassessable and validly issued in compliance with all applicable federal and state securities laws.

d. Except for outstanding options issued pursuant to the Stock Plan, there are no outstanding options, warrants, rights (including conversion or preemptive rights and rights of first refusal or similar rights) or agreements, contingent or otherwise, orally or in writing, for the purchase or acquisition from the Company of any of its material assets or shares of capital stock or securities convertible into or exercisable for its capital stock. There is no commitment by the Company to issue shares, subscriptions, warrants, options, convertible securities or other such rights or to distribute to holders of any of its equity securities any evidence of indebtedness or assets.

2.3 *Authorization.* All corporate action on the part of the Company, its officers, directors and stockholders necessary for the authorization, execution and delivery of this Agreement, and all other agreements executed in connection with the transaction contemplated herein, the performance of all obligations of the Company hereunder and the authorization, issuance and delivery of the Stock and the Common Stock issuable upon conversion of the Stock (together, the "Securities") has been taken or will be taken prior to the Closing, and the Agreements, when executed and delivered by the Company, shall constitute valid and legally binding obligations of the Company.

2.4 *Litigation.* There is no (a) action, suit, claim, proceeding or investigation pending or, to the Company's knowledge after due inquiry, currently threatened against the Company, its properties or assets or any of the Company's officers or directors in their capacity as such that questions the validity of the Agreements or the right of the Company to enter into them, or to consummate the transactions contemplated hereby or thereby, or affects the Company or any of its assets or its properties, at law or in equity, or before any federal, state, municipal or other governmental department, commission, board, bureau, agency or instrumentality, foreign or domestic; or (b) governmental inquiry pending or, to the Company's knowledge after due inquiry, threatened against or specifically affecting the Company (including any inquiry as to the qualification of the Company to hold or receive any license or permit), that could have a material effect on the business of the Company or its financial condition. The Company is not aware that there is any basis for the foregoing. There is no action, suit, proceeding or investigation by the Company currently pending or which the Company intends to initiate. The Company is not in default on any order, judgment or decree of any court or administrative agency.

2.5 *Intellectual Property.* The Company has sufficient title and ownership or license rights to all copyrights, trade secrets, licenses, information, proprietary rights, customer lists, know how and processes and, to the Company's knowledge, all patents, patent applications, trademarks, trademark applications, service marks, service mark applications and trade names (collectively, "Intellectual Property") necessary for its business without any conflict with, or infringement upon, the rights of others. All registered patents, copyrights, trademarks, and service marks held by the Company are in full force and effect and are not subject to any unpaid taxes or maintenance fees. No claim is pending or threatened to the effect that any Intellectual Property owned or licensed by the Company, or which the Company otherwise has the right to use, is invalid or unenforceable by the Company, and to the Company's knowledge there is no basis for such claim.

2.6 *Disclosure.* The Company has fully provided the Purchasers with all the information that the Purchasers have requested for deciding whether to acquire the Stock and all information that the Company believes is reasonably necessary to enable the Purchasers to make such a decision, including certain of the Company's projections describing its proposed business (collectively, the "Business Plan"). No representation or warranty of the Company contained in this Agreement and the exhibits attached hereto, any certificate furnished or to be furnished to Purchasers at the Closing, or the Business Plan (when read together) or the Company's unaudited financial statements contains any untrue statement of a material fact or omits to state a material fact necessary in order to make the statements contained herein or therein not misleading in light of the circumstances under which they were made.

3. ***Representations and Warranties of the Purchasers.*** Each Purchaser hereby represents and warrants to the Company that:

3.1 *Authorization.* Such Purchaser has full power and authority to enter into this Agreement. The Agreement, when executed and delivered by the Purchaser, will constitute valid and legally binding obligations of the Purchaser, enforceable in accordance with its terms.

3.2 *Purchase Entirely for Own Account.* This Agreement is made with the Purchaser in reliance upon the Purchaser's representation to the Company, which by the Purchaser's execution of this Agreement, the Purchaser hereby confirms, that the Securities to be acquired by the Purchaser will be acquired for investment for the Purchaser's own account, not as a nominee or agent, and not with a view to the resale or distribution of any part thereof, and that the Purchaser has no present intention of selling, granting any participation in, or otherwise distributing the same. By executing this Agreement, the Purchaser further represents that the Purchaser does not presently have any contract, undertaking, agreement or arrangement with any person to sell, transfer or grant participations to such person or to any third party, with respect to any of the Securities.

COMMENTARY: *The federal securities laws prohibit the public distribution of securities without the filing of a registration statement with the SEC. An unlawful public distribution could occur if an investor purchases stock from the Company and then resells that stock to numerous other investors. In order to prevent that scenario, the Company has required the Purchasers to represent that they are buying the securities for investment purposes and not with a view to reselling them.*

3.3 *Disclosure of Information.* All of the Company's documents, records and books that have been requested by the Purchaser have been made available to the Purchaser. The Purchaser has had an opportunity to discuss the Company's business, management, financial affairs and the terms and conditions of the offering of the Stock with the Company's management and has had an opportunity to review the Company's facilities. The Purchaser understands that such discussions, as well as the Business Plan and any other written information delivered by the Company to the Purchaser, were intended to describe the aspects of the Company's business which it believes to be material.

COMMENTARY: *This representation is designed to protect the Company from claims by the Purchasers that the Company failed to make important documents and information available to them. While the Company must disclose all material facts about its business and financial condition, there is no requirement that every operational detail or company document be disclosed. Because the Company provides all relevant and material information to the Purchasers, the Purchasers assume the responsibility of deciding whether an investment in the Company is suitable for them.*

3.4 *Restricted Securities.* The Purchaser understands that the Securities have not been, and will not be, registered under the Securities Act, by reason of a specific exemption from the registration provisions of the Securities Act which depends upon, among other things, the *bona fide* nature of the investment intent and the accuracy of the Purchaser's representations as expressed herein. The Purchaser understands that the Securities are "restricted securities" under applicable U.S. federal and state securities laws and that, pursuant to these laws, the Purchaser must hold the Securities indefinitely unless they are registered with the Securities and Exchange Commission and qualified by state authorities, or an exemption from such registration and qualification requirements is available. The Purchaser acknowledges that the Company has no obligation to register or qualify the Securities for resale except as set forth in the Investors' Rights Agreement.

3.5 *No Public Market.* The Purchaser understands that no public market now exists for any of the securities issued by the Company. Further, the Purchaser acknowledges that the Company has made no assurances that a public market will ever exist for the Securities.

COMMENTARY: *By including this representation, the Company is protecting itself from later claims by Purchasers that they are unable to resell the illiquid stock of the company. The Purchasers must wait to resell their shares until the Company goes public or is bought out by another company.*

3.6 *Legends.* The Purchaser understands that the Securities and any securities issued in respect of or exchange for the Securities, may bear one or all of the following legends:

a. "THE SHARES REPRESENTED BY THIS CERTIFICATE HAVE NOT BEEN REGISTERED UNDER THE SECURITIES ACT OF 1933, AND HAVE BEEN ACQUIRED FOR INVESTMENT AND NOT WITH A VIEW TO, OR IN CONNECTION WITH, THE SALE OR DISTRIBUTION THEREOF. NO SUCH SALE OR DISTRIBUTION MAY BE EFFECTED WITHOUT AN EFFECTIVE REGISTRATION STATEMENT RELATED THERETO OR AN OPINION OF COUNSEL IN A FORM SATISFACTORY TO THE COMPANY THAT SUCH REGISTRATION IS NOT REQUIRED UNDER THE SECURITIES ACT OF 1933."

b. Any legend set forth in the other Agreements.

c. Any legend required by the blue sky laws of any state to the extent such laws are applicable to the shares represented by the certificate so legended.

3.7 *Accredited Investor.* The Purchaser is an accredited investor as defined in Rule 501(a) of Regulation D promulgated under the Securities Act.

COMMENTARY: *By restricting the offering to a limited number of accredited investors, the Company does not have to provide any specified disclosure documents. The law presumes that accredited investors have the sophistication to determine what documents they require to analyze the investment and that they have the negotiating power to obtain those documents from the Company.*

4. **Conditions of the Purchasers' Obligations at Closing.** The obligations of each Purchaser to the Company under this Agreement are subject to the fulfillment, on or before the Closing, of each of the following conditions, unless otherwise waived:

COMMENTARY: *This section protects the Purchasers from having to close if material changes occur between the time the Agreement is signed and the time of the closing.*

4.1 *Representations and Warranties.* The representations and warranties of the Company contained in Section 2 shall be true, complete and correct in all material respects on and as of the Closing with the same effect as though such representations and warranties had been made on and as of the date of the Closing.

4.2 *Performance.* The Company shall have performed and complied with all covenants, agreements, obligations and conditions contained in this Agreement that are required to be performed or complied with by it on or before the Closing.

4.3 *Board of Directors.* Effective upon the Closing, the Board of Directors shall have seven (7) members.

5. **Conditions of the Company's Obligations at Closing.** The obligations of the Company to each Purchaser under this Agreement are subject to the fulfillment, on or before the Closing, of each of the following conditions, unless otherwise waived:

> **COMMENTARY:** *This section protects the Company from having to close if material changes occur between the time the Agreement is signed and the time of the closing.*

5.1 *Representations and Warranties.* The representations and warranties of each Purchaser contained in Section 3 shall be true and correct in all material respects on and as of the Closing with the same effect as though such representations and warranties had been made on and as of the Closing.

5.2 *Performance.* All covenants, agreements and conditions contained in this Agreement to be performed by the Purchasers on or prior to the Closing shall have been performed or complied with in all material respects.

6. **Furnishing of Information.** The Company agrees that, as long as the Purchasers hold the Stock, the Company shall furnish to the Purchasers whatever information concerning the business and financial condition of the company that the Purchasers may reasonably request.

COMMENTARY: *This type of clause will ensure that the Purchasers continue to receive current information about the Company after they make their investment.*

7. *Miscellaneous.*

7.1 *Survival of Warranties.* Unless otherwise set forth in this Agreement, the warranties, representations and covenants of the Company and the Purchasers contained in or made pursuant to this Agreement shall survive the execution and delivery of this Agreement and the Closing for a period of two (2) years following the Closing.

7.2 *Transfer; Successors and Assigns.* The terms and conditions of this Agreement shall inure to the benefit of and be binding upon the respective successors and assigns of the parties. Nothing in this Agreement, express or implied, is intended to confer upon any party other than the parties hereto or their respective successors and assigns any rights, remedies, obligations, or liabilities under or by reason of this Agreement, except as expressly provided in this Agreement.

7.3 *Governing Law.* This Agreement and all acts and transactions pursuant hereto and the rights and obligations of the parties hereto shall be governed, construed and interpreted in accordance with the laws of the State of New York, without giving effect to principles of conflicts of law.

7.4 *Counterparts.* This Agreement may be executed in two or more counterparts, each of which shall be deemed an original and all of which together shall constitute one instrument.

7.5 *Titles and Subtitles.* The titles and subtitles used in this Agreement are used for convenience only and are not to be considered in construing or interpreting this Agreement.

7.6 *Notices.* Any notice required or permitted by this Agreement shall be in writing and shall be deemed sufficient upon delivery, when delivered personally or by overnight courier or sent by fax, or two (2) business days after being deposited in the U.S. mail, as certified or registered mail, with postage prepaid, addressed to the party to be notified at such party's address as set forth on the signature page or as subsequently modified by written notice, and if to the Company, with a copy to Robert Heim, Meyers & Heim LLP, 488 Madison Avenue, New York, New York 10022.

7.7 *Finder's Fee.* Each party represents that it neither is nor will be obligated for any finder's fee or commission in connection with this transaction. Each Purchaser agrees to indemnify and to hold harmless the Company from any liability for any commission or compensation in the nature of a finder's fee (and the costs and expenses of defending against such liability or asserted liability) for which such Purchaser or any of its officers, employees, or representatives is responsible. The Company agrees to indemnify and hold harmless each Purchaser from any liability for any commission or compensation in the nature of a finder's fee (and the costs and expenses of defending against such liability or asserted liability) for which the Company or any of its officers, employees or representatives is responsible.

7.8 *Amendments and Waivers.* Any term of this Agreement may be amended or waived only with the written consent of the Company and the holders of at least a majority of the Common Stock issued or issuable upon conversion of the Stock.

7.9 *Entire Agreement.* This Agreement, and the documents referred to herein constitute the entire agreement between the parties hereto pertaining to the subject matter hereof, and any and all other written or oral agreements relating to the subject matter hereof existing between the parties hereto are expressly cancelled.

7.10 *Confidentiality.* Each party hereto agrees that, except with the prior written permission of the other party, it shall at all times keep confidential and not divulge, furnish or make accessible to anyone any confidential information, or confidential knowledge or data concerning or relating to the business or financial affairs of the other party to which such party has been or shall become privy by reason of this Agreement, discussions or negotiations relating to this Agreement, the performance of its obligations hereunder or the ownership of Stock purchased hereunder.

[Signature page follows]

The parties have executed this Preferred Stock Purchase Agreement as of the date first written above.

COMPANY: **PURCHASERS:**

Internet Co., Inc.

By: _____   _____

    (Name) President   Name

    Address: Address:

COMMENTARY: *Additional documents that are typically attached as exhibits to the Stock Purchase Agreement are: (1) a schedule of purchasers; (2) the amended and restated certificate of incorporation; and (3) an investors' rights agreement.*

APPENDIX 3H

Internet Co., Inc.
Voting Agreement

(Date)

COMMENTARY: *A voting agreement allows various shareholders, who might otherwise have divergent interests, to agree in advance as to how their votes will be cast. Investors will often negotiate for provisions in the voting agreement that will give them authority to appoint a certain number of directors to the Company's board. This will allow the investors to monitor the company closely as well as exert a degree of control over the company through the votes of the board members.*

This Voting Agreement (the "Agreement") is made as of the ___ day of ___, 2001 by and among Internet Co., Inc., a Delaware corporation (the "Company") and the holders of shares of Preferred Stock listed on Exhibit A (collectively, the "Investors" and each individually, an "Investor").

Recitals

The Company and the Investors have entered into a Preferred Stock Purchase Agreement (the "Purchase Agreement") pursuant to which the Company has agreed to sell to the Investors and the Investors have agreed to purchase from the Company shares of the Company's Preferred Stock. A condition to the Investors' obligations under the Purchase Agreement is that the Company, the Founders and the Investors enter into this Agreement for the purpose of setting forth the terms pursuant to which the Investors and the Founders shall vote their shares of the Company's stock in favor of certain designees to the Company's Board of Directors. The Company, the Founders and the Investors all desire to facilitate the voting arrangements set forth in this Agreement by agreeing to the terms and conditions set forth below.

Agreement

The parties agree as follows:

1. ***Election of Directors.***

    1.1 *Board Representation.* At each annual meeting of the stockholders of the Company, or at any meeting of the stockholders of the Company at which members of the Board of Directors of the Company are to be elected, or whenever members of the Board of Directors are to be elected by written consent, the Founders and the Investors agree to vote with respect to their shares so as to elect:

    a. one (1) member of the Company's Board of Directors designated by RH Venture Capital, LP ("RHVC") so long as RHVC owns at least five percent (5%) of the Company's capital stock (as calculated using the formula in Section 1.2);

    b. John Smith;

c. Robert Jones until such time as the Board of Directors shall elect a Chief Executive Officer of the Company, and thereafter such Chief Executive Officer;

d. two (2) members of the Board of Directors selected by the unanimous vote of the members of the Board of Directors or otherwise selected pursuant to this Agreement.

COMMENTARY: *Paragraph 1 sets out who will fill certain positions on the board of directors and the mechanism for selecting the additional members. The right to appoint a director to the company's board is a central part of the Voting Agreement and ensures that the preferred stockholders will have a major voice in the operations of the Company. In addition to the board member that is directly appointed by RHVC, the parties have agreed upon two other individuals who are acceptable to both sides to sit on the board.*

1.2 *Calculation of Ownership.* To determine when RHVC owns less than five percent (5%) of the Company's capital stock for purposes of voting under Section 1.1(a), (a) the total number of shares of Common Stock issued or issuable to RHVC shall be divided by (b) the total number of issued and outstanding shares of Common and Preferred Stock of the Company, which number shall not include any capital stock issuable upon exercise of outstanding options or warrants of the Company.

1.3 *Appointment of Directors.* In the event of the resignation, death, removal or disqualification of a director selected by RHVC, RHVC shall promptly nominate a new director, and each Investor and Founder shall vote its shares of stock of the Company to elect such nominee to the Board of Directors.

1.4 *Removal.* Only RHVC may remove its designated director. RHVC may remove its designated director at any time, with or without cause, subject only to the Bylaws of the Company as in effect from time to time and any requirements of law. After written notice to each of the parties hereto of the new nominee to replace such director, each Investor and Founder shall promptly vote its shares of capital stock of the Company to elect such nominee to the Board of Directors.

2. **Additional Representations and Covenants.**

2.1 *No Revocation.* The voting agreements may not be revoked during the term of this Agreement.

2.2 *Change in Number of Directors.* The Founders and the Investors will not vote for any amendment or change to the Certificate of Incorporation and/or Bylaws providing for the election of more or less than seven (7) directors, or any other amendment or change to the Certificate of Incorporation Bylaws inconsistent with the terms of this Agreement.

2.3 *Legends.* Each certificate representing shares of the Company's capital stock held by Founders or Investors or any assignee of the Founders or Investors shall bear the following legend:

"THE SHARES EVIDENCED HEREBY ARE SUBJECT TO A VOTING AGREEMENT BY AND AMONG THE COMPANY AND CERTAIN STOCKHOLDERS OF THE COMPANY (A COPY OF WHICH MAY BE OBTAINED FROM THE

COMPANY), AND BY ACCEPTING ANY INTEREST IN SUCH SHARES THE PERSON ACCEPTING SUCH INTEREST SHALL BE DEEMED TO AGREE TO AND SHALL BECOME BOUND BY ALL THE PROVISIONS OF SAID VOTING AGREEMENT."

COMMENTARY: *Because a Voting Agreement can have a significant influence on the result of shareholder votes, many state laws require that notification of the existence of the Voting Agreement be placed directly on the stock certificates. Such notification will alert potential future buyers of the shares to the fact that they will take the shares subject to the Voting Agreement.*

2.4 *Covenants of the Company.* The Company agrees to use its best efforts to ensure that the rights granted hereunder are effective. Towards that end, the Company agrees to use its best efforts to cause the nomination and election of the directors as provided above.

2.5 *No Liability for Election of Recommended Directors.* Neither the Company, nor the Founders, the Investors or any officer, director, shareholder or agent thereof makes any representation or warranty as to the fitness or competence of the nominee of any party hereunder to serve on the Company's board by virtue of such party's execution of this Agreement or by the act of such party in voting for such nominee pursuant to this Agreement.

2.6 *Specific Enforcement.* It is agreed and understood that monetary damages would not adequately compensate an injured party for the breach of this Agreement by any party, that this Agreement shall be specifically enforceable, and that any breach or threatened breach of this

Agreement shall be the proper subject of a temporary or permanent injunction or restraining order.

3. **Termination.**

3.1 *Termination Events.* This Agreement shall terminate upon the earlier of:

a. A firm commitment underwritten public offering by the Company of shares of its Common Stock pursuant to a registration statement under the Securities Act of 1933, as amended, which would result in aggregate cash proceeds to the Company of at least $10,000,000, after payment of underwriting discounts and commissions; or

COMMENTARY: *A Voting Agreement such as this is strictly for use in a private company and would not be appropriate in a publicly traded company. Therefore, the agreement specifically provides that it will terminate in the event the Company conducts an IPO.*

b. The sale, conveyance or disposal of all or substantially all of the Company's property or the Company's merger into any other corporation (other than a wholly owned subsidiary corporation) or if the Company effects any other transaction or series of related transactions in which more than fifty percent (50%) of the voting power of the Company is disposed of.

3.2 *Removal of Legend.* At any time after the termination of this Agreement, any holder of a stock certificate legended pursuant to Section 2.3 may surrender such certificate to the Company for removal of the legend, and the Company will promptly issue a new certificate without the legend.

4. *Miscellaneous.*

4.1 *Successors and Assigns.* The terms and conditions of this Agreement shall inure to the benefit of and be binding upon the respective successors and assigns of the parties. Nothing in this Agreement, express or implied, is intended to confer upon any party other than the parties hereto or their respective successors and assigns any rights, remedies, obligations, or liabilities under or by reason of this Agreement, except as expressly provided in this Agreement.

4.2 *Amendments and Waivers.* Any term hereof may be amended or waived only with the written consent of the Company, the Founders, and holders of at least a majority (greater than 50%) of the Preferred Stock. Any amendment or waiver effected in accordance with this Section 4.2 shall be binding upon the Company, the holders of Preferred Stock and any holder of Founders' Shares, and each of their respective successors and assigns.

4.3 *Notices.* Any notice required or permitted by this Agreement shall be in writing and shall be deemed sufficient on the date of delivery, when delivered personally or by overnight courier or sent by telegram or fax, or forty-eight (48) hours after being deposited in the U.S. mail, as certified or registered mail, with postage prepaid, and addressed to the party to be notified at such party's address as set forth on the signature page or on Exhibit A hereto, or as subsequently modified by written notice.

4.4 *Severability.* If one or more provisions of this Agreement are held to be unenforceable under applicable law, the parties agree to renegotiate such provision in good faith.

4.5 *Governing Law.* This Agreement and all acts and transactions pursuant hereto and the rights and obligations of the parties hereto shall be governed, construed and interpreted in accordance with the laws of the State of New York, without giving effect to principles of conflicts of law.

4.6 *Counterparts.* This Agreement may be executed in two or more counterparts, each of which shall be deemed an original and all of which together shall constitute one instrument.

4.7 *Titles and Subtitles.* The titles and subtitles used in this Agreement are used for convenience only and are not to be considered in construing or interpreting this Agreement.

The parties hereto have executed this Voting Agreement as of the date first written above.

COMPANY: **INVESTORS:**

Internet Co., Inc.   (Name)

By: _____   By: _____
    (Name), President   Name

Address: Title: _____

Fax Number: (Name)

FOUNDERS: By: _____

_____   Name: _____
    (Name)

_____   Title: _____
    (Name)

APPENDIX 31

Form D

SEC 1972 (6/99)   Potential persons who are to respond to the collection of information contained in this form are not required to respond unless the form displays a currently valid OMB control number.

ATTENTION

Failure to file notice in the appropriate states will not result in a loss of the federal exemption. Conversely, failure to file the appropriate federal notice will not result in a loss of an available state exemption state exemption unless such exemption is predicated on the filing of a federal notice.

UNITED STATES

SECURITIES AND EXCHANGE COMMISSION

Washington, D.C. 20549

OMB APPROVAL
OMB Number: 3235-0076
Expires: May 31, 2002
Estimated average burden hours per response. . . 1

NOTICE OF SALE OF SECURITIES

PURSUANT TO REGULATION D,

SECTION 4(6), AND/OR

UNIFORM LIMITED OFFERING EXEMPTION

SEC USE ONLY		
Prefix		Serial
DATE RECEIVED		

Name of Offering (check if this is an amendment and name has changed, and indicate change.)

Filing Under (Check box(es) that apply):
❑ Rule 504   ❑ Rule 505   ❑ Rule 506   ❑ Section 4(6)   ❑ ULOE

Type of Filing: ❑ New Filing   ❑ Amendment

A. BASIC IDENTIFICATION DATA

1. Enter the information requested about the issuer

Name of Issuer (check if this is an amendment and name has changed, and indiciate change.)

Address of Executive Offices   (Number and Street, City, State, Zip Code)   Telephone Number
(Including Area Code)

Address of Principal Business Operations   (Number and Street, City, State, Zip Code) Telephone Number
(Including Area Code)
(if different from Executive Offices)

Brief Description of Business

Type of Business Organization
❑ corporation   ❑ limited partnership, already formed   ❑ other (please specify):
❑ business trust   ❑ limited partnership, to be formed

                                                          Month   Year
Actual or Estimated Date of Incorporation or Organization: [ ]]   [ ]]   ❑ Actual ❑ Estimated
Jurisdiction of Incorporation or Organization: (Enter two-letter U.S. Postal Service abbreviation for State:
            CN for Canada; FN for other foreign jurisdiction)   [ ][ ]

GENERAL INSTRUCTIONS

Federal:

Who Must File: All issuers making an offering of securities in reliance on an exemption under Regulation D or Section 4(6), 17 CFR 230.501 et seq. or 15 U.S.C. 77d(6).

When to File: A notice must be filed no later than 15 days after the first sale of securities in the offering. A notice is deemed filed with the U.S. Securities and Exchange Commission (SEC) on the earlier of the date it is received by the SEC at the address given below or, if received at that address after the date on which it is due, on the date it was mailed by United States registered or certified mail to that address.

Where to File: U.S. Securities and Exchange Commission, 450 Fifth Street, N.W., Washington, D.C. 20549.

Copies Required: Five (5) copies of this notice must be filed with the SEC, one of which must be manually signed. Any copies not manually signed must be photocopies of manually signed copy or bear typed or printed signatures.

Information Required: A new filing must contain all information requested. Amendments need only report the name of the issuer and offering, any changes thereto, the information requested in Part C, and any material changes from the information previously supplied in Parts A and B. Part E and the Appendix need not be filed with the SEC.

Filing Fee: There is no federal filing fee.

State:

This notice shall be used to indicate reliance on the Uniform Limited Offering Exemption (ULOE) for sales of securities in those states that have adopted ULOE and that have adopted this form. Issuers relying on ULOE must file a separate notice with the Securities Administrator in each state where sales are to be, or have been made. If a state requires the payment of a fee as a precondition to the claim for the exemption, a fee in the proper amount shall accompany this form. This notice shall be filed in the appropriate states in accordance with state law. The Appendix in the notice constitutes a part of this notice and must be completed.

A. BASIC IDENTIFICATION DATA

2. Enter the information requested for the following:

- Each promoter of the issuer, if the issuer has been organized within the past five years;

- Each beneficial owner having the power to vote or dispose, or direct the vote or disposition of, 10% or more of a class of equity securities of the issuer;
- Each executive officer and director of corporate issuers and of corporate general and managing partners of partnership issuers; and
- Each general and managing partner of partnership issuers.

Check Box(es) that Apply: ❏ Promoter ❏ Beneficial Owner ❏ Executive Officer ❏ Director ❏ General and/or Managing Partner

---

Full Name (Last name first, if individual)

Business or Residence Address (Number and Street, City, State, Zip Code)

Check Box(es) that Apply: ❏ Promoter ❏ Beneficial Owner ❏ Executive Officer ❏ Director ❏ General and/or Managing Partner

---

Full Name (Last name first, if individual)

Business or Residence Address (Number and Street, City, State, Zip Code)

Check Box(es) that Apply: ❏ Promoter ❏ Beneficial Owner ❏ Executive Officer ❏ Director ❏ General and/or Managing Partner

---

Full Name (Last name first, if individual)

Business or Residence Address (Number and Street, City, State, Zip Code)

Check Box(es) that Apply: ❏ Promoter ❏ Beneficial Owner ❏ Executive Officer ❏ Director ❏ General and/or Managing Partner

---

Full Name (Last name first, if individual)

Business or Residence Address (Number and Street, City, State, Zip Code)

Check Box(es) that Apply: ❏ Promoter ❏ Beneficial Owner ❏ Executive Officer ❏ Director ❏ General and/or Managing Partner

_____
Full Name (Last name first, if individual)

_____
Business or Residence Address (Number and Street, City, State, Zip Code)

_____
Check Box(es) that Apply: ❑ Promoter ❑ Beneficial ❑ Executive ❑ Director ❑ General and/or
Owner Officer Managing Partner

_____
Full Name (Last name first, if individual)

_____
Business or Residence Address (Number and Street, City, State, Zip Code)

_____
Check Box(es) that Apply: ❑ Promoter ❑ Beneficial ❑ Executive ❑ Director ❑ General and/or
Owner Officer Managing Partner

_____
Full Name (Last name first, if individual)

_____
Business or Residence Address (Number and Street, City, State, Zip Code)

_____
(Use blank sheet, or copy and use additional copies of this sheet, as necessary.)

B. INFORMATION ABOUT OFFERING

1. Has the issuer sold, or does the issuer intend to sell, to non-accredited investors in this offering?

❑ Yes ❑ No

Answer also in Appendix, Column 2, if filing under ULOE.

2. What is the minimum investment that will be accepted from any individual? $_____

3. Does the offering permit joint ownership of a single unit? ❑ Yes ❑ No

4. Enter the information requested for each person who has been or will be paid or given, directly or indirectly, any commission or similar remuneration for solicitation of purchasers in connection with sales of securities in the offering. If a person to be listed is an associated person or agent of a broker or dealer registered with the SEC and/or with a state or states, list the name of the broker or dealer. If more than five (5) persons to be listed are associated persons of such a broker or dealer, you may set forth the information for that broker or dealer only.

_____
Full Name (Last name first, if individual)

_____
Business or Residence Address (Number and Street, City, State, Zip Code)

Name of Associated Broker or Dealer

States in Which Person Listed Has Solicited or Intends to Solicit Purchasers

(Check "All States" or check individual States)   ❑ All States

[AL]	[AK]	[AZ]	[AR]	[CA]	[CO]	[CT]	[DE]	[DC]	[FL]	[GA]	[HI]	[ID]
[IL]	[IN]	[IA]	[KS]	[KY]	[LA]	[ME]	[MD]	[MA]	[MI]	[MN]	[MS]	[MO]
[MT]	[NE]	[NV]	[NH]	[NJ]	[NM]	[NY]	[NC]	[ND]	[OH]	[OK]	[OR]	[PA]
[RI]	[SC]	[SD]	[TN]	[TX]	[UT]	[VT]	[VA]	[WA]	[WV]	[WI]	[WY]	[PR]

Full Name (Last name first, if individual)

Business or Residence Address (Number and Street, City, State, Zip Code)

Name of Associated Broker or Dealer

States in Which Person Listed Has Solicited or Intends to Solicit Purchasers

(Check "All States" or check individual States)   ❑ All States

[AL]	[AK]	[AZ]	[AR]	[CA]	[CO]	[CT]	[DE]	[DC]	[FL]	[GA]	[HI]	[ID]
[IL]	[IN]	[IA]	[KS]	[KY]	[LA]	[ME]	[MD]	[MA]	[MI]	[MN]	[MS]	[MO]
[MT]	[NE]	[NV]	[NH]	[NJ]	[NM]	[NY]	[NC]	[ND]	[OH]	[OK]	[OR]	[PA]
[RI]	[SC]	[SD]	[TN]	[TX]	[UT]	[VT]	[VA]	[WA]	[WV]	[WI]	[WY]	[PR]

Full Name (Last name first, if individual)

Business or Residence Address (Number and Street, City, State, Zip Code)

Name of Associated Broker or Dealer

States in Which Person Listed Has Solicited or Intends to Solicit Purchasers

(Check "All States" or check individual States)   ❑ All States

[AL]	[AK]	[AZ]	[AR]	[CA]	[CO]	[CT]	[DE]	[DC]	[FL]	[GA]	[HI]	[ID]
[IL]	[IN]	[IA]	[KS]	[KY]	[LA]	[ME]	[MD]	[MA]	[MI]	[MN]	[MS]	[MO]
[MT]	[NE]	[NV]	[NH]	[NJ]	[NM]	[NY]	[NC]	[ND]	[OH]	[OK]	[OR]	[PA]
[RI]	[SC]	[SD]	[TN]	[TX]	[UT]	[VT]	[VA]	[WA]	[WV]	[WI]	[WY]	[PR]

(Use blank sheet, or copy and use additional copies of this sheet, as necessary.)

C. OFFERING PRICE, NUMBER OF INVESTORS, EXPENSES AND USE OF PROCEEDS

1. Enter the aggregate offering price of securities included in this offering and the total amount already sold. Enter "0" if answer is "none" or "zero." If the transaction is an exchange offering, check this box ¨ and indicate in the columns below the amounts of the securities offered for exchange and already exchanged.

Type of Security	Aggregate Offering Price	Amount Already Sold
Debt	$_____	$_____
Equity	$_____	$_____
❏ Common ❏ Preferred		
Convertible Securities (including warrants)	$_____	$_____
Partnership Interests	$_____	$_____
Other (Specify _____).	$_____	$_____
Total	$_____	$_____

Answer also in Appendix, Column 3, if filing under ULOE.

2. Enter the number of accredited and non-accredited investors who have purchased securities in this offering and the aggregate dollar amounts of their purchases. For offerings under Rule 504, indicate the number of persons who have purchased securities and the aggregate dollar amount of their purchases on the total lines. Enter "0" if answer is "none" or "zero."

	Number Investors	Aggregate Dollar Amount of Purchases
Accredited Investors	_____	$_____
Non-accredited Investors	_____	$_____
Total (for filings under Rule 504 only)	_____	$_____

Answer also in Appendix, Column 4, if filing under ULOE.

3. If this filing is for an offering under Rule 504 or 505, enter the information requested for all securities sold by the issuer, to date, in offerings of the types indicated, the twelve (12) months prior to the first sale of securities in this offering. Classify securities by type listed in Part C-Question 1.

Type of offering	Type of Security	Dollar Amount Sold
Rule 505	_____	$_____
Regulation A	_____	$_____
Rule 504	_____	$_____
Total	_____	$_____

4. a. Furnish a statement of all expenses in connection with the issuance and distribution of the securities in this offering. Exclude amounts relating solely to organization expenses of the issuer. The information may be given as subject to future contingencies. If the amount of an expenditure is not known, furnish an estimate and check the box to the left of the estimate.

Transfer Agent's Fees . . . . ❏ $_____

Printing and Engraving Costs . . . . ❏ $_____

Legal Fees . . . . ❏ $_____

Accounting Fees . . . . ❏ $_____

Engineering Fees . . . . ❏ $_____

Sales Commissions (specify finders' fees separately) . . . . ❏ $_____

Other Expenses (identify) _____ . . . . ❏ $_____

    Total . . . . ❏ $_____

b. Enter the difference between the aggregate offering price given in response to Part C—Question 1 and total expenses furnished in response to Part C—Question 4.a. This difference is the "adjusted gross proceeds to the issuer." . . . . $_____

5. Indicate below the amount of the adjusted gross proceeds to the issuer used or proposed to be used for each of the purposes shown. If the amount for any purpose is not known, furnish an estimate and check the box to the left of the estimate. The total of the payments listed must equal the adjusted gross proceeds to the issuer set forth in response to Part C—Question 4.b above.

	Payments to Officers, Directors, & Affiliates	Payments To Others
Salaries and fees	❏ $_____	❏ $_____
Purchase of real estate	❏ $_____	❏ $_____
Purchase, rental or leasing and installation of machinery and equipment	❏ $_____	❏ $_____
Construction or leasing of plant buildings and facilities	❏ $_____	❏ $_____
Acquisition of other businesses (including the value of securities involved in this offering that may be used in exchange for the assets or securities of another issuerpursuant to a merger)	❏ $_____	❏ $_____
Repayment of indebtedness	❏ $_____	❏ $_____
Working capital	❏ $_____	❏ $_____
Other (specify): ._____	❏ $_____	❏ $_____
_____	❏ $_____	❏ $_____
_____		
Column Totals	$_____	$_____
Total Payments Listed (column totals added)	❏ $_____	

D. FEDERAL SIGNATURE

The issuer has duly caused this notice to be signed by the undersigned duly authorized person. If this notice is filed under Rule 505, the following signature constitutes an undertaking by the issuer to furnish to the U.S. Securities and Exchange Commission, upon written request of its staff, the information furnished by the issuer to any non-accredited investor pursuant to paragraph (b)(2) of Rule 502.

Issuer (Print or Type)	Signature	Date
Name of Signer (Print or Type)	Title of Signer (Print or Type)	

ATTENTION

Intentional misstatements or omissions of fact constitute federal criminal violations. (See 18 U.S.C. 1001.)

E. STATE SIGNATURE

1. Is any party described in 17 CFR 230.262 presently subject to any of the disqualification provisions of such rule? ❏ Yes ❏ No

See Appendix, Column 5, for state response.

2. The undersigned issuer hereby undertakes to furnish to any state administrator of any state in which this notice is filed, a notice on Form D (17 CFR 239,500) at such times as required by state law.

3. The undersigned issuer hereby undertakes to furnish to the state administrators, upon written request, information furnished by the issuer to offerees.

4. The undersigned issuer represents that the issuer is familiar with the conditions that must be satisfied to be entitled to the Uniform limited Offering Exemption (ULOE) of the state in which this notice is filed and understands that the issuer claiming the availability of this exemption has the burden of establishing that these conditions have been satisfied.

The issuer has read this notification and knows the contents to be true and has duly caused this notice to be signed on its behalf by the undersigned duly authorized person.

Issuer (Print or Type)	Signature	Date
Name of Signer (Print or Type)	Title of Signer (Print or Type)	

Instruction:

Print the name and title of the signing representative under his signature for the state portion of this form. One copy of every notice on Form D must be manually signed. Any copies not manually signed must be photocopies of the manually signed copy or bear typed or printed signatures.

150

APPENDIX

1	2		3	4				5	
	Intend to sell to non-accredited investors in State (Part B-Item 1)		Type of security and aggregate offering price offered in state (Part C-Item 1)	Type of investor and amount purchased in State (Part C-Item 2)				Disqualification under State ULOE(if yes, attach explanation of waiver granted) (Part E-Item 1)	
State	Yes	No		Number of Accredited Investors	Amount	Number of Non-Accredited Investors	Amount	Yes	No
AL									
AK									
AZ									
AR									
CA									
CO									
CT									
DE									
DC									
FL									
GA									
HI									
ID									
IL									
IN									
IA									
KS									
KY									
LA									
ME									
MD									
MA									
MI									
MN									
MS									
MO									
MT									
NE									
NV									
NH									
NJ									
NM									

State	Yes	No		Number of Accredited Investors	Amount	Number of Non-Accredited Investors	Amount	Yes	No
NY									
NC									
ND									
OH									
OK									
OR									
PA									
RI									
SC									
SD									
TN									
TX									
UT									
VT									
VA									
WA									
WV									
WI									
WY									
PR									

http://www.sec.gov/divisions/corpfin/forms/d.htm
Last update: 08/27/1999

APPENDIX 3J

Resources for Locating Potential Investors and Learning About the Venture Capital Industry

LOCATING POTENTIAL INVESTORS

www.Garage.com Garage.com describes itself as a venture capital investment bank that provides funding services for high tech startups. The CEO of Garage.com is Guy Kawasaki, a noted entrepreneur and author of several business books.

https://ace-net.sr.unh.edu/pub This is the site for the Access to Capital Electronic Network (ACE-Net), an organization that is a national securities offering listing service. It allows venture capitalists, and institutional and individual accredited investors to find small, growing companies through a secure Internet database.

www.NYNMA.com This is the site for the New York New Media Association, which describes itself as a not-for-profit industry association founded in 1994 to support and promote the new media industry in New York. For those in the New York area, this is the premier industry association with all aspects of the New Media and e-commerce.

www.MITEF-NYC.org This is the site for the MIT Enterprise Forum of New York City. This group describes itself as a "not-for-profit organization dedicated to promoting and strengthening the entrepreneurial process and assisting entrepreneurs and investors in emerging and growth companies that are technologically oriented."

www.NYBusinessForums.com This organization sponsors very well-attended breakfast meetings that are geared towards financial executives and business people.

VENTURE CAPITAL INDUSTRY ASSOCIATIONS

www.vcinstitute.org is the site for the Venture Capital Institute, an organization that is comprised of venture and private equity professionals throughout the world. This organization sponsors educational programs for those in the venture capital industry and publishes a variety of books and papers relating to finance that entrepreneurs may find helpful.

www.nvca.org is the site for the National Venture Capital Association. This organization is a trade group for venture capitalists and produces useful guides and directories relating to the venture capital industry.

CHAPTER 4

SELECTING AND OPERATING THE BOARD OF DIRECTORS

A company's board of directors, when properly selected, can be an invaluable asset to a business. In fact, it can make the difference between the success and failure of an enterprise. Having talented and experienced individuals on the board can give potential investors confidence in the viability of a new business and its plans, thereby facilitating that company's ability to raise capital. In addition, board members with well-established professional affiliations, legal, accounting and banking connections and friends in the right places can prove very valuable. If board members have been involved with taking a company public, their experience will certainly be very helpful when the time comes to prepare the current company's IPO. In addition, when economic conditions turn tougher, directors who have substantial business experience will be in a unique position to provide guidance and insights into how a company can survive a downturn. A corporate board that has members who have experienced economic downturns can be particularly helpful when the founders and executives of a company are relatively young and inexperienced and may not have been previously exposed to economic cycles. In short, the right combination of board members can give a company a competitive advantage in both good and bad economic times.

The role of the board of directors is to represent the corporation's shareholders and oversee the operation of a company's business. Legally, a corporation's business must be managed under the direction of the board of directors. While the overall management of the corporation is in the hands of the board of directors, typically the board will delegate day-to-day management of the business to the officers of the company. However, the board retains the responsibility for setting long-term goals and ensuring that the shareholders' interests are protected. The board is also charged with approving major corporate transactions such as mergers or acquisitions and is also responsible for approving the issuance of new stock to investors.

When selecting individuals to serve on a company's board, care should be taken to ensure that the board membership will possess a variety of talents. It is highly recommended that the board contain a mixture of members with business and technical experience in the industry in which the company operates. A common mistake that many new companies make is to include only individuals with technical experience on the company's board. This is a mistake because in order to grow to the point that an IPO is a realistic possibility, the board will need some members who can contribute to the business mission of the company. These individuals can offer advice on setting marketing goals and ensuring that appropriate financial and legal controls are in place. Having a board where half the members have a business background and half the members have a technical background in the company's industry would be an ideal mix. When choosing board members, it is important to take into consideration a potential director's current involvements (e.g., whether he sits on any other corporate boards and, if so, whether those companies are competitors or potential competitors). In addition, the potential board member should have enough time available to competently carry out his responsibilities.

The proper size of a corporation's board of directors varies from company to company and depends on the company's stage of development. Many companies have successfully adopted a strategy whereby individuals are recruited to the board of directors based on their unique skills so that the resulting board consists of a team of people, each with his own specialized expertise. Companies that adopt this approach will generally have at least one board member with a technical background in the product or service that the company sells, such as software development, content creation or computer hardware manufacturing. In addition, companies also strive to include on the board individuals with substantial business experience and contacts in the areas of marketing, sales and/or finance. Such individuals can help translate the technical or creative ideas of the other board members into hard-nosed business strategies. By using a team approach to building a board of directors, a company can develop a board that can greatly enhance its chances of success.

In general, the number of board members for new companies ranges from three to nine. It's best to have an odd number of board members to eliminate the possibility of a tie vote. Having more than nine members presents logistical problems—it may become difficult to ensure that there are enough members present for a quorum. In addition, a large board can slow down the decision making process.

Practically speaking, a company's founders will not have the ability to select each of the board members once outside financing is raised from venture capitalists. Often venture capitalists will condition the funding of a company on their right to appoint an individual of their own choosing to the board. This gives the venture capitalists a voice in the management of the company and also allows the venture capitalists to closely monitor the performance of the company.

It is extremely important for the board members to observe corporate formalities in conducting their meetings. This will ensure that no legal issues with respect to their conduct will arise on the company's road to an IPO. The various state statutes set forth the rules regarding how the board members are notified of meetings and how many members constitute a quorum so that business may be conducted. A company must comply with the statutes of the jurisdiction where it is incorporated, even if it does business primarily in another state. Each state's corporate law rules are designed to protect the interests of corporate shareholders. A company must be sure to follow all of the statutory rules.

In addition to the formal rules governing board members, there are important substantive rules in place that are designed to ensure that board members competently carry out their important responsibilities. Each board member owes a duty of care and duty of loyalty to the corporation and its shareholders. A board member who is found to have violated either of these duties can be held personally responsible for substantial monetary damages. It is therefore extremely important to be familiar with these important responsibilities and what steps can be taken to prove compliance.

THE DUTY OF CARE

While the director's duty of care has been defined many ways, most formulations require that a director's duties be performed with such care, including reasonable inquiry, as an ordinarily prudent person in a like position would use under similar circumstances. One of the basic requirements of the duty of care is that directors make their decisions on an informed basis. In other words, all relevant information must be presented to the board members and considered by them prior to making any decision. The duty of care does not require directors to know everything about the everyday operation of the corporation or everything about a particular transaction that management is proposing. However, it does require directors to have a reasonable amount of knowledge about a company's activities as well as any transaction that is under consideration. If a board decision is made hastily and without due consideration, directors can be held personally liable for the resulting damage to the corporation.

Attorneys must ensure that their clients understand that the duty of care places an affirmative responsibility upon directors to carry out their responsibilities. Particularly in technology and new media companies, where important decisions are often made within a very tight time frame, directors must be aware that they still have a duty to act on an informed basis. Therefore, directors should insist on being presented with as much information and analysis as they believe is necessary to allow them to act on an informed basis. It is particularly important for directors of new media companies not to allow the informal procedures under which many new media companies operate to lessen the degree of care that they use in carrying out their responsibilities. Directors are not shielded from liability for board decisions merely because they did not attend a board meeting or did not participate in the deliberations. The courts have clearly stated that if a person is unable or unwilling to take an active role in carrying out the responsibilities of a director, then that person should not be a director. Attorneys can help ensure that directors meet the duty of care standards when carrying out their responsibilities by advising them to take the following actions:

1. ***Regularly Attend Board Meetings.*** One of the most basic requirements imposed upon directors by the duty of care is to regularly attend board meetings. While at a board meeting, directors must be prepared to participate in the meeting and deliberate about the matters that come before them. If a director fails to become involved in board meetings or fails to consider important facts in making decisions, the director can be held to have violated the duty of care. As noted above, failing to attend board meetings will not relieve a director from responsibility for the actions taken at those meetings.

2. ***Obtain Sufficient Information to Make Informed Decisions.*** As a result of the affirmative obligations imposed on directors by the duty of care, the directors must take reasonable steps to ensure that they are receiving sufficient information from the corporation's officers and other parties, such as bankers and attorneys, to allow them to make informed decisions. If the required information is not forthcoming, directors have a duty to push for it. Directors also must never allow corporate officers to dictate to them the final decisions of the board.

3. ***Understand the Business of the Corporation.*** Another fundamental responsibility that each director has is to understand the corporation's business. Board members are responsible for the management of the corporation's affairs on behalf of the shareholders. While this requirement may pose a challenge to board members who are associated with high tech or e-commerce companies, the fundamental responsibility is the same as in other types of companies. Prior to assuming the position of a director, an individual must be educated about the company's basic business, products and services, competition and other important matters. Without at least a basic understanding of a company's business, it is hard to see how a director can effectively carry out his responsibilities.

4. ***Understand the Corporation's Financial Statements.*** Board members must also be very concerned about the corporation's ongoing financial condition. This requires that each director review the financial statements of the corporation on a regular basis. A working knowledge of the corporation's financial statements is often required when making board decisions. In addition, board members must be constantly alert for any signs of irregularity in the preparation of the corporation's financial statements. Even large corporations are not immune from serious accounting irregularities.

THE IMPORTANCE OF PROPER DECISION MAKING PROCEDURES

The experience of Internet and new media companies in the 1990s demonstrated that new companies can grow extremely rapidly into large business operations. As a result, they often do not have in place the types of systems and procedures that a more seasoned company of its size would have. Moreover, frequently the senior officers and directors of new media companies are quite young and do not have any previous experience to draw upon when making important business decisions. Therefore, it is not uncommon for officers of new media companies to fly by the seat of their pants when operating the company. However, this can be a dangerous way to make decisions at the board of directors' level because a court could find that such haphazard decision making constitutes a violation of the director's duty of care. Therefore, in addition to the substantive requirements set forth above, attorneys can perform a valuable service to the company's board by establishing specific procedures designed to assist the board in making informed decisions and carrying out its duty of care. Having specific procedures in place will assist the board in fighting off later claims that they breached their duty of care.

First, attorneys must ensure that the board is not acting with undue haste. While there are certainly circumstances that call for quick decision making, the board must be on the alert for artificial deadlines imposed by the company's officers. Unreasonably short deadlines can mean that hasty decisions were made. They can also be evidence that the board lacked sufficient time to gather and review all of the information needed to make an informed decision. In short, if a decision has to be made quickly, the board must have a good reason why—and an artificial deadline is not considered a good reason.

Second, attorneys should recommend that board members be prepared for each meeting at which important matters will be decided. Towards this end, written materials should be prepared and given to board members prior to the meeting. If the board will be deliberating about an important transaction or agreement, the terms of the proposed transaction should be disseminated in writing prior to the meeting. The actual agreements, if available, and any related agreements should also be provided to board members prior to the meeting so that they can be read. If experts such as investment bankers have prepared written reports, board members should be provided with these reports. Board members are required to take reasonable steps to ensure that any information they receive is accurate, even if the information is provided by experts such as investment bankers, attorneys or accountants. The board cannot act in blind reliance on materials given to them. However, board members are given some protection in this area by statute. For example, Section 141(e) of Delaware's General Corporation Law protects directors who reasonably rely on reports of officers or outside experts.[1] However, Section 141 requires that the board members act in good faith and take reasonable steps to ensure that reports are accurate and adequate. Also, the statute requires that any expert relied on be selected with reasonable care.

Third, attorneys should encourage the board members to ask questions during board meetings. There have been cases that have criticized board members for failing to ask questions about the actions that they were being asked to take.[2]

Fourth, counsel should always make sure that there is a paper record to document the board's actions in carrying out its duty of

---

[1] See Del. Gen. Corp. L. § 141(e).

[2] See, e.g., Mills Acquisition Co. v. Macmillan, Inc., 559 A.2d 1261 (Del. 1988).

due care. Copies should be retained of all material that the board was provided with both before and during the board meeting. Minutes of meetings should be kept to record the deliberations and questions. Needless to say, all expert reports furnished to the board must be retained.

As the suggestions above make clear, one of the valuable roles an attorney can play in this area is to ensure that a proper "atmosphere" is created and maintained. When the proper atmosphere for informed decision making is established, courts will often find that the board has carried out its responsibilities in accordance with the duty of care. For example, courts have held that directors have fulfilled their duty of loyalty when the board as a whole considered in detail any contracts they were being asked to approve, when the board had adequate written information concerning its proposed course of action, and when the board did not act with undue haste.[3] Courts have also credited board members with fulfilling their duty of loyalty when the board deliberately engaged in long-term corporate planning and examined a significant amount of information concerning alternative courses of action.[4] In contrast, courts have held that the board did not meet its duty of care when it did not have advance notice of the purpose of a special board meeting, the board completely relied upon a short oral presentation by the CEO in making its decisions, no questions were asked by any of the board members, an extension of a very short deadline in which to make the decision was not requested, the agreement that the board was asked to approve was not fully read or understood, and no outside professional advice was sought by the board.[5]

---

[3] Unocal v. Mesa Petroleum Co., 493 A.2d 946 (Del. 1985).

[4] Moran v. Household International, Inc., 490 A.2d 1059 (Del Ch.), *aff'd* 500 A.2d 1346 (Del. 1985).

[5] Smith v. Van Gorkom, 488 A.2d 858 (Del. 1985).

Limiting the Exposure of Directors

In light of the substantial liability that can be imposed on directors, attorneys are frequently asked what can be done to limit the financial exposure that directors personally face. First, an attorney must know of whether the jurisdiction in which the corporation is incorporated provides for any statutory options. For example in Delaware, Section 102(b)(7) of the General Corporation Law permits a Delaware corporation to include in its certificate of incorporation a provision limiting or eliminating the personal liability of a director to the corporation or its stockholders for violations of the duty of care.[6] This section, however, will not protect a director in certain circumstances, including when the director does not act in good faith, knowingly violates the law or derives an improper personal benefit. In addition, state corporate statutes often allow the corporation's certificate of incorporation and bylaws to provide for indemnification of board members. In New York, these provisions can be found at Sections 721-726 of the Business Corporation Law.[7] Another form of protection can be provided by Directors and Officers insurance, commonly known as D&O insurance. A common initial demand of potential new directors is that the corporation maintain sufficient D&O insurance coverage. What constitutes a sufficient amount of insurance depends on a number of factors, including the size of the corporation, whether it is a public or private company and the industry.

With the foregoing guidelines in mind, attorneys for growing companies can guide corporate directors in carrying out their responsibilities under the duty of care and, ultimately, help to ensure that the best corporate decisions are made.

---

[6] See Del. Gen. Corp. L. § 102(b)(7).

[7] N.Y. Bus. Corp. L. §§ 721-726.

THE DUTY OF LOYALTY

Each member of a corporation's board of directors has a duty of loyalty that flows directly to the corporation and its shareholders. Essentially, the duty of loyalty requires a director to act in good faith and make all corporate decisions in the best interest of the corporation and its shareholders, without regard to the director's own personal interests. Directors, as representatives of the corporation's shareholders, have an important obligation to act in the best interests of those shareholders. Particularly in large corporations where individual shareholders have minimal amounts of control over the policies and operations of the corporation, shareholders trust the directors to protect their interests and vigilantly supervise the officers of the corporation. Shareholders have a right to expect directors to carry out these important responsibilities in good faith, free of any personal or financial conflicts.

Directors Cannot Engage in Undisclosed Self-Dealing

At its most basic level, the duty of loyalty requires a director to abstain from undisclosed self-dealing with the corporation. A classic example of self-dealing involves participating in board approval of a corporate transaction that brings undisclosed financial gain to one of the directors voting on the matter. Courts have long held that "[c]orporate officers and directors are not permitted to use their position of trust and confidence to further their private interests."[8]

At common law, a corporate transaction involving an interested director—that is, a director who will personally gain from a corporate transaction—was voidable. However, modern-day corporate statutes have abolished the common law rule and permit

---

[8] Guth v. Loft, 5 A.2d 503, 510 (Del. 1939).

transactions with interested directors if certain conditions are met. Typically, state statutes require either approval of the transaction by a majority of disinterested directors who have been informed of the interested director's conflict or a demonstration that the transaction is fair to the corporation. The statutory changes arose from practical considerations of allowing corporations to engage in fair and beneficial transactions that were accomplished after full disclosure to the disinterested directors. For Delaware corporations, Section 144 of the General Corporation Law sets forth the requirements that must be met for approval of transactions involving interested directors.[9] The Delaware statute is typical of the statutes of many states and includes requirements that the interested director disclose his interest to the other members of the board and that the board approve the transaction in good faith and with a majority vote of the disinterested directors.

The duty of loyalty also requires directors to deal "fairly" with all shareholders when directors have an interest in a corporate transaction. As a result, the obligations imposed by the duty of loyalty can arise under numerous circumstances and the proper course of conduct can, at times, be unclear. For instance, questions regarding the duty of loyalty can arise in transactions involving a parent corporation and its subsidiary when their board members overlap, and also in mergers or reorganizations that treat minority shareholders differently than majority shareholders.

When a company is contemplating a transaction that could be deemed to involve an interested director, counsel must make sure that two questions are adequately addressed: (1) Has sufficient disclosure been made to the disinterested directors who will be approving the transaction? and (2) Is the transaction, as a whole, fair to the corporation and its shareholders? In practice, it is the second

---

[9] See Del. Gen. Corp. L. § 144.

question—whether the transaction as a whole is fair—that is of primary concern to shareholders. Often, this question boils down to whether the corporation received adequate financial consideration in a sale, merger or other transaction. Establishing whether a particular transaction is "fair" can be complicated, especially if the transaction is a large one with an intricate structure. In those circumstances, the board is well-advised to obtain a fairness opinion from a qualified, independent third party such as an accounting firm or investment bank. Such an opinion can go a long way in demonstrating that the board members complied with their duty of loyalty.

Directors May Not Take Corporate Opportunities

The duty of loyalty prohibits a director from taking a business opportunity that rightfully belongs to the corporation. This prohibition arises from the rule that a fiduciary may not take for personal gain an opportunity that arises in connection with the fiduciary's exercise of his responsibilities. Whether a business opportunity rightfully belongs to the corporation is determined on a case-by-case basis and is highly fact dependent. Courts have generally focused on three factors in deciding whether an opportunity belonged to the corporation:

1. Is the opportunity in the corporation's line of business?[10]

2. Did the corporation have an actual or expectant interest in the opportunity?[11]

3. Is it "fair" to say that the opportunity belonged to the corporation in light of what is equitable under the circumstances?[12]

---

[10] See, e.g., Guth v. Loft, N.8 *supra*.

[11] See, e.g., Morad v. Coupounas, 361 So.2d 6 (Ala. 1978).

[12] See, e.g., Weiss v. Kay Jewelry Stores, Inc., 470 F.2d 1259 (D.C. Cir. 1972).

Delaware courts generally look to the first two factors, and if the business opportunity meets either test it is deemed to be a corporate opportunity.[13] However, if a business opportunity presents itself to a director, the opportunity is not one which is essential or desirable for the corporation to embrace and the opportunity is one in which the corporation has no actual or expectant interest, the director may treat the opportunity as his own—so long as the corporation's assets are not used to exercise the business opportunity.[14] A director may also avail himself of a corporate opportunity for his own if there has been a knowing waiver of the opportunity by a majority of the company's disinterested directors.

There is an often overlooked aspect of a director's duty of loyalty. It is the prohibition against a director entering into a business opportunity with a company or individual that is in direct competition with the corporation to whom the duty is owed. However, once a director has left a corporation, he is permitted to engage in activities that are in competition with his old corporation, barring an agreement to the contrary.

In circumstances when directors must unavoidably have personal financial dealings with the corporation, such as in setting their compensation levels or engaging in transactions that affect their personal stockholdings, directors should take special care to demonstrate that their actions are fair. The directors must base their compensation on the reasonable value of the services that they are providing to the company. Setting compensation levels too high can result in a breach of the duty of loyalty. Likewise, when purchasing or selling the company's stock, directors must ensure that they are not misusing confidential information. Misuse of confidential

---

[13] See Equity Corp. v. Milton, 43 Del. Ch. 160, 221 A.2d 494, 497 (Del. 1966).
[14] *Id.*

information is a breach of the duty of loyalty as well as possibly a violation of insider trading laws if the information is material.

Special Situations Faced by Directors of Technology Companies

Directors of technology companies often face two special scenarios that raise thorny issues relating to the duty of loyalty. First, it is common for the same individual to sit on the boards of several technology companies. Individuals with exceptional business backgrounds are often courted by numerous start-up companies to sit on their boards. Frequently, potential directors are offered attractive equity and stock option packages to induce them to sit on each company's board. Prominent individuals may choose to increase their chances of substantial financial gain by sitting on numerous corporate boards. However, sitting on multiple boards can present significant legal issues. Questions can arise when a business opportunity comes along which may be appropriate for more than one of the corporations. How does the director decide with which corporations, if any, to share the opportunity?

Another problem arises if two of the companies decide to enter into a transaction together. In these circumstances, Delaware courts have held that the individual owes the same duty of loyalty to both corporations. The director must exercise the duty in light of what is best for both corporations. While the formulation of the duty in these circumstances is straightforward, its application is not. Difficult questions can arise relating to how the director should handle confidential information obtained from each company. Also, questions arise concerning whether the director may participate in board discussions or vote on the transaction for either company. In these circumstances, the board of each corporation should set up independent negotiating teams, each free of the interested director, to hammer out the details of any proposed transaction. Some courts have stated that the director with a seat on each board may be required to abstain from any participation in the matter. However, even then questions can be raised as to whether total abstinence from the matter can shield the director from liability, particularly in light of the duty of care that would otherwise require careful participation.

Another issue that frequently arises with technology companies concerns what duties a director owes when that director has been designated by a particular shareholder. This issue comes up quite often when companies begin accepting investments by venture capitalists. Typically, sophisticated venture capitalists will require as a condition of their investment that the company grant them the right to appoint an individual of their choosing to the board. Such an appointee can easily be confused about where his duty of loyalty lies—to the shareholder who appointed him or to all of the corporation's shareholders. In these circumstances, courts have held that the director's duty is to the corporation and its shareholders as a whole and not to the particular individual or entity that designated him as director. Directors faced with a conflict between their duty to the corporation and their allegiance to the entity that designated the director should immediately disclose the conflict to the other board members. If necessary, the director may be required to abstain from participation in a matter for which there is a significant conflict.

With the foregoing advice in mind, attorneys can help to ensure that directors carry out their responsibilities under the duty of loyalty and, ultimately, that the corporation and its shareholders have the benefit of the directors' unbiased good judgment.

THE BUSINESS JUDGMENT RULE

In both good and bad economic times, attorneys can expect to be called upon to assist corporate directors in evaluating their responsibilities and the liabilities they may face as a result of proposed decisions and actions. Corporate directors often wish to know what legal protections are available to them if their business decisions, in hindsight, appear to be wrong or misguided. It is in just such situations that the business judgment rule applies.

The business judgment rule operates to protect directors when they carry out their corporate decision making responsibilities in good faith and with due care. Fundamentally, the business judgment rule recognizes that the business of a corporation is managed by its directors. Therefore, without evidence of bad faith, fraud or lack of due care, courts will respect the business judgment of corporate directors and give their decisions significant deference. When the business judgment rule applies, it provides two distinct types of protections. First, it prevents directors from being held personally liable for decisions that later turn out to be unprofitable or misguided. Second, it protects the integrity of decisions made by a corporation's board from challenges by shareholders or third parties. In other words, those who disagree with a decision made by the board will not be permitted to invoke the power of the court to reverse a business decision made by the directors. In essence, the business judgment rule prevents a court from substituting its own judgment regarding what is in the best interest of the corporation for the judgment of the corporation's directors.

The Public Policies Behind the Business Judgment Rule

The business judgment rule embodies the public policy of granting substantial deference to the business decisions made by corporate directors. It requires courts to respect the decisions made by directors so long as those decisions can be supported by a rational business purpose.

Courts have articulated several policies behind the business judgment rule. First is the recognition that courts are not well-equipped to perform a meaningful review of a director's business decisions. One court stated:

> "After the fact litigation is a most imperfect device to evaluate corporate business decisions. The circumstances surrounding a corporate decision are not easily reconstructed in a courtroom years later, since business imperatives often call for quick decisions, inevitably based on less than perfect information. The entrepreneur's function is to encounter risks and to confront uncertainty, and a reasoned decision at the time made may seem a wild hunch viewed years later."[15]

Therefore, the business judgment rule prevents courts from reexamining the business decisions of corporate directors even if such decisions are challenged by third parties or turn out, in hindsight, to be misguided.

The second policy behind the business judgment rule is that courts do not want to unnecessarily hamper directors from taking reasonable and necessary risks in the operation of their business. It is the responsibility of corporate directors, not the courts, to weigh the relative risks and rewards of a particular course of action. Courts have recognized that the potential for making great profits often requires the corporation to take great risks—risks that could result in great losses. "Because potential profit often corresponds to the potential risk, it is very much in the interest of shareholders that the law not create incentives for overly cautious corporate decisions."[16]

Third, the business judgment rule protects directors from being held personally liable in damages for honest mistakes of

---

[15] Spiegel v. Buntrock, 571 A.2d 767, 774 (Del. 1990).

[16] Joy v. North, 692 F.2d 880, 886 (2d Cir. 1982).

judgment—this protection encourages talented people to serve on corporate boards.[17] Courts recognize that competent people would be severely discouraged from serving as directors if they were subject to liability for business decisions that, in hindsight, turned out to be unprofitable. Since the business people have the information and skills they need to make well-reasoned judgments, courts should be reluctant to second-guess their decisions when they appear to have been made in good faith.[18]

When Will Business Judgment Rule Protection Not Apply?

Although the business judgment rule gives directors broad latitude to conduct the affairs of the corporation as they see fit, it does not protect directors from liability in all circumstances. It is only when directors act with due care and in the best interests of the corporation that the business judgment rule will shield them from liability. The exercise of a director's authority is governed by the fiduciary duties owed by a director to the corporation. Specifically, a director owes the corporation a duty of care and a duty of loyalty. The duty of care requires that directors make all decisions on an informed basis. The duty of loyalty requires directors to act in the best interests of the corporation free from any conflict with their personal financial interests. It is only when directors fulfill both of these duties that they will be afforded the protections of the business judgment rule.

The business judgment rule can be thought of as a presumption by the courts that a director's decision was made in good faith, with an informed basis and in the honest belief that the action taken was in the best interest of the company.[19] When the business

---

[17] Unitrin, Inc. v. American Gen. Corp., 651 A.2d 1361, 1374 (Del. 1995).

[18] Solash v. Telex Corp., C.A. Nos. 9518, 9528 and 9525, slip op. at *1 (Del. Ch. Jan. 19, 1988).

[19] Aronson v. Lewis, 473 A.2d 805, 812 (Del. 1984).

judgment rule applies, there is a rebuttable presumption that the board's action is proper. A plaintiff who challenges the board's decision bears the burden of overcoming this presumption.[20] The courts will require the plaintiff to provide evidence that the directors, in reaching their decision, did not act in accordance with their fiduciary duties of good faith and due care.[21] In other words, the burden is on the plaintiff to provide evidence that the directors should not have the protections of the business judgment rule because they acted in violation of their fiduciary duties. This is a difficult burden to meet because if there is any rational basis for the directors' decision, courts will likely uphold it. Directors who make honest mistakes in judgment will not be deprived of protections offered by the business judgment rule, particularly when, at the time, the directors' judgments appeared to be rational.[22]

However, in situations where the plaintiff can prove that the director's decisions were made in breach of their fiduciary duties, the business judgment rule presumption will be overcome. If the plaintiff proves that the directors' actions were taken primarily in bad faith or primarily to advance their own personal interests, the courts will no longer defer to the directors' decisions. In such cases, the burden will shift to the directors to show that their decisions and actions were fair and done in the best interest of the corporation.[23] In instances where there is a change in corporate control, courts are more likely to scrutinize the conduct of directors because there may be a conflict between the directors' interests in retaining their positions and the interest of the corporation in

---

[20] See, e.g., Smith v. Van Gorkom, 488 A.2d 858, 872 (Del. 1985).

[21] Cede & Co. v. Technicolor, Inc., 634 A.2d 345, 361 (Del. 1994).

[22] Moran v. Household International, Inc., 490 A.2d 1046, 1074 (Del. Ch.), aff'd 500 A.2d 1346 (Del. 1985).

[23] See Shamrock Holdings, Inc. v. Polaroid Corp., 559 A.2d 257 (Del. Ch. 1989).

consummating a favorable transaction. Similarly, in circumstances involving a sale of a corporation's assets, courts will scrutinize the conduct of directors to determine whether proper actions were taken to ensure that the corporation received the maximum value from the sale.[24]

It is also important to note that the business judgment rule protects directors' deliberate actions. It does not protect them in the case of their neglect or inaction. The business judgment rule does not protect directors when they have either abdicated their functions or, absent a conscious decision, failed to act.[25]

By informing directors of the protections offered by the business judgment rule, counsel can help reassure directors that their actions, if taken in good faith and on an informed basis, will receive protection from judicial scrutiny and second guessing. Such reassurances should help directors make decisions that are in the best interest of the corporation and its shareholders during these challenging and uncertain times.

[24] Revlon v. MacAndrews & Forbes Holdings, Inc., 501 A.2d 1239 (Del. Ch. 1985), *aff'd* 506 A.2d 173 (Del. Ch. 1986).

[25] Aronson v. Lewis, 473 A.2d 805, 813 (Del. 1984).

APPENDIX 4

Potential Director Information Sheet

Name: _____

Address: _____

Telephone Number: _____

Other Contact Information (e.g., e-mail address, cellular number, fax number, etc.):

_____

_____

Summary of Relevant Business Experience:

_____

_____

Summary of Relevant Industry Experience:

_____

_____

Has this person served on a corporate board before? _____

If yes, name each company.

_____

_____

Were any of those companies publicly traded?

_____

Is this person currently on the board of a company? _____

If yes, name each company.

_____

_____

Are any of these companies publicly traded?

_____

Work History (or attach résumé):

_____

_____

_____

Educational History (or attach résumé):

_____

_____

_____

How did the company learn of this individual?

_____

_____

Any other relevant information:

_____

_____

_____

CHAPTER 5

SELECTING AN UNDERWRITER AND UNDERSTANDING THE UNDERWRITING PROCESS

Once a company has decided that it is appropriate to go public, the officers of the company must begin the process of approaching various underwriters and selecting the firm that is best able to handle the distribution of the company's securities to public investors. There are a substantial number of firms that underwrite the issuance of stock and these firms vary widely in their size, geographic coverage and distribution capability. If a company has obtained financing from a venture capital firm, the venture capital firm will most likely be in a position to introduce the company to potential underwriters. If the company has not received venture capital financing it may still find an underwriter for its securities if it has a solid business plan and strong growth prospects. In either case, the officers of a company must have a working knowledge of the underwriting process in order to ensure that the company's IPO is handled successfully.

Essentially, the function of an underwriter is to distribute the company's securities to a significant number of investors once the sale of such securities has been registered with the Securities and Exchange Commission (SEC). Typically, the investors will be clients of the underwriting firm, which is itself a registered broker-dealer. In addition to actually distributing the company's securities in the IPO, the underwriter will assist the issuer in setting the proper price for the securities based on current market conditions and the anticipated demand. The underwriter's attorneys will also work closely with the issuer's attorneys in preparing the registration statement for filing with the SEC.

Selecting an Appropriate Underwriter

There are many factors that go into selecting an appropriate underwriter for a company's securities. First, the issuer should consider the size of the underwriter, in terms of capitalization and number of customers, to ensure that it has the capability to effectively distribute all of the securities that will be offered in the IPO. Firms such as Merrill Lynch, Goldman Sachs and Morgan Stanley Dean Witter have a huge number of retail and institutional customers and can handle even the largest IPOs effectively. However, not every company will be in a position to have its securities underwritten by such large and prestigious firms. In fact, most large underwriters usually don't show interest in small IPOs seeking to raise less than $50 million. To maximize the chances for success, a company should approach underwriters who have handled IPOs similar in size to the one the company is contemplating. In fact, there are a number of smaller regional firms that actively underwrite the securities of smaller companies. The issuer must carefully review the size of the offerings that the potential underwriters have handled in the past to ensure that the underwriting firm under consideration can successfully handle the contemplated IPO.

Another important factor that an issuer must consider is the level of support and coverage that a potential underwriter can provide for the issuer's securities once the IPO is completed and aftermarket trading of the company's stock begins. Once a company's stock begins publicly trading, the management of the company must closely follow the stock's market price. Although many factors affect the price of a company's stock, having high visibility in the financial press and analyst coverage can increase demand for a particular company's stock. For this reason, in recent years issuers have looked closely at the underwriter's analysts when choosing an underwriter. Companies prefer to work with underwriters who employ analysts who understand and cover their industry. If an underwriter employs a high-profile analyst who will be covering the company's securities, such coverage virtually guarantees that the company's stock will be of great interest to the investing public. Conversely, if an underwriter can only offer limited aftermarket coverage of a company's securities, the company and its stock can easily fall into obscurity. Very often a lack of visibility in the financial press can lead to a low level of investor demand for the stock and a relatively illiquid market for those who desire to purchase or sell the company's stock. Therefore, when choosing an underwriter, a company must research the type of post-IPO coverage the underwriter will provide. A good starting point is to research publicly traded companies in the same industry and learn which analysts tend to be the most respected by both institutional and individual investors.

When a company considers the effect that an analyst may have on the aftermarket visibility of a company's securities, it must keep in mind that the analyst is supposed to be objective when providing his or her opinions about the value of a company and whether the stock should be purchased or sold. In fact, every reputable underwriting firm maintains a Chinese Wall between the analysts and the investment bankers. Analysts will not be aware of any of the nonpublic information about a company that the investment banking division possesses as part of its underwriting role. Although analysts do not use nonpublic information when making their evaluations, they do face enormous pressure from the issuer, and sometimes by the underwriting firm itself, to generate positive research reports about a company that is a client of the firm. The potential conflicts faced by analysts have made analyst independence a hotly debated topic.

When a company is considering a public offering it will typically meet with several potential underwriters. In these meetings, the potential underwriters will make a presentation to the company in an attempt to convince the management to retain their firm to perform the underwriting. While underwriters compete on size, geographic coverage, prestige and aftermarket coverage, one thing they generally don't compete on is price. Generally speaking, the underwriting fee consists of the difference between the price at which the underwriter purchases the securities from the issuer and the price at which the underwriter sells the shares to its customers. The underwriting fee is usually set at 7% of the offering price regardless of which underwriter is ultimately retained. In addition to the 7% fee, the issuer must also pay other expenses, including legal, accounting and printing fees, as discussed later in this chapter.

Underwritings in the United States are generally of two types—firm commitment underwritings and best-efforts underwritings. In a firm commitment underwriting, the underwriter commits to the issuer that it will purchase a specified number of shares at a specified price. The underwriter will then resell those shares to its customers at a higher price. In contrast, in a best-efforts underwriting, the underwriter only commits to using its best efforts in selling an issuer's stock and the issuer assumes the risk that not all of the shares can be sold. A more detailed description of each type of underwriting follows.

Firm Commitment Underwriting

The firm commitment underwriting is the most prevalent type of underwriting in the United States and is the type used for virtually every significant IPO. In a firm commitment underwriting, the issuer sells all of the securities offered in the IPO to an underwriter at a predetermined price. The underwriter then resells the stock to customers who have previously been solicited to purchase in the IPO and who have indicated an interest in doing so. The advantage of a firm commitment underwriting is that the company knows that it will get a set amount of money for its stock, and the risk that the entire offering can't be sold at the IPO price is shifted from the company to the underwriter. In practice, the underwriters do not formally commit to purchasing the securities until a few hours prior to the actual offering to the public. This leaves only a short window in which the underwriter is at risk in the event of a market decline.

The stock is always sold to the underwriter's customers at a higher price than the price paid by the underwriter. The difference between what the underwriter paid for the stock and what the underwriter sells the stock to its customers for is known as the "spread." The spread represents the underwriter's compensation for distributing the company's stock. As mentioned above, underwriters charge a standard 7% spread on all IPOs.

In the early twentieth century, it was common for only one underwriter to handle the entire distribution of a company's securities. But as the size of securities offerings became larger, underwriters began to form groups, known as "syndicates," that would share the risk of purchasing a company's securities in an IPO and reselling those securities to their respective customers. By acting as part of a group, no one underwriter was required to put up all of the capital required for a firm commitment IPO. The use of underwriting syndicates also enabled the issuer's securities to be distributed to an extremely broad base of investors. The formation of underwriting syndicates is used extensively today in firm commitment underwritings. Although procedures can vary among the major underwriters, typically a lead underwriter will enter into a letter of intent with the issuer, which will begin the IPO process. The lead underwriter will be responsible for conducting due diligence on behalf of the syndicate and will also work with the issuer's counsel in preparing the SEC registration statement. Usually the lead underwriter will invite other underwriters to participate in the syndicate immediately after the issuer's registration statement is filed with the SEC. If an underwriter chooses to participate in the syndicate it will do so by entering into the agreement among underwriters for that particular IPO. That agreement among the underwriters usually appoints the lead underwriter as the representative of the syndicate for purposes of structuring and pricing the offering and for other dealings with the issuer. The lead underwriter, on behalf of the syndicate, will ultimately enter into an underwriting agreement with the issuer in which the syndicate formally commits to purchasing the issuer's securities at a particular price.

Once a firm commitment underwriting agreement has been signed, the underwriter, with limited exceptions, is committed to purchasing the securities of the issuer at the stated price—even if the market demand for the securities drops off before the entire offering can be sold. In order to protect the syndicate from changing market demand, the underwriting agreement is generally signed only hours before the SEC registration statement is declared effective. This limits as much as possible the amount of time between the underwriter's irrevocable commitment to purchasing the securities and its resale of the securities to investors.

To reduce their risks in firm commitment underwritings even further, underwriters developed what is known as a "market out" clause, which is inserted in most underwriting agreements with an issuer. The market out clause allows the underwriting syndicate to withdraw from the underwriting agreement prior to the IPO if trading in the company's securities is suspended, a material adverse change affects the issuer or other such occurrences make it impractical for the securities to be sold at the agreed-upon price. Counsel for a company that is preparing to enter into an underwriting agreement must carefully review the market out clause to determine what conditions will allow the underwriting syndicate to withdraw from its commitment to purchase and distribute the company's securities. A market out clause that is overly broad will eviscerate the concept of a firm commitment underwriting because such a clause will permit the underwriter to cancel the underwriting agreement for virtually any reason. Broad market out clauses will, in effect, keep the risk of being unable to sell the securities with the company.

In *First Boston Corp.,* the SEC weighed in on the issue of overly broad market out clauses and stated that they are inappropriate in firm commitment underwritings.[1] In the *First Boston* release the SEC stated that a market out clause in a firm commitment underwriting is inappropriate if it allows the underwriter to terminate its agreement with the issuer on the basis of either: (1) the occurrence of nonmaterial events affecting the issuer or the securities market in general; or (2) its inability to market the issuer's securities. Such overly broad market out clauses have the effect of changing a firm commitment underwriting into a best-efforts underwriting.

In addition to the market out clause, underwriting agreements also will condition the syndicate's obligation to purchase the issuer's securities on a number of contingencies, including the receipt of an opinion letter from the issuer's attorney and a "comfort letter" from the issuer's accountant stating that the accountant in not aware of any material changes in the issuer's financial statements. The attorney's opinion letter will confirm that the securities offered in the IPO have been duly authorized and validly issued.

The managing underwriter may engage selling dealers in order to ensure that the issuer's securities will be rapidly resold to investors. Selling dealers are registered broker-dealers that are brought into the distribution process solely to assist in placing the securities with investors. Selling group members do not risk their own capital as the underwriters do. It is the responsibility of the managing underwriter to allocate shares in the IPO to each member of the underwriting syndicate, each selling group member and, in many

---

[1] See First Boston Corp., CCH Fed. Sec. L. Rep. ¶78,152 (SEC Sept. 2, 1985).

cases, to the institutional investors who place their orders directly with the lead underwriter. In making this determination, the lead underwriter will look at each participant's distribution capabilities, geographic location and other factors.

Overallotment Option

Managing underwriters typically allocate more shares to each syndicate member than they are obligated to purchase pursuant to the terms of the Underwriting Agreement. This overallotment is designed to protect against cancellations of orders by the syndicate member's customers. The lead underwriter will usually include a clause in the underwriting agreement that permits the underwriter to purchase additional shares from the issuer to cover such overallotments. However, pursuant to NASD Rule 2710(c)(6)(B)(ix), an overallotment option may not exceed 15% of the number of securities being offered in the IPO.[2] Securities attorneys also refer to the overallotment option as the "Green Shoe" option—Green Shoe was the name of the issuer in which an overallotment option was first used.

Best-Efforts Underwriting

In a best-efforts underwriting, the underwriting firm does not commit to buy any of the securities offered by an issuer. Instead, the underwriter merely agrees to use its best efforts to find purchasers for the company's stock. Unlike a firm commitment underwriting where the underwriter acts as a principal and purchases and sells the issuer's stock for its own account, in a best-efforts underwriting the underwriter acts only as an agent and receives a commission for any securities that are sold. Technically, a best-efforts underwriting is not an underwriting in the traditional sense of the word because the firm handling a best-efforts offering

---

[2] See NASD Rule 2710(c)(6)(B).

never owns the stock it is selling and therefore never runs the risks of owning securities that it can't sell. In contrast, a traditional underwriter purchases stock from an issuer and then resells the stock to its customers. If the underwriter in a traditional IPO can't sell all of an issuer's stock, it will be the owner of the stock. However, the term "best-efforts underwriting" is a long-standing expression and is certainly a viable option for a company that can't attract the interest for a traditional underwriting.

Best-efforts underwritings can be utilized by less well-established companies in situations when underwriters do not want to take the chance of getting stuck with securities they cannot sell. In addition, a best-efforts underwriting can also be a viable option in bad economic times for any company that may be having trouble finding a traditional underwriter. When the IPO market is not active, traditional underwriters will be very reluctant to underwrite any new issues until conditions improve and the underwriter can be assured of strong demand for an issuer's stock. However, many companies require capital right away and do not have the luxury of waiting until the IPO market bounces back and underwriters are again willing to bring companies public. A best-efforts underwriting will allow the company to work with an experienced underwriter without the danger that the underwriter will be left with stock it cannot resell. Accordingly, a best-efforts underwriting is a valuable option for companies to consider, particularly in bad economic times when a more traditional underwriting is impossible to arrange.

There are several varieties of best-efforts underwritings. One variety is known as an "all-or-none" offering. In this scenario, the underwriter undertakes to use its best efforts to sell all of the securities registered with the SEC in a particular period of time. The time frame in which the securities must be sold is set through discussions between the underwriter and the issuer. Typically, the time frame for completing the offering is 90 to 120 days from when solicitations first begin. If all of the securities are not sold within the agreed-upon time period, the issuer must return any funds collected from investors. In the case of an all-or-nothing distribution of securities, SEC Rule 15c2-4 requires that all investor funds be deposited into either a separate bank account or into a bank escrow account until such time as all of the securities are sold.[3] Once all of the securities are sold, the money held in the separate bank account or escrow account may be released and transferred to the issuer. Rule 10b-9 is an antifraud rule that also applies to all-or-none offerings.[4] In essence, Rule 10b-9 says that it is unlawful to state that securities are being sold on an all-or-none basis unless the issuer will promptly return all of the investors' money in the event that all of the securities offered are not sold.

Another type of best-efforts underwriting is known as a "minimum/maximum" offering, also known as a "mini/max." In this type of offering, the issuer must sell a certain minimum number of securities before any investor's money is released, but the minimum is less than the full amount registered with the SEC. Other alternatives to a traditional underwriting, such as a direct public offering and a reverse merger, are discussed in Chapter 9. The methods discussed in Chapter 9 can all be used in bad economic times.

Responsibilities of the Underwriter

Whether an issuer's IPO is being conducted as a firm commitment underwriting or a best-efforts underwriting, the underwriter has several important responsibilities to carry out. One critical responsibility that falls on the underwriter is to ensure the accuracy of all of the material statements contained in the SEC registration

---

[3] 17 C.F.R. § 240.15c2-4.

[4] 17 C.F.R. § 240.10b-9.

statement, which includes the prospectus that is sent to investors. Under Section 11 of the Securities Act of 1933 (the "Securities Act"), an underwriter will be liable for any material misrepresentations contained in the registration statement, unless the underwriter had reasonable grounds to believe the statements contained therein after reasonable investigation.[5] This due diligence defense is set forth in Section 11(b)(3) of the Securities Act.[6] To ensure that the registration statement is accurate, the underwriter will perform an extensive amount of due diligence on the company prior to filing the registration statement with the SEC.

Another important responsibility the underwriter has is to properly price the securities that are offered in the IPO. At the end of the day, each member of the underwriting syndicate and each selling group member will charge its customers the same retail price for the stock that was issued in the IPO. The lead underwriter sets the final IPO price for the company's securities in the weeks leading up to the IPO. Setting this price is a critical responsibility of the lead underwriter.

Pricing the securities of companies that are going public for the first time is notoriously tricky. This is especially true with regard to Internet and technology companies, many of which do not have the traditional revenues and book values used to price companies in other industries. If the underwriter prices the securities too high, investors will not be eager to purchase the securities and the underwriter will have difficulty selling the entire offering. If the price of the IPO securities is set too low, then there will be an immediate and large spike in the stock's price in aftermarket trading. If there is a huge spike in the price of a company's stock in the first day of trading, then the issuer will not receive the full value of the securities that it sold. Generally, underwriters attempt

---

[5] 15 U.S.C. § 77k.

[6] 15 U.S.C. §§ 77k *et seq.*

to price the stock so that there will be a small increase in the price during the first day of trading.

In addition to these substantive responsibilities, the underwriter must also comply with the provisions of NASD Rule 2710, known as the Corporate Financing Rule.[7] This rule was promulgated by the NASD and regulates the type and amount of compensation that an underwriter may charge. It also sets out the NASD filing and fee requirements.

Costs

Conducting an IPO is an expensive process whether a company conducts a firm commitment underwriting or a best-efforts underwriting. While the costs associated with going public vary from company to company and depend heavily on the size and complexity of the offering, certain generalizations may be made. For example, if a smaller IPO is designed to raise $20 million, the greatest cost will be the underwriter's discount of 7% of the offering price. In addition, certain expenses will be incurred by the company in connection with the preparation of the IPO documents. Legal fees on an offering of this size will run between $150,000 and $250,000. Accounting fees will generally be $100,000 to $150,000, including the price of an audit. If any problems are encountered with the audit, the accounting fees can go up substantially. Printing costs will be about $100,000. There will also be fees for registering the securities with each of the states, as well as SEC and NASD fees and other fees for arranging for a stock transfer agent. All of these additional fees can total between $60,000 and $90,000, depending on how many shares of stock are issued and in how many states the offering must be registered.

---

[7] See NASD Rule 2710.

The Letter of Intent

Once a company has selected an underwriter that is interested in conducting the company's IPO, typically that underwriter will prepare a letter of intent. While the letter of intent does not obligate the underwriter to underwrite the company's IPO, it does outline the basic terms of the underwriting agreement and it gives the company enough certainty to begin incurring the expenses necessary to prepare for going public. The terms of the letter of intent will become legally binding when the underwriting agreement is signed by the issuer and the underwriter.

Many important topics are addressed in the letter of intent, including the contemplated offering price for the company's stock, the underwriter's discount and the overallotment option. Often the underwriter may also request and receive the right to participate in future corporate financings. However, counsel for the issuer should attempt to negotiate a limit on the future preferential financing rights sought by the underwriter. Generally underwriters will agree to a three- or four-year limit on their preferential financing rights. While the letter of intent will often require an issuer to pay certain fees of the underwriter in connection with the proposed financing, including attorneys' fees, the attorney for the issuer should ensure that the company will not have to pay any of the underwriter's fees in the event that the underwriter unilaterally decides not to proceed with the IPO. The attorney for the issuer should also ensure that the issuer's reimbursement obligations for underwriter expenses are capped at a specific dollar amount.

APPENDIX 5A

Analysis of a Sample Letter of Intent Between an Underwriter and an Internet Company

Internet Co., Inc.
488 Madison Avenue
New York, NY 10022

Ladies and Gentlemen:

This will serve to memorialize the discussions held between Internet Co., Inc. (the "Company") and Smith and Jones Capital, Inc. (the "Underwriter") regarding a proposed public offering of 200,000 shares of common stock, no par value, of the Company (the "Shares").

On the basis of these discussions, the reports and information submitted by the Company, and other information, the Underwriter and the Company have come to the following understanding concerning the proposed public offering of the Shares:

1. ***Authorized and Outstanding Shares.*** Prior to the effective date of the registration statement referred to below, the aggregate number of shares that the Company will be authorized to issue will consist of:

   a. Not less than 500,000 shares of common stock, no par value, of which 150,000 shares are to be sold to the public as set forth in Paragraph 4 below, 300,000 shares are to be issued to the present stockholders, and a sufficient number of shares will be reserved for issuance on conversion of the preferred shares and exercise of warrants as contemplated in this letter; and

b. 50,000 shares of preferred stock, no par value, each paying cumulative dividends at the rate of 6% per annum and convertible into shares of common stock of the company on a share-for-share basis at any time after January 1, 2004, to be issued to the present stockholders.

COMMENTARY: *Paragraph 1 sets forth the capital structure of the Company as it exists on the effective date of the offering. This is a very important paragraph because it ensures that the company is aware that it may have to amend its certificate of incorporation to increase the number of shares that are authorized and available for issuance. The Company must also ensure that its certificate of incorporation authorizes the issuance of preferred stock on the terms set forth in the underwriting agreement. Often, various underwriting scenarios are discussed between a company and its underwriter. Paragraph 1 sets forth the parties, understandings and their agreement on the final result of their negotiations.*

2. **Registration Statement.** The Company, with all convenient speed, will prepare and file with the Securities and Exchange Commission a registration statement under the Securities Act of 1933, as amended, covering the proposed sale of the Shares. The registration statement will contain appropriate financial statements audited by XYZ or any other independent certified public accountants satisfactory to the underwriter

covering the period ending September 30, 2001. The registration statement will become effective upon a date to which the underwriter consents and, in any event, no later than 90 days after the filing of the registration statement.

COMMENTARY: *Paragraph 2 makes clear that the obligation for preparing the registration statement that will permit the public sale of securities lies with the Company and not the Underwriter. Typically, the Underwriter will reserve the right to approve the Company's choice of an independent accountant. In the majority of cases, a Big 5 accounting firm will be used to audit the financial records of a company that is preparing to go public. The choice of a Big 5 accounting firm will allow the Underwriter to sell the shares to investors more easily than if the Company was audited by just any accounting firm.*

3. ***Underwriting.*** On the basis of the foregoing, the Underwriter hereby confirms in principal its interest in forming an underwriting group of securities firms to be headed by the Underwriter (the "Underwriters") to underwrite, on a firm commitment basis, a public offering of the Shares in accordance with the terms and conditions set forth below.

COMMENTARY: *This Paragraph confirms that the Underwriter will be engaged to underwrite the securities on a firm commitment basis, as opposed to a best-efforts basis. In doing so, the Underwriter will commit to buying the Company's securities for its own account and having the responsibility to resell the securities to public investors.*

Once the Underwriter commits to purchasing the shares, the Underwriter, and not the Company, assumes the risk that not all of the shares can be sold to investors.

4. **Public Offering.** The Shares will be sold to the public at an initial public offering price of $6 per share or another mutually agreed-upon price.

COMMENTARY: *This Paragraph memorializes the parties' general understanding with respect to the price of the stock sold in the IPO. The final price, however, will not be set until immediately before the registration statement becomes effective. This will allow the Underwriter to predict more accurately the demand for the securities being offered.*

5. **Underwriter's Discount.** The gross discount to the Underwriters will be 10% of the total public offering price.

COMMENTARY: *The discount is the reduction in price at which the Underwriter will purchase the securities from the Company. The difference between the price at which the Underwriter purchases the securities from the Company and the price it resells the securities to investors is called the "spread." The spread represents the Underwriter's profit on the transaction.*

6. ***Reimbursement of Underwriting Expenses.*** Upon consummation of the transaction contemplated in this letter, the Underwriters will be reimbursed for their expenses (in an amount up to $30,000) and for compensation of their counsel. These expenses and compensation may be deducted at the closing of the proposed public offering.

> **COMMENTARY:** *In order to track and control costs associated with the underwriting, the Company must ensure that there is either a cap on the Underwriter's reimbursable expenses or that prior approval from the Company is required in connection with expenses over a specified amount. The Company should also condition the reimbursement of the Underwriter's expenses on the closing of the underwriting.*

7. ***Purchase Warrants Reserved for the Underwriter.*** The Company will authorize and the Underwriters or their designees will be entitled to purchase 37,000 warrants (the "Warrants") at the closing of the proposed public offering. The purchase price of the Warrants will be $0.01. The Warrants will expire five years after the effective date of the registration statement covering the proposed issuance and sale of the Shares. Each of the Warrants will entitle the holder to purchase one share of common stock, no par value, of the Company at an exercise price of $6.60 per share. The Company will register the Warrants and the common stock which can be purchased upon exercise of the Warrants in accordance with the requirements of the Securities Act of 1933, as amended, and will maintain the effectiveness of the registration during the five-year period during which the Warrants are exercisable.

COMMENTARY: *This Paragraph provides for warrants to be issued to the Underwriter. The Underwriter will use these warrants to purchase additional shares of stock from the Company in the event that demand from investors for the Company's stock is greater than the supply of the original stock issued in the IPO. In the case of high investor demand, the Underwriter will exercise its option and acquire additional shares of stock from the Company for resale to investors. The terms of the warrants, including the expiration date and exercise price, should be spelled out clearly, as they are in this Paragraph.*

8. **Expenses of Issuance.** The Company will bear all costs and expenses in connection with the issuance, purchase, sale, and delivery of the Shares, the Warrants and the common stock which can be purchased upon the exercise of the Warrants, including all expenses and fees incident to the registration of these securities with the Securities and Exchange Commission, the costs of qualification under state securities laws including counsel fees, fees and disbursements of counsel and accountants for the Company, the cost of printing and preparing registration statements and as many prospectuses as the Underwriters may deem necessary, and related exhibits, including all amendments and supplements to the registration statements and prospectus.

9. **Representations of Financial History of the Company.** The Company's financial history for purposes of the registration statement covering the proposed issuance of the sale of the Shares will be substantially as represented previously to the Underwriter. The Underwriter must be satisfied with its investigation of the Company and its prospectus so that,

among other things, the Underwriter can anticipate earnings for the Company of at least $300,000 after taxes for the Company's fiscal year ending December 31, 2001 and earnings of approximately $100,000 before taxes for the Company's fiscal quarter ending March 31, 2002, based on generally accepted accounting principles applied on a consistent basis. If, in the opinion of the Underwriter, the financial condition of the Company and its outlook do not fulfill the Underwriters' expectations, the Underwriter will have the right, in its sole discretion, to review and determine its interest in the proposed underwriting.

COMMENTARY: *Paragraph 9 provides the Underwriter with a way to avoid its obligations to underwrite the Company's stock in the event that the financial condition of the Company changes substantially from the time the letter of intent is signed until the time the registration statement is filed.*

10. ***Examination of Corporate Books and Records.*** The Company will supply the Underwriters with whatever financial statements, contracts and other corporate records and documents that the Underwriters deem necessary, and will supply counsel for the Underwriters with all corporate papers, contracts, documents, and information they may require in connection with their activities related to the proposed underwriting. The Underwriters will be entitled to receive transfer sheets, interim financial statements and other information from the Company upon reasonable request after consummation of the transaction contemplated in this letter.

COMMENTARY: *Paragraph 10 gives the Underwriter the right to conduct a thorough due diligence investigation. Underwriters will always perform an extensive investigation of the Company prior to the time the shares are sold to the public. The due diligence process will include a review of the Company's accounting records and policies, its material contracts, corporate governance documents and other important information.*

11. ***Formal Agreement Contemplated.*** It is understood that this letter is merely a statement of intent, and, while the Company and the Underwriter agree in principle to the contents of this letter and propose to proceed promptly, and in good faith, to work out the arrangements with respect to the proposed public offering, any legal obligations between the Company and the Underwriter will be only as set forth in a duly negotiated and executed underwriting agreement (the "Underwriting Agreement"). The Underwriting Agreement shall be in form and content satisfactory to all parties, including other underwriters, if any, to be associated with the Underwriter in the proposed public offering and to counsel for the Underwriters. The Underwriter's obligations under the Underwriting Agreement shall be subject, among other things, to there being, in the opinion of the Underwriter, (a) no material adverse change in the condition or obligations of the Company, and (b) no market conditions that might render the purchase and sale of the Shares inadvisable.

COMMENTARY: *Paragraph 11 sets out the parties' agreement that they do not intend to be bound by the terms of the letter of intent. Instead, a formal underwriting agreement will be drafted and executed that will bind the parties. Although a letter of intent does not bind either party, it is an extremely useful way to set forth in writing the basic underlying terms of the contemplated underwriting. A letter of intent can pave the way for a mutually beneficial underwriting agreement between the Company and the Underwriter.*

12. ***Preferential Financing Rights.*** The Underwriting Agreement shall provide that the Company shall grant to the Underwriter preferential financing rights for a period of five years after the effective date of the registration statement covering the proposed issuance and sale of the Shares for any public offerings or exempt offerings contemplated during that period by the Company or any of its affiliates.

COMMENTARY: *Underwriters will often seek preferential financing rights from a company that they take public. The underwriting agreement should specify in detail the type of preference to be granted to the Underwriter and should also contain a date on which such preferential rights expire. The Company should ensure that any such clause will not bar it from using another underwriter if the original underwriter declines to assist the Company in a financing transaction.*

13. ***Disclaimer of Responsibility if Financing Is Not Consummated.*** If the financing is not consummated, the Underwriter shall not be responsible for any expenses incurred by the Company in connection with the proposed underwriting. In addition, the Underwriter shall not be liable for any claims or charges relating to the proposed financing if the financing is not consummated.

> **COMMENTARY:** *Paragraph 13 alerts the Company to the fact that it is responsible for all of its own expenses incurred in connection with the underwriting, even if the underwriting is never completed.*

If the foregoing correctly states our agreement, please sign below and return a copy of this letter to the Underwriter.

Very truly yours,

Underwriter

Agreed to:
Internet Co., Inc.

_____
(Name and title)

APPENDIX 5B

Checklist of Steps to Take
in Selecting an Appropriate Underwriter

1. Examine research reports and investor surveys to determine who the most popular analysts are in the company's industry. Find out with which underwriter those analysts are associated.

2. Research recent IPOs of companies that are in the same industry and determine who the underwriters were. Also research how successful each underwriter was in selling the issuers' stock to investors at the price originally set.

3. After determining which underwriters are most active in the company's industry, find the underwriters that participated in deals that were about the same size as the company's proposed IPO.

4. Research the level of post-IPO support that the underwriters provide to the companies they underwrite. Do the underwriters enthusiastically support and stand behind the companies they bring to market? Or do they simply underwrite each company and then move on to the next deal?

5. Begin interviewing potential underwriters and be sure to cover the following topics:

   ➢ Why does each underwriter think it will be best for the company?

➤ What makes each underwriter unique and better than its competitors?

> ➤ What are the underwriter's typical expenses for an underwriting that is the same size as the company's proposed underwriting? What are the typical fees of the underwriter's counsel? (Note: The underwriter's expenses and the counsel's fees are paid by the company at the completion of the underwriting.)

> ➤ What type of lockup provisions will each underwriter seek? (A lockup provision restricts company insiders from selling their shares for a specified period of time, usually from 30-120 days. Companies will want to push for a shorter lockup period.)

> ➤ Will the underwriter require the company to give it preferential rights to participate in future corporate financing transactions? If so, how long will the preferential rights extend?

APPENDIX 5C

An Overview of the
Underwriting Process

1. The company interviews several underwriting firms to determine which underwriter will be best to participate in the IPO.

2. It then provides the contemplated underwriters with preliminary financial and operational data.

3. The company should negotiate the terms of the proposed underwriting with a number of underwriters. Terms negotiated include lockup provisions, limits on underwriter's expenses and timing for the IPO.

4. The company and the underwriter enter into a letter of intent.

5. The underwriter begins the due diligence process. During this process the underwriter will review the company's financial statements, material contracts, corporate governance documents and other important information.

6. While the due diligence process is under way, a registration statement will be prepared by the company and its attorneys. During preparation of the registration statement no offers of securities can be made and attempts to condition the market for the securities are prohibited.

7. Once the registration statement is completed, it is submitted to the SEC for review and comment. At this point, the price of the securities has not yet been finalized.

8. Once the registration statement is filed with the SEC, the underwriter begins accepting indications of interest from investors. However, no sales are made during this time period.

9. The SEC's comments are incorporated into the registration statement and it is resubmitted to the SEC.

10. The lead underwriter will form a syndicate with other underwriters to ensure wide distribution of the company's securities and to spread the risk of the underwriting among several firms.

11. When the SEC has indicated that it has no further comments on the registration statement, an amendment is filed setting forth the per share offering price of the securities.

12. The registration statement is then declared effective and the underwriters purchase the securities from the issuer and immediately begin reselling the securities to investors.

Due Diligence and the Preparation of the Registration Statement

Once the letter of intent between the issuer and the underwriter is signed, the preparation of the registration statement can begin. A registration statement must be filed with the SEC and be declared effective before any securities can be sold to the public. Federal and state laws heavily regulate the sale of securities in the United States. At the federal level, the Securities and Exchange Commission is the primary agency responsible for enforcing the securities laws enacted by Congress. At the state level, all fifty states have some form of statutory or common law rule that affects the sale of securities. The state securities laws are also known as Blue Sky laws.

The primary statute that regulates the offer and sale of securities is the Securities Act of 1933 (the "Securities Act").[1] Section 5 of the Securities Act—which has been described as the heart of the statute—establishes a regulatory scheme whereby a detailed registration statement for the securities offering is prepared by the issuer and its counsel and then submitted to the SEC for review prior to any sales of securities.[2] Substantial legal liabilities can be imposed against the issuer and others involved with the underwriting process if any material misrepresentations are contained in the registration statement. To guard against this, the underwriter and its counsel conduct a thorough investigation of

---

[1] 15 U.S.C. §§ 77a *et seq.*

[2] 15 U.S.C. § 77e.

the issuer, its business and the senior officers before the registration statement is filed. This chapter examines in detail the process of preparing the registration statement for filing with the SEC and what restrictions a company must be aware of before a registration statement is declared effective by the SEC.

THE SECURITIES ACT

Congress enacted the Securities Act in 1933 in the wake of the Great Depression. At the time, it was felt that a contributing cause of the country's economic crisis was the unregulated sale of stock in businesses that had highly questionable prospects. The purpose behind the Securities Act was to provide the investing public with full disclosure of all material information about the issuer and the securities that were being offered for sale. The Securities Act was also designed to protect the public from fraud and to promote honesty and ethical standards through the imposition of civil liabilities on issuers of securities and others.[3] In essence, the Securities Act, through the imposition of strict disclosure requirements, removed the concept of "buyer beware" from the securities markets. The issuer bears the burden of ensuring that all material information is disclosed to those offered the opportunity to purchase securities.

The Securities Act accomplishes its purpose of full disclosure by requiring that a detailed registration statement be filed with and reviewed by the SEC. The registration statement is a publicly available document that can be reviewed by potential investors, securities analysts and other industry participants. An important part of the registration statement is the prospectus that potential investors will receive. The aim of the Securities Act is to provide an investor with sufficient written information about an issuer and its

---

[3] See, e.g., Ernst & Ernst v. Hochfelder, 425 U.S. 185, 96 S.Ct. 1375, 47 L.Ed.2d 668 (1976).

securities so that the investor can make an informed decision about whether to purchase the securities.

While the purpose behind the Securities Act is the protection of investors, it is important to note that the Securities Act is exclusively a disclosure statute and not a merit-based regulatory scheme. In other words, the likelihood of success of a particular company or business venture is irrelevant assuming that all material facts are disclosed to potential investors. In fact, the SEC requires a statement in each prospectus that informs investors that the agency has not approved or disapproved the securities being offered, nor has the SEC passed upon the accuracy or adequacy of the prospectus. It is a violation of Section 23 of the Securities Act for an issuer or any individual to state that the SEC has endorsed the securities being offered.[4]

An important side effect of the full disclosure system is that issuers will often put in place substantive, investor-friendly measures designed to help the offering sell. This is an intended benefit of the full disclosure philosophy behind the Securities Act. Merely shedding light on business practices that are detrimental to investors is enough to eliminate such practices. In addition, during the process of preparing the registration statement the issuer will take numerous steps to improve its business processes. Typically, the issuer will upgrade its accounting procedures and formalize its accounting policies. The issuer will also put important contracts in writing and the company's books and records will be put in order. Also, prior to the offering of securities, companies will recapitalize to ensure that enough new shares are available for the IPO.

Under Section 5 of the Securities Act, the registration of securities is broken down into three time periods: (1) the prefiling period which occurs before the registration statement is filed with the

---

[4] 15 U.S.C. § 77w.

SEC; (2) the waiting period which occurs after the statement is filed with the SEC but before it has been declared effective; and (3) the post-effective period which occurs after the registration statement has been declared effective and buying and selling of the security begins. The types of promotional and sales activities that an issuer can engage in is dependent to a great extent on which time period the registration process is in. Therefore, an issuer and its counsel must pay careful attention to the offering's stage in the registration process.

THE PREFILING PERIOD

Before a registration statement has been filed with the SEC absolutely no offers of securities can be made by the issuer or any underwriter working on the offering. Allowing companies and their agents to make offers to sell securities prior to the preparation and filing of a registration statement would run completely counter to the goal of full written disclosure of all material information to investors. Without detailed written disclosure, investors may succumb to a company's hype regarding its business or securities.

The prohibition against making offers of securities during the prefiling period is contained in Section 5(c) of the Securities Act. The term "offer" is broadly defined in Section 2(a)(3) of the Securities Act and includes "every attempt or offer to dispose of, or solicitation of an offer to buy, a security or an interest in a security for value."[5] As a result of the broad definition of what constitutes an offer to sell securities, issuers of securities must be very careful not to inadvertently make an offer to sell in violation of Section 5 of the Securities Act. A wide variety of activities have been deemed to constitute offers to sell securities in violation of Section 5. For

---

[5] 15 U.S.C. § 77b.

example, a newspaper ad that offered securities to the public was deemed to be an offer to sell,[6] as was a press release describing an offering that was to be made in the future.[7] The broad interpretations of what constitutes an offer to sell securities also prohibit a company from making offers through public Internet postings or e-mail solicitations. However, important language in Section 2(a)(3) exempts preliminary negotiations or agreements between an issuer and an underwriter from the broad ban on offers to sell securities prior to the filing of a registration statement.

Actual sales of securities are, of course, also prohibited from occurring during the prefiling period. Sales of securities can only occur after the SEC declares the registration statement to be effective. The prohibition against sales is contained in Section 5(a) of the Securities Act.[8] Preliminary negotiations or agreements between an issuer and an underwriter are excepted from the broad ban on offers to sell securities prior to the filing of a registration statement. In addition, if an issuer desires to make a registered offering of its securities to its own employees, special SEC rules allow for advance notification without the risk that such notification will constitute an offer. SEC Rule 135(a)(5) allows an issuer to provide notification that it proposes to make a public offering of securities if the notice states that the offering will be made only by means of a prospectus and the notice contains no more than the following information: (1) the name of the employer; (2) the class or classes of employees to whom the securities are proposed to be offered; (3) the offering price; and (4) the period during which the offering is to be made.[9] Although advance notification is permitted in these circumstances, actual sales must wait for the registration statement to become effective.

---

[6] SEC v. Chinese Consolidated Benevolent Ass'n, 120 F.2d 738 (2d Cir. 1941).

[7] SEC v. Arvida Corp., 169 F. Supp. 211 (S.D.N.Y. 1958).

[8] 15 U.S.C. § 77e.

[9] 17 C.F.R. § 230.135.

Other than engaging in preliminary negotiations with an underwriter and the employee notification that is allowed under Rule 135, an issuer must carefully avoid any other activities designed to generate interest in the securities that are the subject of the upcoming registration statement. Specifically, an issuer should not engage in any efforts to locate or contact potential investors. An issuer should also refrain from using any publicity designed to generate demand for its securities by potential investors. An issuer that engages in promotional activities prior to the time that its registration statement is declared effective can seriously jeopardize the success of its upcoming offering. This early, improper publicity for the sale of securities is known as "gun jumping."

Gun Jumping

Gun jumping occurs when an issuer, or people affiliated with it, illegally attempts to generate demand for its securities through advance publicity. Such publicity is intended to create an early demand for the company's securities by potential investors and can condition the market for a successful IPO. Because the SEC views gun jumping as a serious violation of Section 5 of the Securities Act,[10] the issuer of securities must refrain from publicizing its upcoming securities offering before the registration statement is declared effective.

The rationale for banning publicity for an issuer's upcoming security offering is clear. Advance publicity for a securities offering can create hype among investors and the information used to create the hype may be misleading. Any activities that could be construed as an attempt to generate interest in an issuer's securities among investors must be avoided. The clear aim of the

---

[10] 15 U.S.C. § 77e.

Securities Act is to inform investors about the merits of an offering through a detailed prospectus.

Officers of companies that plan to sell shares to the public in the near future must be aware of the prohibitions on "conditioning" the market for the companies' securities. Accordingly, care must be taken with regard to speeches, press releases and interviews with reporters so that nothing is done or said that can be construed as improperly attempting to generate demand for an issuer's upcoming offering. If the SEC believes that a gun jumping violation has occurred, it may insist that the issuer delay its offering until the market has had time to put the hype in perspective. In extreme cases, the SEC could also take enforcement action against an issuer, which could include the imposition of significant fines.

Because the SEC takes gun jumping so seriously, corporate officers are often extremely careful not to do anything that could delay the company's offering. In the past, some companies have gone so far as to shut down the flow of public information out of fear that the SEC would otherwise find a gun jumping violation. Underwriters who were working with an issuer would also be concerned about their own research or reports being construed as improper publicity for an upcoming offering.

To help alleviate concerns that the gun jumping prohibition was impeding the legitimate flow of corporate information into the marketplace, the SEC issued a release that provided guidance on what types of public communication could be made without fear of violating the rule against gun jumping.[11] In the release, the SEC stated that corporate communications are permitted during the prefiling and waiting periods, but the communications must not be veiled attempts to condition the market and generate demand for

---

[11] SEC Rel. No. 5180 (Aug. 16, 1971).

the company's stock. The SEC provided fairly specific guidance to issuers. It stated that factual information should not be withheld and companies with securities in the registration process are allowed to:

1. Continue to advertise products and services.

2. Continue to distribute quarterly, annual and periodic reports to shareholders.

3. Continue to publish proxy statements and send out dividend notices.

4. Continue to make announcements to the press with respect to factual business and financial developments such as the receipt of a contract, the settlement of a strike, the opening of a plant or similar events of interest to the community in which the business operates.

5. Answer unsolicited telephone inquiries from stockholders, financial analysts, the press and others concerning factual information.

6. Observe an open door policy in responding to unsolicited inquiries concerning factual matters from securities analysts, financial analysts, security holders and participants in the communications field who have a legitimate interest in the company's affairs.

7. Continue to hold stockholder meetings as scheduled and to answer shareholders' inquiries at such meetings relating to factual matters.[12]

Throughout this release the SEC emphasized that the dissemination of accurate financial information by companies was to be

---

[12] Id.

encouraged. An issuer and its counsel should therefore review all public communications by corporate officers and directors any time that the company is contemplating preparing a registration statement. The issuer and its counsel should specifically examine public communications to ensure that the information disseminated is primarily factual in nature and not designed to create interest in an upcoming securities offering or IPO.

THE REGISTRATION STATEMENT

Full disclosure of material information to investors, the primary purpose of the Securities Act, is accomplished by filing a detailed registration statement with the SEC. The registration statement sets out in detail all of the material facts about the company and its business. It also includes copies of the company's financial statements. The basic registration statement that is used by companies going public for the first time is Form S-1, although small business issuers can use shorter forms that are known as Forms SB-1 and SB-2.

The SEC has recently undertaken a major initiative to ensure that registration statements filed in connection with an IPO are written in plain English and not legalese. As of October 1, 1998, companies filing registration statements under the Securities Act of 1933 must:

➤ Write the first part of the registration statement in plain English;

➤ Write the remaining portions of the registration statement in a clear, understandable manner; and

➤ Design the registration statement to be visually inviting and easy to read.[13]

---

[13] Final Rule: Plain English Disclosure, SEC Rel. No. 33-7497 (Jan. 28, 1998).

In accordance with the SEC's plain English rules, technical jargon and long, complex sentences should be avoided when preparing the registration statement. Instead, the registration statement should contain short, clear sentences that concisely communicate the required disclosure information. The SEC's plain English rules do not sacrifice thorough disclosure for simplicity. Indeed, the SEC still requires a company to make complete disclosure of all material information relating to its business, even if the business is extremely complex. However, such disclosure must now be made in understandable, easy-to-read language.

In addition to information relating to the company and its business, all registration statements must contain risk disclosures that provide meaningful cautionary language to investors. Risk factors loosely fall into three broad categories:

➤ *Industry Risk*—risks companies face by virtue of the industry they are in. For example, many new media companies that manufacture computer hardware run the risk that, despite careful planning, they will be subject to computer chip shortages.

➤ *Company Risk*—risks that are specific to the company. For example, a new media company has suffered significant losses in the past and will have to expend substantial amounts of capital to achieve profitability.

➤ *Investment Risk*—risks that are specifically tied to a security. For example, in a debt offering, the debt being offered is the most junior subordinated debt of the company.[14]

When drafting risk factors, a company should be sure to specifically link each risk to its industry, company or investment, as

---

[14] *Id.*

applicable. Too often, companies include only generic, boilerplate risk disclosures that do not alert investors to the specific risks that they face by investing in the company.

In addition to the foregoing general rules, the SEC has promulgated several regulations that address in fairly specific detail the type of information that a company must disclose in a registration statement. Counsel for an issuer that is preparing a registration statement must consult these regulations to ensure that all of the required information is provided. In general, SEC Regulation C[15] governs all registration statements filed under the Securities Act—unless a specific provision of a form or SEC Regulation S-K[16] differs. Regulation C is primarily concerned with the form of the filings made with the SEC, and covers such matters as the size of the paper to be used, the number of copies and the type of binding required for registration statements. Counsel should consult SEC Regulation S-T for information concerning how filings are made electronically using the SEC's EDGAR system.[17] For guidance on substantive disclosure issues in the narrative portion of the prospectus, counsel must consult Regulation S-K.[18] For guidance related to financial statement disclosure, counsel must consult Regulation S-X.[19]

After considering the foregoing regulations as well as the instructions for the Form S-1, SB-1, or SB-2, counsel may begin to prepare the registration statement. An examination of Form S-1 is instructive as to the type of information the SEC will expect to be disclosed. The Form S-1 is divided into two parts. Part I is the

---

[15] 17 C.F.R. §§ 230.400 *et seq.*

[16] 17 C.F.R. §§ 229.101 *et seq.*

[17] 17 C.F.R. §§ 232.10 *et seq.*

[18] See N.15 *supra.*

[19] 17 C.F.R. §§ 229.101 *et seq.*

prospectus that will be given to potential investors while Part II contains additional information about the company and the offering that is not required to be included in the prospectus. Generally speaking, Part I of Form S-1 is answered with narrative responses while Part II seeks responses to specific items called for by applicable SEC rules.

Part I of Form S-1, the prospectus, is the document that investors will receive regarding the offering. Therefore, it is critical that the prospectus contain all of the material information about the issuer. The issuer and its counsel should ensure that the prospectus is written in a clear and direct manner so that an ordinary investor can understand the disclosures being made.

In general, the prospectus will contain the following:

➤ A summary of the information presented in the prospectus.

➤ A discussion of risk factors.

➤ A description of the company, including what business it is in, its corporate name and operating history.

➤ Information regarding corporate property.

➤ Information regarding management.

➤ Information regarding any promoters.

➤ Summary information on corporate earnings.

➤ A description of the company's capital structure.

➤ A description of the stock being registered and other securities being registered.

➤ The plan of distribution.

➤ An explanation of how the proceeds are to be used.

➤ A list of sales being made for other than cash.

➤ A list of the principal holders of securities along with the number of shares owned by each principal holder.

> Disclosures of any interests management has in certain transactions.

> A statement setting forth the compensation of officers and directors.

> Disclosure of any options to purchase securities, including the number of options outstanding and their exercise price.

> Disclosure of any pending legal proceedings.

> Any legal opinions of counsel.

> Management's discussion and analysis of the company's financial condition and results of operations.

> Financial Statements.

It should be noted that the issuer's financial statements are among the most important information contained in the registration statement. In addition to Regulation S-X, the SEC has published numerous releases to help guide issuers in ensuring that financial performance is presented accurately. The registration statement must include a balance sheet of the issuer as of a date not more than ninety days prior to the date of filing showing all assets and liabilities of the issuer and the nature of each. In addition, a profit and loss statement must also be included in the registration statement.

Part II of the registration statement contains information that is not required to be part of the prospectus. It includes:

> A list of the expenses associated with the issuance and distribution of the securities.

> Disclosure of any relationship with experts named in the registration statement.

> Listing of sales to special parties.

> Disclosures of any recent sales of unregistered securities.

> Information about the registrant's subsidiaries.

> A discussion of the effect of any charter provision or bylaw under which an officer or director is indemnified against liability which he may incur in his capacity as such.

> Any exhibits, including any material contract not made in the ordinary course of business.

> Disclosures of certain undertakings that the issuer must perform after the conclusion of the offering.

> Signatures of the company's officers and directors to confirm that they have read and approved the registration statement.

> Consent of the certified public accountant to the use of its auditing reports in the registration statement.

Exhibits include the underwriting agreement, a copy of the issuer's certificate of incorporation and bylaws and the opinion of counsel relative to the issuance of securities. Although the information contained in Part II is not part of the prospectus, it is publicly available from the SEC.

THE SEC REVIEW PROCESS

Once a registration statement is filed with the SEC by an issuer, it is sent to the appropriate review group for the industry in which the issuer operates. After an initial review, the SEC will provide the issuer's counsel with written comments on the registration statement, including directions to make certain changes. The company will usually receive the SEC's written comments about three weeks after the registration statement is first submitted. The SEC's comments can address any items in the registration statement. Some of the supplemental information that the SEC may request on a registration statement incudes: (1) additional company specific risk disclosures; (2) additional disclosures related to the company's business; and (3) more disclosures related to how future corporate transactions could affect the shareholders. Depending on the number of SEC comments, the company generally will take one to two weeks to revise its registration statement and then refile it with the SEC. If the company desires to discuss particular comments with the SEC, the staff is generally available for a conference call with the company's attorneys. The SEC also issues comments to ensure that registration statements are written in plain English. The following is an example of language that has been revised to conform to the plain English requirements:

INITIAL VERSION: **ABC 10-K**	PLAIN ENGLISH VERSION: **ABC/EFG's Merger Proxy**
The Company primarily designs, produces and markets an integrated family of advanced predictive maintenance products and services for use in large scale, continuous run manufacturing facilities. The Company's Reliability-Based Maintenance products and services help customers detect potentially disruptive conditions in the operation of their machinery before damage or complete mechanical failure occurs, thereby allowing maintenance to be scheduled at the most appropriate time.	*ABC's primary business is the design, manufacture, and sale of a family of high-tech instruments that help companies determine when their industrial machines are in need of repair or adjustment. ABC also offers services to help its customers better manage the maintenance of their equipment. ABC's products and services help its customers keep their production lines running and maintain the quality of their products which may be adversely affected by an improperly functioning production line machine. ABC's customers are primarily large manufacturing, processing or power-generating companies.*

If the SEC believes that the registration statement is deficient and the issuer intends to proceed anyway, Section 8 of the Securities Act allows the SEC to commence what is known as a "stop order" proceeding which prohibits the registration statement from becoming effective.[20] This procedure is rarely used. Instead, the SEC generally relies on the review and comment process. Even when using the review and comment process, the SEC still maintains a great deal of control over the registration statement. Section 8 of the Securities Act states that a registration statement, or any amendment thereto, will not be effective until twenty days after the filing unless the Commission accelerates the time. In practice, the review and comment process works well because issuers rely on the SEC to accelerate the effectiveness of the final amendments to the registration statement. Once the issuer satisfies all of the SEC's disclosure concerns, the SEC will accelerate the twenty days and declare that the registration statement is immediately effective. This allows the issuer and the underwriter to begin selling the securities to the public.

THE WAITING PERIOD

Once the registration statement has been filed with the SEC it goes through a review process. The time period between when the registration statement is filed with the SEC and the time that the registration statement is declared effective is known as the "waiting period."

During the waiting period, the underwriter may legally begin to make oral offers to sell the securities that are the subject of the registration statement. The solicitation of offers is also known as taking "indications of interest" from investors who are interested

---

[20] 15 U.S.C. § 77h.

in purchasing the securities once the registration statement becomes effective. Also during the waiting period, the underwriter will set up "road shows." The company and its management will travel to different cities to meet with institutional investors who may be interested in purchasing the company's stock in the IPO. In recent years, more and more road shows have been conducted electronically over the Internet. This, of course, can save corporate officers a great deal of time and can open up the road show process to more institutional investors. The SEC specifically approved use of the Internet to conduct road shows in a series of no-action letters.[21]

While indications of interest may be taken during the waiting period, binding contracts for sale are not yet permitted. Accordingly, an underwriter is not permitted to accept funds for any securities during the waiting period because such activities can be construed as evidence that a sale took place before the registration statement was declared effective.

While issuers and underwriters may make oral offers and take indications of interest during the waiting period, there are still strict limits placed on the type of written information that can be provided to customers. Only certain specified types of written information may be provided in connection with the offering. In practice, the only written information that can be sent to a potential investor is a preliminary prospectus, which is a nonfinal copy of the prospectus that was filed with the SEC as part of the registration statement. The preliminary prospectus is also known as a "red herring" because of the red legend contained on the first page informing investors that the document is subject to completion or amendment and that a registration statement

---

[21] Private Financial Network, publicly available Mar. 12, 1997; Net Road Show, publicly available Sept. 8, 1997; Net Roadshow II, publicly available Jan. 30, 1998.

relating to the securities has been filed with the SEC. The legend must also disclose that the preliminary prospectus is not an offer to sell or the solicitation of an offer to buy. The principal difference between the preliminary prospectus and the final version is the omission of information relating to the price of the securities, underwriters' compensation and other information that depends on the price of the security. This information is omitted because the price is not set until the day that the prospectus is declared effective. With the exception of the pricing information, the preliminary prospectus contains a great deal of information about the securities being offered as well as information about the issuer. Investors rely heavily on the preliminary prospectus in deciding whether to purchase securities in the IPO.

SEC rules also allow the underwriter to take out what is known as a "tombstone ad," which provides basic information about the offering. Rules 134 and 135 strictly limit what can be placed in a tombstone ad.[22] The only information allowed is the name of the issuer, the price, the name of the entities that will take purchase orders and the identification of who will provide a prospectus to the investor. The Securities Act and the SEC rules allow a summary prospectus to be used. However, in practice, this is not used very often because investors desire to see the entire preliminary prospectus.

During the waiting period, underwriters and issuers are not permitted to use any other written material to help sell the offering. Providing potential investors with selling literature, such as brochures or sales letters, is a violation of Section 5.[23]

---

[22] 17 C.F.R. §§ 230.134, 230.135.

[23] 15 U.S.C. § 77e.

POST-EFFECTIVE PERIOD

Once the registration statement is effective, offers and sales of securities may be made freely, and supplemental selling literature can be used in addition to the prospectus. Typically, an investor will receive a copy of the final prospectus when the securities purchased in the public offering are delivered.

The SEC also allows issuers and underwriters to deliver prospectuses electronically to a customer's computer. In a no-action letter, the SEC stated that customers could voluntarily chose to receive an electronic prospectus if the following conditions were met: (1) the electronic prospectus and the paper prospectus contained the same information; (2) the electronic prospectus could be converted to a paper format; and (3) a paper copy of the prospectus would be forwarded to customers upon timely request.[24]

---

[24] Brown & Wood, 1994-1995 CCH Fed. Sec. L. Rep. ¶77,000 (avail. Feb. 17, 1995).

CHAPTER 7

MARKETING AND COMMUNICATIONS FOR COMPANIES THAT WANT TO GO PUBLIC

A company that desires to go public must make marketing and communications a high priority no matter what stage of development the company is in. The term "marketing" does not refer just to promoting the company's products and services; rather, it encompasses how the company communicates its overall message and vision. This chapter focuses on marketing and communications strategies as they relate to the company's financial growth and development. The goals of a company's marketing efforts will change as the company develops and becomes larger. A start-up company will focus its marketing efforts on getting its message to potential investors in order to raise capital. As the company develops and becomes publicly traded, it will focus its marketing and communications efforts on financial analysts and reporters since they can "create" market value for its shareholders. Finally, the marketing efforts of a seasoned publicly traded company are likely to focus on keeping the financial markets and the company's shareholders apprised of all material developments in order to maintain and increase the company's market value.

Effective corporate marketing and communications are important in both good and bad economic times. While the company's message may have to be modified to take into account current economic conditions, the goal will still be to communicate effectively the company's message to customers, investors and other interested parties. When economic times are bad, a company will often focus on how its business strategies have changed to cope with the new challenges. While many companies will focus on how they plan to stay afloat in a challenging economy, other companies will look at bad economic times as an opportunity to gain market share from competitors.

At any given time, growing companies have numerous constituencies with which they have to effectively communicate, such as potential investors, shareholders, the financial press and the financial markets. Before the company engages in any communications efforts, its management must determine what the company's message should be in order to present that message in a consistent and compelling light. Also, in every stage of the company's development, the management must focus on who the target audience is for the company's message. Once the target audience is identified, the company's message can be tailored to meet the unique needs and interests of that audience. All successful marketing efforts require a great deal of advance planning and in-depth analysis of the objectives that the company is trying to accomplish. This chapter discusses proven marketing strategies that growing companies can employ in each stage of their development.

MARKETING AND COMMUNICATIONS FOR A START-UP COMPANY

The primary focus of a start-up company's marketing efforts will be on raising capital. In fact, the entire process of successfully starting and developing a company involves marketing the company's business idea and its likelihood of success to new investors and the financial community. As every entrepreneur knows, raising capital for a new business is an extremely competitive endeavor. There are always new companies in the marketplace seeking capital investments from potential investors. Moreover, it is a fact of life that most requests for funding are rejected by potential investors, particularly when economic times are challenging. Often, good marketing and communications skills can make the difference between success and failure when raising capital. To be successful in this competitive environment a company must do everything possible to maximize its chances of reaching and impressing potential investors, and convincing them to invest. One of the critical steps that a company can take to maximize its chances of success with investors is to create a compelling message that will succinctly communicate why an investor should invest in the company.

The first step in every good marketing effort is to think about the target audiences and their concerns. Special efforts must be made by the company's management to identify and address the concerns of potential investors. Otherwise, the company's presentations will lack critical elements and will not be as persuasive as they could be.

When they are raising capital for a new company, many entrepreneurs make the mistake of focusing all of their energy on telling potential investors about the company's great products or services, or the market opportunity and the company's competitive advantages. While all of these topics are important and must be discussed with potential investors, executives of early stage companies must be sure to focus primarily on the investors' primary concern—namely, how the investor's are going to make money by investing in the company.

Most investors will be aware that an investment in a new company is illiquid, and that it can take over two years before they realize any return on their money. However, the investors will also want to have specific information on how the company plans on providing them with a return on their investment that is commensurate with the risk they are incurring in funding the new venture. In general, early stage investors who provide seed capital to a business will

237

want to know whether the company plans on going public and, if so, the potential time frame for the IPO. The investors will also want to know about what factors could cause the company to delay the IPO, such as technological setbacks or other obstacles. Instead of an IPO, some new media and technology companies anticipate that they will grow to the point where they can be acquired by a larger company. Typically, before a company becomes an attractive acquisition candidate it must have demonstrated that its business model is viable. In fact, many larger companies will not consider acquiring a smaller company until a minimum amount of revenue is being generated through business operations. IPOs and buyouts are sometimes referred to as "liquidity events" because at such points early investors in the company first receive a return on their money. Investors will also refer to the various liquidity events as "exit opportunities" because they are a mechanism by which the investors can recover their initial investment and, hopefully, also realize a significant return. The executives of a company must be well-prepared to discuss the possible exit strategies when they meet with potential investors.

In addition to exit strategies, potential investors will also want to discuss less obvious topics with the entrepreneur. For instance, potential investors will want to know whether the founders of the company have invested any of their own money in the company, and, if so, how much. Knowing that company founders have invested their own money in a business venture will give potential investors comfort that they are not being asked to fund a venture that the founders are not confident enough to fund themselves. Therefore, entrepreneurs should make a point to discuss with investors the financial commitments that they have made to the business. In fact, when a company's founders and management have made a substantial investment in a company, that information can be used to help persuade new investors that the company is a good investment opportunity. Persuading potential investors to invest in a start-up company requires a great deal of selling skill. Executives will want to emphasize all of the positive aspects of investing in the company.

On occasion, the founders of a new company will make their contributions to the business not so much in money but in time and services. Giving up a steady job for the opportunity to work in a new venture with lower pay and benefits can be just as persuasive to potential investors—if it is presented right—as a substantial financial interest. Accordingly, the founders of a company should be prepared to discuss the alternative business opportunities they have given up in order to work in the new venture. Knowing that an entrepreneur is committed to the company and its success, whether that commitment is demonstrated in terms of dollars or time and services, will give investors substantial comfort. However, if an investor is being asked to give money to a venture that does not have any financial backing or time commitment by the founders, this raises a major red flag—making capital raising substantially more difficult.

One area that new entrepreneurs often overlook is the importance of maintaining good financial and legal controls in an early stage company. All too often, those managing the new company view professional accounting and legal advisors as a drain on scarce corporate assets. The services provided by accountants and attorneys are too often dismissed as unimportant and overly formal for a start-up company. In addition, they view the time spent on accounting and legal issues as being diverted from time that could have been spent on developing the business. However, these views are a prime example of entirely overlooking the concerns of potential investors. More experienced entrepreneurs know that potential investors will want to be sure that there are strong financial and accounting policies in place to ensure that their substantial investment will be used appropriately and will be accounted for. The failure of a company to have a solid accounting system in place will be a major hindrance to raising capital. The accounting systems at a new company do not have to be elaborate or overly expensive. However, there should be clear policies and systems in place to account for all receipts and disbursements of money and to accurately track all assets and liabilities. In addition, the accounting system should be computerized so that it can be scaled up as the company grows. Good financial controls will also require more than one corporate officer to approve in writing any substantial expenditures of corporate money. By retaining an accountant early on, a start-up company can put good financial controls in place from the beginning. It is much easier to start a company off with good financial controls than to go back and fix financial problems that come up later.

In a similar manner, executives should also ensure that appropriate legal steps have been taken from the start. It is important to ensure that the company has been properly incorporated and that the necessary corporate formalities have been complied with during the course of the company's existence, such as keeping minutes of directors, meetings and records of all corporate actions. Professional investors will want to know whether the company is in compliance with all legal requirements, including necessary filings, licensing arrangements and tax payments before they make their investment. In addition, if consulted early on, counsel can help ensure that all of the company's intellectual property is properly protected with copyrights, trademarks and patents. When an investor is prepared to invest in the company, an attorney should be retained to review the transaction, draft the appropriate contracts and ensure that the transaction complies with all federal and state laws. A securities attorney who is familiar with the special issues faced by start-ups can do the required legal work in a cost-effective manner.

Hiring the appropriate professional advisors sends a strong signal to investors that the company is serious about protecting its corporate interests and the investors' money. In fact, if a company's

240

attorneys and other advisors are well-known this can add a great deal of credibility to the company and its venture, particularly in the early stages of development when it is most needed.

THE KEYS TO EFFECTIVE MARKETING FOR A START-UP COMPANY

Certain marketing steps have proven valuable to numerous start-up companies as they set out to raise capital and communicate their corporate message. These steps are set forth and discussed below.

1. ***Prepare in Advance.*** There is no substitute for advance preparation when it comes to maximizing a company's chances of success in raising capital. Prior to meeting with any potential investors, the executives of a company must work on preparing a clear message that tells investors why they should invest in their company as opposed to the many other companies that may have approached the investors. It is important for the company's message to communicate what makes the company unique. The challenge for executives is to make their message compelling and persuasive while, at the same time, keeping the message relatively short and succinct. The attention of potential investors must be caught right from the beginning and the key elements of the company's message must be communicated before the investor loses interest. Advance preparation can help executives target which investors to approach.

2. ***Target Your Message to the Right Audience.*** Most early stage investors, whether they are individuals or venture capital firms, have clearly defined preferences about the type of companies that they invest in. Some investors will only invest in software companies while others will invest only in hardware companies. Many investors also have a preference in terms of the stage of development at which they will invest. By learning

as much as possible about the preferences of potential investors, a company can target its marketing efforts to focus on investors that are likely to have the most interest in the company. Speaking with professionals in the investment field who can advise companies about the preferences of potential investors, and who can make appropriate introductions, will significantly increase the company's chances of raising capital. If a company is fortunate enough to obtain an introduction to a potential investor or venture capitalist, the first thing that the potential investor will ask for is a copy of the company's business plan. Because the business plan may be the first real contact that a potential investor has with a new company, it is important that the business plan be well-written and persuasive. Writing an effective business plan is discussed in detail in Chapter 3.

3. **Set Up an In-Person Meeting.** Once a potential investor receives the company's business plan he will usually ask for an in-person meeting with the executives of the company. The in-person meeting will often make the difference between an investment and a pass. It is important for all of the key officers of the company to be present at the meeting. Bringing the key officers to the meeting will show the investor that the company has a management team in place. Investors are likely to have questions that span a range of topics, including marketing, finance and legal. Having more than one officer at the meeting will increase the likelihood that the investors' questions can be fully answered.

4. **Develop Succinct and Persuasive Messages.** When the meeting with an investor gets under way, the company should strive to make a compelling presentation to the investor about why he should invest in the company. There is certainly an element of selling present in these meetings. The company's message should be as persuasive as possible. Investors will be

much more likely to invest in the company when officers discuss specific facts and figures to support their view that the company presents a good investment opportunity. Discussing facts and details also shows that the company's management has done its homework and has thoroughly researched the business opportunity and its chances of success. Charts and graphs are a great way to clearly communicate facts and figures as well as show any trends that may be reflected in the figures. The company should also plan to address how current and future economic conditions will impact its business plan.

5. ***Avoid Too Much Technical Jargon.*** One mistake that entrepreneurs make over and over again in their presentations to investors is to use technical jargon and concepts without explaining at a basic level the ideas that are being presented. It is important to remember that if the investor does not understand the presentation he is unlikely to invest in the company. Although potential investors may have invested in other companies in the same industry, do not assume that they are familiar with the technical ideas and jargon. The chances of offending an investor by explaining basic terms are slight. The greater danger is that the potential investor will not understood the presentation and therefore decide not to invest. If any technical concepts must be used, executives should make sure to fully explain them at a basic level. In fact, when the company's management educates potential investors, this can go a long way towards establishing the credibility of the management.

6. ***Anticipate Investor Questions and Concerns.*** At the end of any presentation to a potential investor, time should be left to answer whatever questions the investor may have. The company's management should be prepared to answer tough questions from investors regarding their business model and operations to date. Often, investors will want to know exactly

how their money will be spent by the company and how that spending will create value. Management must be prepared to explain the reasonableness of their salaries. Potential investors prefer to see the management team take most of its compensation in the form of stock or options rather than cash. This type of arrangement preserves money for the company's use and also provides the managers with a strong incentive to make the company a success. Another tough area that investors will explore is whether there are any special transactions between the company and its management team. Special transactions include situations where the company rents office space from an officer or shareholder, the existence of any promissory notes or other agreements between the company and any of its officers, and other similar transactions. These types of arrangements should be disclosed up front so that it does not appear that the company is hiding anything. However, investors will often probe deeper into these areas after the management team makes its presentation. If the company is getting fair value in return for any special transactions, such as the use of office space at fair market value, that point should be emphasized to the potential investor.

7. **Rehearse the Presentation.** Unfortunately, it is easy for potential investors to spot when corporate officers are unprepared or unfamiliar with the process of raising capital. To ensure a smooth presentation, the management team should rehearse, preferably with a person who is knowledgeable about the process of raising capital. Attorneys who have worked with start-up companies or professional investors who have previously invested in start-up companies are good individuals with whom to rehearse. Seeking professional advice before any meetings can greatly increase the quality of the information and enhance the presentation. It is a good idea to rehearse not only management's presentation, but also the question and answer

segment so that the management team can practice answering tough questions from potential investors.

8. ***Obtain Feedback and Incorporate It into the Next Presentation.*** Each time the company's executives make a presentation to a potential investor, they should pay close attention to which parts of the presentation seemed to interest the investors and which parts did not. By studying the reactions of potential investors during the course of the meeting, the management team can gain valuable feedback about the impact of its presentation. This type of feedback can help management hone its presentation and message as the team speaks with other potential investors. If the potential investors ask many questions about material covered in the presentation, it may be a sign that the message and information is not being communicated in a clear manner. Perhaps the officers have not explained the concepts in basic enough terms or perhaps too much technical jargon was thrown in. Any feedback can be helpful in fine-tuning the message. Even if the potential investor does not ultimately invest in the company, a lot can be learned from the meeting.

SPECIAL MARKETING CONCERNS RELATING TO VENTURE CAPITAL INVESTORS

When a company meets with a venture capital firm about a potential investment, several special concerns arise that will not usually be present during meetings with the individual investors who supply the early stage seed financing. The first thing to be aware of is that venture capital firms are not passive investors— they invest with a view to being closely involved growing the company. Most individual or angel investors are usually not as actively involved with the management of the company. The nature of a venture capital investment makes it even more important for a company to prepare in advance what its message will be and how it will negotiate with the venture capital firm.

First, executives must be aware that there will likely be significant corporate changes after a venture capitalist makes an investment. The venture capitalist will want a seat on the company's board of directors so that it can closely monitor and control the company's corporate strategy. Second, a venture capitalist will generally not accept shares of common stock in return for its investment. Rather, a venture capitalist will want preferred stock that often has superior rights to common stock. For instance, in the event of a liquidation the preferred stockholders would be paid in full prior to any money going to the holders of common stock. In addition, preferred stockholders generally have rights to dividend payments that the common stockholders do not have.

By being aware of the types of issues that concern venture capitalists, the company's executives can tailor their presentation to address all of these critical concerns. Advance preparation regarding board representation and the type of securities the company will sell will also make the officers of a company more effective negotiators. If any type of venture capital investment is contemplated, the company should retain a securities attorney to review all of the terms of the proposed financing and explain the implications of the various rights the venture capitalist will want.

By becoming aware of and addressing the issues that a venture capitalist will bring to the table, the company's management will make a positive impression and appear to be experienced and knowledgeable. While venture capitalists often possess superior bargaining power over a new company because they hold the money, they are often willing to be flexible on some issues. In fact, if the company has an effective marketing and communications strategy, it may have interest from more than one venture capital fund. If that is the case, the company will be in a much better position than it would otherwise be in for negotiating purposes. The desire to invest in the company that was generated by the company's marketing efforts will often lead competing investors to negotiate away points on which they otherwise would have held firm.

WHAT TO DO IF YOUR COMPANY HAS BEEN UNSUCCESSFUL AT RAISING MONEY

What if your company has done the best it can to implement the marketing and communications guidelines set out above and still can't raise capital? Are there any other options? Yes there are. If the company has been unsuccessful in raising capital it should strongly consider using a professional advisor who is retained primarily for the purpose of introducing the company to potential investors. The truth is that it can be extremely difficult for a company to raise capital from professional investors without an introduction from a respected source. There are firms and individuals that will work with companies and help them to raise capital. Sometimes these companies and individuals are referred to as "finders" because they help the company find capital. Finders will rely on their professional networks and relationships to locate potential investors that a company may be unable to locate on its own. Moreover, even if the company could locate these potential investors on its own, the investors are often unlikely to invest without the recommendation of a trusted colleague.

Selecting an appropriate firm or individual to work with requires careful consideration of a number of factors. The backgrounds, experience and success rates of different finders vary wildly. The challenge of selecting an appropriate finder to work with is compounded by the fact that there are only minimal regulations regarding who can be a finder. While some states require finders to register as broker-dealers, most do not. Finders avoid having to register with the SEC as broker-dealers so long as their responsibilities only relate to locating potential investors and making an introduction. Finders that are not registered as broker-dealers are not allowed to make recommendations to potential investors regarding whether they should or should not invest in a particular company. The responsibility for evaluating the investment opportunity rests solely with the potential investor.

When evaluating a potential finder, determine whether the finder has been successful in locating funding for other companies, particularly those in the same industry as your company. An experienced and successful finder will have a well-established track record of locating financing for other companies. One of the most important services that a professional finder can provide is an objective and knowledgeable evaluation of the company's business plan. There are two aspects to the finder's review of a company's business plan. First, the finder will examine whether the company's business model is something that is likely to be funded by a professional investor. A finder can make very valuable contributions to the company by suggesting ways that its chances for funding can be increased. For instance, the finder may suggest that the company focus on increasing its revenues, or the finder may suggest that it would be most valuable for the company to focus on increasing its profit margins. On occasion, the finder may believe that more objective evidence may be needed to show that there is a demand for a company's products or services. In such cases, it may be worthwhile for the company to retain a professional marketing firm to do market research, such as focus groups or surveys, to demonstrate in an objective manner that there is a sufficiently strong demand for the company's products or services. If needed, this type of market research should be done before any potential investors are approached. If it is cost-effective and appropriate to do so, the finder may also have the company prepare a prototype of its product and have a test run to demonstrate consumer interest. For example, with a new media company involved in e-commerce, developing a small-scale version of its Web site to show that customers will actually purchase products from the site can go a long way towards persuading potential investors that the business model is valid.

In addition to the foregoing services, the finder will also review the company's written business plan and marketing materials to make sure that they are well-written and communicate the appropriate message. It is not uncommon for a finder to insist on substantial revisions to the company's written business plan so as to present the company in a more compelling manner. In general, a company will be quite receptive to these types of changes, particularly if it has been unsuccessful in raising capital on its own.

The finder, of course, will want a fee for the work he will perform on behalf of the company. There are usually two components to a finder's fee: one is an up-front retainer and the other is a success fee that is paid only upon the successful closing of the financing. Fairly structuring the finder's fee will be an important concern to the company as well as to the finder. In general, a company that has a well-known network of investors and a good track record of raising capital will insist on a significant up-front retainer. The retainer can be as high as $75,000 for the most prestigious firms. Less well-known finders will charge a substantially smaller up-front fee. Some finders will not charge any up-front fee and will be paid only upon the successful completion of financing. The retainer paid by the company will generally be used to pay for the time the finder must take to rework the company's business model and prove that the business concept is viable.

However, for all finders, the success fee makes up most of the compensation. The success fee is calculated based on a percentage of the money raised and is usually paid as a combination of cash and securities at the time of the closing. The structure of a finder's success fee varies widely from finder to finder. The fee itself also varies depending on what stage of development the company is in.

Finders reasonably argue that it is harder to locate investors willing to invest in new start-up companies than more established ones. Therefore, they believe they should be entitled to a larger success fee for locating investors who are willing to invest in a new venture. One common formula for calculating the success fee is what is known as the "Lehman Formula." This formula gives the finder a success fee of 5% of the first million raised, 4% of the second million, 3% of the third million, 2% of the fourth million and 1% of every million thereafter. However, many finders believe that the Lehman Formula will not adequately compensate them for their efforts, particularly when it comes to new companies that are harder to fund. Therefore, it is not uncommon for finders to insist on success fees of between 7% and 12% of the money raised, paid in a combination of cash and securities. It is important for companies to disclose the amount of any finder's fee to potential investors because it is their money that will likely be used to pay the finder's fee.

It is strongly recommended that a company that decides to work with a finder have a written agreement prepared that covers all of the terms of the engagement. Contracts relating to finder's fees should be clear about when the retainer must be paid by the company and when the success fee must be paid. Also, how the success fee is calculated should be clearly set forth, including what percentage of the fee will be paid in cash and what percentage will be paid in securities. The contract should also explicitly state whether the finder is being engaged as the exclusive finder for the company or whether other finders may be retained. The term of the contract with the finder should also be set forth. It is a good idea for companies to require in the contract that the finder submit all introductions of potential investors in writing. This type of written record will avoid disputes in the event that the company approaches potential investors on its own and the finder claims that he introduced the investor to the company. A sample finders fee agreement is attached as the appendix to this chapter. See Appendix 7 below.

MARKETING CONSIDERATIONS FOR A COMPANY PREPARING FOR AN IPO

A company's marketing and communications strategies will change dramatically when preparing for an IPO, as will its constituencies. Whereas once the company could focus its marketing on professional investors and venture capitalists, now it must be prepared to effectively communicate with a large number of nonprofessional shareholders, the financial press, securities analysts and other market participants such as stockbrokers. In addition, important SEC regulations affect how a company may market itself to investors and require the disclosure of certain information. The SEC rules relating to what a company can and cannot say during the IPO process are discussed in detail in Chapters 3 and 4. While the audience for the company's message becomes wider the same basic principle applies of creating a compelling message that clearly and succinctly communicates with a target audience. However, with a wider audience comes the challenge of making sure that the company's message is consistent across each of its constituencies and relevant to the audience that it reaches.

As a company prepares for its IPO, the underwriter will schedule a series of meetings between the company's management and institutional investors who may invest in the IPO. These meetings are held in major cities throughout the United States and, in some cases, around the world. The meetings with professional investors, also called road shows, are designed to generate interest in the company's IPO among the institutions that may buy the company's securities. All of the information discussed above relating to meetings with potential investors is equally applicable to the presentations given at road shows. Because the company will be working with a professional underwriter who has a financial incentive to sell all of the securities offered in the IPO, the underwriter will often provide a significant amount of guidance and preparation to the executives of the company who will be participating in the road show presentations. The road shows often only last for an hour, so management must strive to present a persuasive and succinct message to the institutional investors about why they should purchase the securities offered in the company's IPO. Remember, as with any investor, the institutional investors will want to know how they will profit from their investment.

MARKETING CONSIDERATIONS FOR A PUBLICLY TRADED COMPANY

Once a company has completed its IPO and becomes publicly traded, the focus of its marketing and communications will shift from locating potential new investors to keeping current shareholders and the financial marketplace informed about ongoing developments at the company. The target audience for the company's message will be much broader than it was when the company was private. First, the number of shareholders that a company has will grow exponentially once it is publicly traded. In addition, the company will have to communicate effectively with securities analysts, financial reporters and other market professionals. The company will also have to comply with important SEC disclosure rules that will affect how it can craft its message. Many companies choose to bring in professional marketing advisors who specialize in financial public relations to help them prepare for the IPO and operations after the IPO is completed.

WORKING WITH PROFESSIONAL FINANCIAL PUBLIC RELATIONS FIRMS

Once a company becomes publicly traded it is essential for the company to retain the services of a public relations firm that specializes in financial public relations. The press and the public will be paying more attention to the company and its ongoing business developments. In addition, regular news flow from the company is important to keep it in the public eye. Firms that specialize in financial public relations have an extensive network of contacts within the financial news community and are experienced at communicating important business developments to the public company's many constituencies. Financial public relations firms can help a company to develop and maintain good working relationships with the financial news media. When important events occur, such as mergers, acquisitions or consolidations, financial public relations firms can help the company communicate these events and the impact that they will have on the company's business and the financial markets. The PR people can also help prepare earnings announcements and other important communications to assure that the information is conveyed quickly, accurately, and in the best possible light for the company.

Managers of publicly traded companies must also be prepared to answer questions by reporters about important events. Financial public relations firms can help executives prepare for interviews with reporters and coach them on how to effectively answer any questions that reporters may ask. Reporters can be aggressive and their questioning techniques can sometimes lead an interviewee to say things that he may later regret. The PR people provide tips on handling reporters and other members of the news media. Executives with limited exposure to reporters particularly benefit from PR guidance.

Financial public relations firms can help a publicly traded company effectively communicate its message by carrying out a number of important tasks. They can draft professional quality press releases that disclose important developments. This must be done on an ongoing basis. The PR people can also prepare a one-page profile of the company, its business and its executive officers. This profile can be given to anybody interested in the company. They can also prepare detailed company kits to be distributed to the news media and professional investors. A financial public relations firm can also help the company prepare a professional annual report for distribution to its shareholders. It will also arrange for regular conference calls between management and securities analysts and help management make professional presentations to investors and the news media. In general, a financial public relations firm will help the company be proactive in getting its message out to a large number of people. Some financial public relations firms have departments that specialize in crisis management so that whatever crisis the company may face, the PR firm is there to take care of the company's image and prevent its problems from spiraling out of control in the minds of the public and governmental regulators.

A financial public relations firm can also help with developing and communicating an overall corporate strategy. Once of the most important things that any financial PR firm can do is to help the company craft its overall vision and mission statement. The right corporate vision will clearly set forth the company's strong points and what it hopes to accomplish in its business. To effectively communicate the company's vision, the financial public relations firm must thoroughly understand the company, its industry and the trends that are shaping the competitive landscape. The right corporate vision can help to distinguish a company from its competitors and create significant shareholder value.

Creating shareholder value is one of the most important functions of a public relations firm. Effectively communicating with Wall Street requires a combination of public relations skills and business acumen. Wall Street often has specific expectations for newly public companies, such as steadily increasing quarterly earnings. Balancing the company's long-term strategic interests with Wall Street's concern for short-term earnings increases is always a challenge, even for the most seasoned public companies and their advisors. Financial public relations firms can be very helpful in providing earnings announcements to Wall Street and helping analysts interpret those results. A financial public relations firm can also help a company and its stock receive this broad coverage by these securities analysts and the financial press. Broader interest in the company and its stock often leads to more demand for the company's stock among investors and, consequently, a higher stock price. In addition, when major personnel shifts and other situations occur, financial public relations firms can help ensure that the developments are accurately and quickly communicated to the financial markets.

One often overlooked service that financial public relations firms can provide is identifying current market perceptions of a company's products, services or people. Financial public relations firms will uncover these perceptions through surveys, in-person interviews and other techniques. Oftentimes, such surveys reveal unexpected opinions about the company in the marketplace. This information can lead a company to make changes in its strategy or undertake renewed efforts to correct troublesome impressions.

Important corporate developments, whether good or bad, must be disclosed. A company that ignores bad news or fails to disclose it on a timely basis will hurt its credibility in the marketplace and with investors. This can lead to a lack of confidence in the company's management and a depressed share price. To counteract these negative effects it is important for a company to maintain a free flow of information about developments as they occur. PR firms can help the company maintain this flow of information and help to present it in the best possible light.

One of the advantages of using a financial public relations firm instead of the typical public relations firm is that the financial PR people are knowledgeable about and familiar with the rules of the SEC and the exchanges on which a company's stock trades. A financial public relations firm hired to work with a company prior to its IPO will be familiar with the SEC rules that govern the types of

255

communications that can be made to potential investors and the market. Improper publicity prior to the time a company files a registration statement with the SEC can lead to charges of gun jumping. As a result, the company's IPO can be delayed and fines imposed. Financial public relations firms also must be familiar with the SEC rules that govern the timely disclosure of corporate information by publicly traded companies, including SEC's Regulation FD[1] which prohibits a publicly traded company from disclosing material information to only a select group of analysts or other market professionals. Financial public relations firms can help the company navigate the complex disclosure regulations and still ensure that the company's announcements reach its target audience.

Even if a company remains relatively small in terms of market size after its IPO, financial public relations firms can provide valuable services. Oftentimes, small public companies want to increase and maintain their stock price, increase the liquidity of the market for their securities, generate interest in the stock among institutional buyers, and increase the geographic interest in the company. An experienced financial PR firm can help a smaller company accomplish these goals by communicating the company's message to a broader audience, including securities analysts and the financial press. Generating a broader base of interest in the company's stock can lead to a healthy, stable market for the company's shares.

Companies that engage financial public relations firms must ensure that they are working with an ethical, compliance-oriented firm. Smaller publicly traded companies are sometimes targeted by unscrupulous stock promoters who promise to help push up a company's stock price. While there is nothing improper about

---

[1] 17 C.F.R. Parts 210, 240.

retaining a firm to generate increased awareness among investors and market professionals, certain practices are clearly illegal. First, the company should read each press release prior to its issuance to ensure that all of the facts contained in it are 100% accurate. Improperly pumping up a company's stock through misleading press releases is a violation of the antifraud provisions of the federal securities laws. Publicly trading companies should also be aware that Section 17(b) of the Securities Act of 1933[2] requires the disclosure of any compensation received in exchange for recommendations to purchase a stock. Issues regarding disclosure of compensation under Section 17(b) of the Securities Act often arise when stock promoters work with newsletters or Web sites which recommend that investors purchase a particular stock. If a newsletter or Web site receives compensation in connection with its recommendations to purchase a stock, that compensation must be disclosed. Good practice dictates that the amount of the compensation, the form it takes (such as cash or stock), and the date the compensation was received be fully disclosed. The purpose behind Section 17(b) of the Securities Act is to protect investors who may think they are receiving objective investment advice, when in fact the securities recommendations are bought and paid for by the company itself. Those who recommend a company's securities should also disclose whether they own any of the company's securities. This will allow potential investors to weigh the conflict of interest inherent in the recommendations because the stock price may increase as the result of a positive recommendation. Finally, under no circumstances should any compensation be paid to stockbrokers in exchange for their soliciting their customers to purchase a company's securities. When such payments are not disclosed to the broker's customers, a violation of the antifraud rules occurs.

---

[2] 15 U.S.C. §§ 77q(b).

THE USE OF THE INTERNET FOR MARKETING AND COMMUNICATIONS

The Internet should be a central part of any company's marketing and communications strategy because it offers a unique opportunity to communicate directly with shareholders, financial reporters, customers and other visitors to the site. Through its Web site, a company can communicate with its various constituencies in a way that is not filtered by the news media or the opinions of others. In order to promote its site, a company can include its web address on correspondence and press releases. By promoting its Web site through traditional marketing and public relations materials a company can dramatically increase the number of visitors to its Web site. However, once those visitors arrive at the Web site it is important to provide them with information they will find useful and an incentive to return to the site. Many companies keep complete versions of their recent press releases on their Web sites so that visitors can quickly learn about recent developments at the company. This is an effective way to communicate and keep people updated. Keeping all of the company's press releases on the Web site ensures that new information is regularly added to the site and may give visitors an incentive to return to the site often.

Another important way that a company's Internet site can be used for effective marketing is to maintain complete background information about the company and its executives on the Web site. Maintaining this type of information on the Web site is inexpensive and can be easily updated as the company grows and personnel change. In addition, significant postage and shipping costs can be avoided by directing people to the company's Web site for basic background, particularly if there are large numbers of people interested in receiving information about the company. Many investors now obtain most of their research information from the Internet, and a company's Web site can be a convenient way for them to locate the latest financial statements or annual report. Because of the large numbers of people who may visit a company's Web site, its potential in marketing and communications should not be overlooked by any new company.

CONCLUSION

No matter what stage of development it is in, effective corporate and marketing strategies can make the difference between success and failure for a company. Executives can prepare for success by thinking through the concerns that will be important to the company's various constituencies. Properly marketing and communicating the management's vision for the company is just as important for success as marketing the company's products and services.

APPENDIX 7

Finder's Fee Agreement

> **COMMENTARY:** *This Agreement can be used by a company when retaining an individual or firm to help the company find potential investors. The terms of the relationship between the company and finder are clearly set forth, including the amount and calculation of the finder's fee.*

THIS AGREEMENT entered into this _____ day of _____, 2001 (the "Effective Date"), by and between _____, Inc. of _____, (the "Company") and Jonathan Smith ("Finder") of New York, New York.

WHEREAS the Company desires to locate individuals and entities that would consider either investing in the Company or consummating a transaction whereby majority voting control or substantially all of the assets of the Company are transferred;

WHEREAS Finder desires to assist Company in finding such individuals and entities;

FOR AND IN CONSIDERATION OF the mutual promises and benefits of the parties, they do hereby agree to the following:

1. ***Agreement to Act as Finder.*** Finder hereby agrees to attempt to locate entities and individuals ("Potential Investors") that would consider either: (i) making an investment in Company, through the purchase of equity in the Company or the lending of money to the Company; or (ii) consummating a transaction or series of transactions whereby, directly or indirectly, majority voting control or substantially all of the assets of the Company are transferred for consideration, including, but not limited to, a sale or exchange of stock or assets, a merger or consolidation, a tender or exchange offer or any similar transaction ("Transaction").

> **COMMENTARY:** *This paragraph sets forth the responsibilities of the finder and specifically states that the finder is retained to locate equity investors as well as potential acquirors for the company.*

2. ***Introductions by Finder.*** If Finder locates a Potential Investor interested in consummating a Transaction, Finder may, in his discretion, submit in writing the name of the Potential Investor to Company for consideration and negotiation. If Finder chooses to submit the name of a Potential Investor to the Company such submission must be in writing. Company acknowledges that Finder is not a registered broker-dealer or investment advisor and does not purport to give any investment advice. Finder's role under this Agreement is limited strictly to making introductions of Potential Investors to Company, and Finder shall not provide any advice as to whether an investment in Company is appropriate for any Potential Investor. A Potential Investor shall be responsible for negotiating all of the terms and conditions of any investment or transaction directly with Company.

COMMENTARY: *This paragraph gives the finder discretion in making an introduction. However, if the finder chooses to introduce a potential investor to the company, that introduction must be set forth in a writing. Requiring a written record of all introductions will help avoid disputes with the company over whether a particular investor was introduced by the finder. This paragraph also makes clear that the finder is not acting as a securities broker, which would require registration with the SEC and the states in which he acts as a finder.*

3. **Finder's Fee.** If Company consummates a Transaction with any Potential Investor who was introduced to Company by Finder, Finder shall receive a fee payable from Company simultaneously with the closing of the Transaction by the Potential Investor ("Finder's Fee"). The Finder's Fee shall consist of 10% of the total amount invested by any party or parties introduced, directly or indirectly, by Finder or, in the case of a change in control or asset purchase, 10% of the total purchase price, payable as follows: (i) a payment shall be due at the closing of any Transaction equal to 5% of the total amount invested by the Potential Investor or, in the event of a change in control or asset purchase, 5% of the total purchase price, and (ii) the remaining 5% of the Finder's Fee shall be paid by Company at the closing of any Transaction through the grant of Company stock. The number of shares of Company stock payable to Finder at the Closing shall be calculated by multiplying the total amount invested by the Potential Investor or, in the event of a change in control or asset purchase, by multiplying the total purchase price by 0.05 and then dividing that figure by the per share price of Company stock as determined at the closing of the Transaction.

COMMENTARY: *The finder's fee in this agreement consists of 10% of the total money raised, with 5% of the fee payable in cash and 5% of the fee payable in stock. The last sentence of the paragraph establishes that the per share value of the finder's stock is the same as the price at which the investors will purchase the stock.*

4. ***Piggyback Registration Rights.*** If at any time or from time to time, the Company shall determine to register any of its securities, either for its own account or the account of any other security holder or holders ("Holders") on a registration statement under the Securities Act of 1933 (the "Act"), the Company will (i) promptly give Finder written notice thereof; and (ii) include in such registration (and any related qualifications under blue sky laws or other compliance requirements) and in any underwriting involved therein all shares of the stock granted pursuant to Paragraph 3 of this Agreement.

COMMENTARY: *Finders will often insist on a clause that gives them piggyback registration rights for the shares they receive as part of the success fee. Piggyback registration rights require the company to register the finder's shares for public sale in the event that the company conducts an IPO. Without piggyback registration rights, the finder could end up holding stock that could not be resold even if the company conducts an IPO. Piggyback registration rights require the company to register the finder's stock with the SEC at the time of the Company's IPO so that the finder can publicly sell his shares.*

5. **Nonexclusive Arrangement.** Company acknowledges that Finder acts and will act as a finder of investors for other corporations and businesses. Finder also acknowledges that he is acting on a nonexclusive basis for the Company and that the Company may use other finders during the term of this Agreement.

COMMENTARY: *Whether the relationship between the company and the finder is exclusive or not should be set forth in the Agreement. This will prevent misunderstandings from arising in the event that a potential investor is located by either the company or another finder.*

6. **Chain of Introductions.** Finder shall be entitled to a Finder's Fee not only from a Transaction consummated by a party he introduced to Company, but on any Transactions consummated with any party that result from his original introduction.

7. **Term.** The Term of this Agreement shall be eighteen (18) months from the Effective Date. Notwithstanding the foregoing, Finder shall be entitled to the Finder's Fee as set forth above for any introductions to Potential Investors made during the term of this Agreement, even if a Transaction is not consummated with Company until after the term of this Agreement has expired. Notwithstanding anything to the contrary in this Agreement, in no event shall Finder be entitled to the Finder's Fee for any transactions consummated between Company and any party, including a Potential Investor introduced by Finder, after twenty-four (24) months from the Effective Date.

8. ***No Oral Modifications.*** This Agreement may not be modified without a writing signed by each of the parties hereto.

9. ***Governing Law.*** This Agreement shall be governed by the laws of the State of New York, exclusive of its choice of law provisions.

In witness whereof, the parties have signed this Agreement as of the Effective Date set forth above.

Corporate Name: _____

By: _____

Title:_____

_____

Jonathan Smith

CHAPTER 8

BEING PUBLIC—POST-IPO RESPONSIBILITIES

Once a company has successfully completed its IPO and its stock becomes publicly traded, important obligations and responsibilities are imposed on the company as well as on the individual officers, directors and shareholders who own more than 10% of the company's stock ("principal shareholders"). Many of the legal responsibilities placed on publicly traded companies are designed to ensure that investors receive full disclosure about the company's business and financial condition as well as the activities of its officers, directors and principal shareholders. The Exchange Act of 1934 (the "Exchange Act"),[1] and the rules promulgated by the SEC thereunder, constitute the primary source of regulation for companies once their IPOs have been completed. The Exchange Act embodies a philosophy of full disclosure of all material information through periodic filings with the SEC. When adopting the Exchange Act, the House of Representatives' Committee on Interstate and Foreign Commerce believed that investors needed to know important corporate information so that they could make informed judgments about the value of a company's securities. The periodic disclosure requirements are extremely important because they insure that investors are aware of current material developments that affect the company. The House Committee stated:

> "No investor, no speculator, can safely buy and sell securities upon the exchanges without having an

---

[1] 15 U.S.C. §§ 78a *et seq.*

intelligent basis for forming his judgment as to the value of the securities he buys and sells. The idea of a free and open public market is built upon the theory that competing judgments of buyers and sellers as to the fair price of a security brings about a situation where the market price reflects as nearly as possible a just price. . . . There cannot be honest markets without honest publicity. Manipulation and dishonest practices of the marketplace thrive upon mystery and secrecy. The disclosure of information materially important to investors may not instantaneously be reflected in market value, but despite the intricacies of security values truth does find relatively quick acceptance on the market."[2]

Under Section 12 of the Exchange Act[3] an issuer must register every nonexempt security that: (1) is listed on an exchange; or (2) is an equity security held by at least 500 people and the issuer has total assets exceeding $10 million.[4] Section 12(g)'s registration requirements apply only to equity securities and not to debt securities such as nonconvertible bonds.[5] The registration requirements imposed by the Exchange Act are separate and distinct from those imposed by the Securities Act. However, the SEC has made great efforts to integrate the disclosure requirements under each statute so that companies do not have to file duplicative information. In addition to the disclosure requirements imposed under federal securities laws, the securities markets such as Nasdaq and the various stock exchanges also have promulgated important rules that listed companies must follow under the terms of their listing agreements. The rules of the stock

---

[2] H.R. Rep. No. 1383, 73d Cong., 2d Sess. 5, 11-12 (1934).

[3] 15 U.S.C. § 78l.

[4] See SEC Rule 12g-1, 17 C.F.R. § 240.12g-1.

[5] E.H.I. of Florida, Inc. v. Insurance Company of North America, 652 F.2d 310, 313-315 (3d Cir. 1981).

exchanges and Nasdaq often incorporate higher standards of public disclosure and corporate governance than the securities laws require. It is important to note that the statutory and contractual obligations imposed on a public company frequently overlap. For this reason, it is often the case that a single event or occurrence gives rise to obligations under more than one statutory provision, or to both statutory and contractual obligations. Violations of the securities laws can result in significant liability, including fines and criminal penalties. Therefore, publicly traded companies and their officers and directors should have a working knowledge of the periodic disclosure requirements.

REPORTING AND DISCLOSURE OBLIGATIONS OF THE COMPANY

The following discussion covers the primary reporting obligations of a publicly traded company. After the company's obligations are examined, we turn to the obligations of the individual officers, directors and principal shareholders.

Reports to the SEC

A publicly traded company whose shares are registered under Section 12(g) of the Exchange Act becomes subject to Section 13 of the Exchange Act, which imposes a duty to file certain reports with the SEC. All such reports must now be filed electronically through the SEC's Electronic Data Gathering, Analysis, and Retrieval ("EDGAR") system. General guidance for the preparation of periodic disclosure forms can be found in SEC Regulation S-K.[6] The following documents are the most important ones for the company to be aware of:

---

[6] 17 C.F.R. §§ 229.101 *et seq.*

Annual Report to Shareholders. The annual report to shareholders is an extremely important document and most companies spend a good deal of time and money to ensure that the report is properly prepared and well-packaged. Usually the annual report to shareholders is printed on glossy paper and contains a fair amount of color and photographs. The annual report to shareholders must accompany or proceed the proxy solicitation material for an annual or special meeting of shareholders at which directors will be elected. Annual reports are mailed in accordance with both the company's bylaws and the rules of the exchange on which the company's stock trades. A copy of the annual report must also be filed with the SEC for informational purposes. The information contained in an annual report includes the company's financial statements and management's discussion and analysis ("MD&A") of the company's business operations and prospects. The SEC encourages companies to present information in an understandable manner and to use graphics and charts.

Annual Reports to the SEC on Form 10-K.[7] The company must file the Form10-K with the SEC annually within ninety days after the end of the company's fiscal year. It must include, among other things, a description of the company's business, audited financial statements, management's discussion and analysis of the company's financial condition and the results of the company's operations. The form must also discuss any material legal proceedings in which the company is involved and the compensation of the CEO and the four most highly paid officers earning over $100,000 per year. The discussion and analysis of the company's results and future prospects is one of the most important parts of the Form 10-K. Analysts and investors rely on that section to learn what the management of the company thinks about the company's future. Item 303 of Regulation S-K requires

---

[7] Form 10-K is set forth as Appendix 8A *infra.*

the MD&A section to analyze the results of operations and discuss important events and trends. The MD&A section must also discuss known risks and future uncertainties that might cause future performance to differ from past performance.[8] Rule 12b-11(b) requires that the Form 10-K be signed by the company's principal executive, as well as financial and accounting officers and a majority of the company's directors.[9] The SEC added this requirement in 1980 to ensure that management, directors, accountants and attorneys would devote sufficient attention to the periodic disclosure requirements.

Quarterly Report on Form 10-Q.[10] The Form 10-Q must be filed by the company within forty-five days after the end of each of its first three fiscal quarters of each fiscal year. It does not have to be filed after the fourth quarter because the Form 10-K covers that time period. The Form 10-Q quarterly report must contain, among other things, condensed financial statements as well as an analysis by management of the company's financial condition and results of operations. The Form 10-Q may also discuss legal proceedings, changes in the number of securities issued and other information. The company must also report any sales of securities that occurred during the quarter that were exempt from registration, unless such sales were made to off-shore investors under Regulation S.[11] Sales of securities under Regulation S are reported on the Form 8-K current report.[12] The management's discussion and analysis section of the Form 10-Q focuses on the results of the quarter and often compares those results for the same quarter from the prior year.

---

[8] Caterpillar Sec. Rel. No. 30532 (Mar. 31, 1992).

[9] 17 C.F.R. § 240.12b-11(b).

[10] Form 10-Q is set forth as Appendix 8B *infra*.

[11] 17 C.F.R. §§ 230.901 *et seq*. Regulation S is a rule promulgated by the SEC that allows publicly traded companies, if they comply with certain specified conditions, to sell stock to off-shore investors without going through the typical registration process.

[12] Form 8-K is set forth as Appendix 8C *infra*.

Current Report on Form 8-K. The Form 8-K is required to be filed with the SEC on the occurrence of certain specified events. This requirement is designed to keep investors informed of material information prior to the time that such information would otherwise have to be disclosed on the Form 10-Q. Events that are required to be disclosed on the Form 8-K include changes in control of the company, material acquisitions or dispositions of assets and the filing for bankruptcy or receivership. All of these occurrences must be disclosed on the Form 8-K within fifteen calendar days following the event. Changes in the company's public accountants or the resignation of a director of the company must be disclosed on the Form 8-K within five business days of the event. The company may also use Form 8-K to disclose any other events that it deems important.

Notification of Late Filing. If a company is unable to meet the filing deadline for its Form 10-K or Form 10-Q, it must file a Form 12b-25 with the SEC.[13] The Form 12b-25 must disclose in reasonable detail why the company was unable to file its required reports on time. The Form 12b-25 must be filed within one day of the due date of the Form 10-K or Form 10-Q which should have been filed.

Proxy and Other Solicitation Materials. A proxy allows shareholders of a company to designate another person who will vote their shares for them at the meeting of shareholders. Most shareholder voting is done through a proxy, rather than in person. The rules governing the solicitation of proxies are set forth in Section 14 of the Exchange Act.[14] Generally, no proxy solicitation may be made unless the stockholders are furnished with written statements containing the information contained in Schedule 14A of the proxy rules. A wide variety of information must be included on the proxy statements.

---

[13] SEC Rule 12b-2, 17 C.F.R. § 240.12b-25.

[14] 15 U.S.C. § 78n.

Such information includes: (1) disclosures related to the beneficial ownership of the company's shares; (2) disclosures related to the company's directors and officers; (3) information on related party transactions; and (4) information on executive compensation.

Preliminary copies of the solicitation materials must be filed with the SEC at least ten days prior to the date when the definitive copies of such materials are first sent to stockholders. However, if at the stockholder meeting the stockholders are only electing directors, approving the selection of the company's accountants or acting on a stockholder proposal, then preliminary copies of the solicitation materials need not be filed with the SEC. Definitive copies of the proxy materials and all other soliciting materials must be filed with the SEC no later than the date such materials are first sent or given to any stockholder. The SEC reserves the right to review and comment upon all proxy and other solicitation materials.

Accounting and Bookkeeping Records. Sections 13(b)(2) and 30A of the Exchange Act[15] impose important accounting and bookkeeping standards on publicly traded companies. New media companies must be particularly mindful of these accounting standards because often such companies have not been in existence long enough to have mature, well-tested accounting systems. The informal business environment that is maintained at many new media companies must not be allowed to carry over into the company's accounting systems.

Specifically, Section 13(b)(2)(A) of the Exchange Act requires publicly traded companies to "make and keep books, records, and accounts, which, in reasonable detail, accurately and fairly reflect the transactions and dispositions of the assets of the [company]." In addition, Section 13(b)(2)(B) of the Exchange Act requires that a publicly traded company

---

[15] 15 U.S.C. §§ 78m, 78dd-1.

"[D]evise and maintain a system of internal accounting controls sufficient to provide reasonable assurances that

"(i) transactions are executed in accordance with management's general or specific authorization;

"(ii) transactions are recorded as necessary (I) to permit preparation of financial statements in accordance with generally accepted accounting principles or any other criteria applicable to such statements, and (II) to maintain accountability for assets;

"(iii) access to assets is permitted only in accordance with management's general or specific authorization; and

"(iv) the recorded accountability for assets is compared with the existing assets at reasonable intervals and appropriate action is taken with respect to any differences."

New media companies must work closely with their accountants to ensure that the record keeping and accounting standards contained in Section 13(b)(2) of the Exchange Act are complied with. Publicly traded new media companies often face strong pressure from investors and Wall Street analysts to meet aggressive earnings projections. The pressure to "make the numbers" can, unfortunately, lead managers to engage in questionable accounting tactics in order to make it appear that the company is doing better than it really is. Obviously, improper accounting must be avoided at all costs because when such tactics are uncovered they can lead to a substantial devaluation in the company's stock as well as enforcement proceedings brought by the SEC.

The record keeping requirements imposed on all publicly traded companies are part of the Foreign Corrupt Practices Act of 1977 ("FCPA").[16] The FCPA was enacted by Congress in response to

---

[16] 15 U.S.C. §§ 78(m)(b)(2), 78dd-1.

startling disclosures by United States companies that off-the-books accounts had frequently been used to make questionable payments to foreign entities and individuals in attempts to facilitate business transactions. The FCPA makes it a criminal act for a public company, or any of its officers, directors or employees to pay money or anything of value to induce a foreign official or foreign government to: (1) use personal influence with the foreign government; (2) influence the enactment of legislation or regulation by that foreign government; or (3) refrain from performing any official responsibility, in each case for the purpose of obtaining or retaining business. Significant fines can be imposed on any company or individual who violates the FCPA. Accordingly, if a new media company enters into a contract in another country, it is highly recommended that the employees or agents who acted on behalf of the company make written representations to the company that they have fully complied with the FCPA.

Antifraud Rules

In addition to the reporting requirements discussed above, a newly public company is subject to the antifraud provisions of the Securities Act, the Exchange Act and the rules of the SEC and various rules relating to the public disclosure of corporate information.[17] The antifraud rules can be a minefield for newly public companies, so it is critical for officers and directors to understand what the antifraud rules require, particularly with respect to the disclosure of corporate information.

Decisions regarding whether information is material, and if so, how to properly disclose such information, are often judgment calls that must be made in conjunction with the advice of counsel.

---

[17] The general antifraud provisions of the Securities Act are found in Section 17(a). See 15 U.S.C. § 77q. The general antifraud provisions of the Exchange Act are found in Section 10(b). See 15 U.S.C. § 78j.

Typically, information is considered to be material if it is the type of information that a reasonable investor would want to know about when making an investment decision. Examples of material information could include an upcoming merger or acquisition, new product launches, and unexpected earnings shortfalls. Issues surrounding the timely disclosure of material corporate information has received a great deal of attention from the SEC and other regulatory bodies as of late.

Distributing Information to the Public

Publicly traded companies have an obligation to keep their shareholders and the marketplace informed about all material developments that impact their business. Accordingly, important information, both good and bad, should be publicly released as soon as practical. The usual manner by which public companies release information to the public is by means of a press release. Typically, companies will issue press releases that contain announcements about earnings developments, mergers, stock splits and other corporate developments that shareholders would want to know about such as new product launches. The company should send the press release to the Dow Jones News Service and also to Reuters Economic Services. In addition, the company may also deliver the press release to *The Wall Street Journal* and *The New York Times*. Every press release should include the name and telephone number of an officer of the company who will be available to confirm or clarify the release.

It is just as important for publicly traded companies to promptly issue press releases about any material bad news that may develop. This could include lower earnings projections, the loss of a key client or the resignation of a senior-level employee. When a company tries to delay such bad news announcements or attempts to put an unwarranted positive spin on bad news, the reputation of the company's management can be damaged. In a similar vein, companies must exercise good judgment in wording all press releases so that the credibility of the company is not doubted. Therefore, companies should stick closely to the facts in their press releases and avoid exaggeration and overly optimistic projections about future performance. How often a company should issue press releases is determined entirely by how frequently material corporate developments occur. Although the marketplace expects timely releases of all material information, the release of essentially the same information over and over will cause investors and analysts to pay less attention to the company's press releases. This can be detrimental in the long run because the company will find it harder to obtain broad exposure for truly important announcements.

Additionally, the company will likely be required to notify representatives from the stock exchange on which its securities trade prior to the release of major announcements to the media. Some period of delay should occur after the release of material information before any trading is done by corporate insiders. This delay allows the market to absorb the new information, and presumably the company's share price will change accordingly. In the case of particularly important disclosures, the markets on which the company's shares trade may halt trading pending the announcement.

There will be occasions when a company is unwilling to make public disclosure of certain information about its affairs, for example, when disclosure would be premature and possibly contrary to a company's business interests. Oftentimes, sensitive negotiations must be kept confidential until a final agreement is reached. Timing can play an important part. Withholding certain information is justified where the premature announcement of events could be construed as misleading, especially if there is a risk that the events will fail to materialize.

Companies are well-advised to establish a "need-to-know" policy that is intended to restrict to as small a group as possible access to information about material developments. A company should recognize, however, that if information about material developments goes beyond this group, it should be prepared to make prompt and complete disclosure. Prior to the announcement of a material development, it is important for a company to limit disclosure on a "need-to-know" basis and to take other precautions to guard against leaks and other premature disclosure.

Insider Trading

As a means of preventing transactions by officers, directors and other corporate insiders based on material nonpublic information, the company should adopt written policies and procedures designed to restrict communication and monitor dissemination of nonpublic information. In addition, the company should establish guidelines for prompt and complete disclosure to stockholders and the financial community of all material developments that, if known, might reasonably be expected to influence the market price of the company's securities or the investment decision of a reasonable investor. Officers, directors, employees and anybody else with access to material nonpublic information should receive regular written reminders of their obligation not to trade on inside information. The proscriptions against insider trading are primarily designed to prevent corporate insiders, such as officers, directors and principal shareholders, from unfairly taking advantage of their access to material nonpublic information. Lawyers, accountants, investment bankers and others with a duty of trust or confidence to the company are also covered by the insider trading rules. Insider trading is prohibited by Section 10(b) of the Securities Exchange Act of 1934, Rule 10b-5 thereunder and other statutes.[18]

---

[18] 15 U.S.C. § 78j; 17 U.S.C. § 240.10b-5.

Also, insiders must not pass along "tips" to others concerning material information that the company has not disclosed to the public. As previously noted, material information is information that a reasonable investor would view as important in making a decision to buy or sell a security.

A person who violates the prohibitions on insider trading can be required to disgorge any profits made from such purchases and sales and is also subject to other fines and penalties. A publicly traded company can protect itself from liability even if an employee engages in improper insider trading by adopting, promulgating and enforcing clear policies that prohibit insider trading. Clear policies in this area will help prove that a company is not encouraging, allowing or participating in these improper activities. In addition, a publicly traded company should also have internal policies that inform employees about what corporate information is confidential and nonpublic. Employees should be told that they are only permitted to use such confidential information for proper business purposes, and at no time are they to use the corporation's confidential information for personal benefit.

The SEC has publicly announced that it is on the lookout for violations of the insider trading provisions by Internet companies and their employees. The SEC believes that the casual work environment of many Internet companies—with open offices and open lines of communication between top management and rank and file employees—can easily result in numerous employees having access to material, nonpublic information about upcoming corporate transactions or announcements. Therefore, it is particularly important to ensure that all employees of newly public Internet companies are aware of the restrictions against insider trading.

Regulation FD

Regulation FD[19] prohibits publicly traded companies from making selective disclosures of material information to favored analysts or institutional investors. Regulation FD (for "Fair Disclosure") is an attempt by the SEC to level the playing field between large investors that have close ties to a company's management and the individual investor. Prior to the SEC adoption of Regulation FD on October 23, 2000, it was common for many public companies to disclose material information, such as advance notice of earnings results, to certain analysts or institutional investors prior to its general release to the public. The danger, of course, is that those who were the recipients of the new information could purchase or sell the company's securities, thereby either earning a profit or avoiding a loss prior to the time that all investors became aware of the new information. This gave those early recipients an unfair advantage over the general public. Their actions, if they own a substantial block of stock, can certainly have an impact on the stock prices.

In adopting Regulation FD, the SEC stated that it believes that "the practice of selective disclosure leads to a loss of investor confidence in the integrity of our capital markets. Investors who see a security's price change dramatically and only later are given access to the information responsible for that move rightly question whether they are on a level playing field with market insiders."[20] It further noted that:

> "Regulation FD (Fair Disclosure) is a new issuer disclosure rule that addresses selective disclosure. The regulation provides that when an issuer, or person acting on its behalf, discloses material nonpublic information to certain enumerated persons (in general, securities market

---

[19] 17 C.F.R. Parts 210, 240.

[20] SEC Rel. Nos. 33-7919, 34-43602.

professionals and holders of the issuer's securities who may well trade on the basis of the information), it must make public disclosure of that information. The timing of the required public disclosure depends on whether the selective disclosure was intentional or non-intentional; for an intentional selective disclosure, the issuer must make public disclosure simultaneously; for a non-intentional disclosure, the issuer must make public disclosure promptly. Under the regulation, the required public disclosure may be made by filing or furnishing a Form 8-K, or by another method or combination of methods that is reasonably designed to effect broad, non-exclusionary distribution of the information to the public."[21]

The SEC also was concerned that company management could use selective disclosure of information as a way to gain favor with particular securities analysts. It was not unheard of for a company to exclude particular analysts from important conference calls or meetings where new material information was disclosed after those analysts had issued unfavorable reports about the company.

One of the key factors in the SEC's decision to adopt Regulation FD was the fact that technological developments have made it much easier for companies to widely disseminate disclosure of any material developments. The SEC specifically noted that in addition to traditional press releases, public companies could also avail themselves of Internet webcasting and teleconferencing to disclose information.

Essentially, Regulation FD provides that when an issuer makes an intentional disclosure of material nonpublic information to a person covered by the regulation, generally to securities markets professionals such as analysts and institutional investors, it may not do so selectively. Disclosure must be made in a manner that

---

[21] *Id.*

provides for disclosure to the general public, rather than selective disclosure. In instances when a company makes a selective disclosure that is nonintentional, the company must publicly disclose the information promptly after it learns that the information selectively disclosed was both material and nonpublic. Regulation FD does not apply to disclosures of information to persons who have a duty of trust or confidence to the company such as an investment banker or a lawyer. Any use of material nonpublic information by those persons is already covered under the insider trading prohibitions.

Regulation FD sets forth four categories of persons to whom selective disclosure may not be made absent a specified exclusion. The first three are securities market professionals: (1) broker-dealers and their associated persons, (2) investment advisors, certain institutional investment managers and their associated persons, and (3) investment companies, hedge funds, and affiliated persons. These categories are very broad and include sell-side analysts, many buy-side analysts, large institutional investment managers, and other market professionals who may be likely to trade on the basis of selectively disclosed information. The fourth category of persons included in Regulation FD is any holder of the issuer's securities under circumstances in which it is reasonably foreseeable that such person would purchase or sell securities on the basis of the information.

Regulation FD is a new and important regulation, and publicly traded companies are still adjusting to its restrictions. One of the concerns that opponents of Regulation FD expressed is the potential chilling effect that it could have on corporate disclosures. Opponents were concerned that publicly traded companies would restrict the amount of information that was publicly disclosed for fear that an unintentional violation of the regulation could occur. The SEC attempted to allay these concerns by protecting issuers from liability in the event that an unintentional selective disclosure of information occurred, provided that the issuer makes a public disclosure promptly after it learns of the selective disclosure. However, only time will tell whether an appropriate balance has been struck between full public disclosure and the potential chilling effect that Regulation FD may have on corporate communications.

Exchange and Nasdaq Disclosure Requirements

In addition to the SEC rules relating to the disclosure of corporate information, the marketplace where a company's stock trades will also have disclosure rules that a company must follow. Oftentimes, the marketplace rules imposed by the exchanges and Nasdaq have more stringent disclosure requirements than the federal securities laws. For example, NASD Rules 4310(c)(16) and 4320(e)(14) require that, except in unusual circumstances, Nasdaq issuers disclose promptly to the public through the news media any material information which would reasonably be expected to affect the value of their securities or influence investors' decisions.[22] These rules further require that Nasdaq issuers notify Nasdaq of the release of any such information prior to its release to the public through the news media. Nasdaq recommends that Nasdaq issuers provide such notification at least ten minutes before such release. The NASD rules also provide that, under unusual circumstances, issuers may not be required to make public disclosure of material events—for example, where it is possible to maintain confidentiality of those events and immediate public disclosure would prejudice the ability of the company to pursue its legitimate corporate objectives.

In addition, Nasdaq also encourages companies to use the Internet to disclose information to the public. Nasdaq has stated:

---

[22] See NASD Rules 4310(c)(16), 4320(e)(14).

"While Nasdaq requires that its listed issuers disseminate material press releases over one of the major news wires, Nasdaq recognizes the increased utilization of the Internet as a vehicle for additional news dissemination. The Internet is a valuable disclosure resource that can enhance the orderly dissemination of material information for all shareholders and market participants. Issuers can and should provide shareholders direct access to corporate disclosures via their Internet home pages and web sites. To ensure a level playing field for all investors in Nasdaq companies, however, this policy on disclosure of corporate information requires that the use of the Internet to disseminate material press releases is appropriate provided the information is not made available over the Internet before the same information is transmitted to, and received by, the traditional news vendor services. Issuers must still notify Nasdaq at least ten minutes prior to the release of any information that would reasonably be expected to affect the value of securities or influence investors' decisions, as indicated in this policy."[23]

The Nasdaq also has a specific rule that requires a company to address marketplace rumors. The rule states:

"Whenever unusual market activity takes place in a Nasdaq issuer's securities, the issuer normally should determine whether there is material information or news which should be disclosed. If rumors or unusual market activity indicate that information on impending developments has become known to the investing public, or if information from a source other than the issuer becomes known to the investing public, a clear public announcement may be

---

[23] NASD Rule 4120-1.

required as to the state of negotiations or development of issuer plans. Such an announcement may be required, even though the issuer may not have previously been advised of such information or the matter has not yet been presented to the issuer's Board of Directors for consideration. It may also be appropriate, in certain circumstances, to publicly deny false or inaccurate rumors which are likely to have, or have had, an effect on the trading in its securities or would likely have an influence on investment decisions."[24]

Likewise, companies listed on the NYSE are also required to address marketplace rumors. NYSE Rule 202.03 states:

"The market activity of a company's securities should be closely watched at a time when consideration is being given to significant corporate matters. If rumors or unusual market activity indicate that information on impending developments has leaked out, a frank and explicit announcement is clearly required. If rumors are in fact false or inaccurate, they should be promptly denied or clarified. A statement to the effect that the company knows of no corporate developments to account for the unusual market activity can have a salutary effect. It is obvious that if such a public statement is contemplated, management should be checked prior to any public comment so as to avoid any embarrassment or potential criticism. If rumors are correct or there are developments, an immediate candid statement to the public as to the state of negotiations or of development of corporate plans in the rumored area must be made directly and openly. Such statements are essential despite the business inconvenience which may be caused and even though the matter may not as yet have been

---

[24] *Id.*

presented to the company's Board of Directors for consideration.

"The Exchange recommends that its listed companies contact their Exchange representative if they become aware of rumors circulating about their company. Exchange Rule 435 provides that no member, member organization or allied member shall circulate in any manner rumors of a sensational character which might reasonably be expected to affect market conditions on the Exchange. Information provided concerning rumors will be promptly investigated."[25]

The NYSE also has two other rules relating to the disclosure of information to the public. Rule 202.05 addresses the timely disclosure of material news developments. That rule states that a "listed company is expected to release quickly to the public any news or information which might be reasonably expected to materially affect the market for its securities."[26] Rule 202.05 also requires listed companies to act quickly to dispel unfounded rumors that result in unusual market activity in the company's stock. Such rumors often relate to mergers and earnings results, two areas where the company has unique access to information to either confirm or deny such rumors.

RULES RELATED TO CORPORATE GOVERNANCE PROMULGATED BY THE STOCK EXCHANGES AND NASDAQ

The exchanges and Nasdaq also have requirements that affect corporate governance. This is in marked contrast to the federal securities laws, which do not generally regulate internal corporate

---

[25] NYSE Rule 202.03.

[26] NYSE Rule 202.05.

governance. The stock exchanges and Nasdaq implement their corporate governance rules through the listing agreements that all companies are required to sign prior to the start of trading on an exchange or Nasdaq.

An examination of Nasdaq's corporate governance requirements that relate to independent directors and audit committees is instructive in learning about the types of corporate governance rules that are in place because it is fairly typical of the rules that are also in place at the exchanges. In December 1999, Nasdaq instituted a significant change in its corporate governance policies by promulgating rule changes requiring stronger corporate audit committees and strengthening the independence requirements for directors who sit on the audit committee. The Nasdaq's new rules recognize the importance of a strong audit committee in ensuring the integrity of a company's financial statements.

Independent Director Requirements

Nasdaq's rules specify the relationships that will disqualify a director from being considered "independent" for purposes of serving as a member of a company's audit committee. A director will not be considered independent if:

> He has been employed by the corporation or its affiliates in the current year or past three years;

> He has accepted any compensation from the corporation or its affiliates in excess of $60,000 during the previous fiscal year (except for board service, retirement plan benefits, or nondiscretionary compensation);

> An immediate family member is, or has been in the past three years, employed by the corporation or its affiliates as an executive officer;

> He has been a partner, controlling shareholder or an executive officer of any for-profit business to which the corporation made, or from which it received, payments (other than those which arise solely from investments in the corporation's securities) that exceed 5% of the organization's consolidated gross revenues for that year, or $200,000, whichever is more, in any of the past three years; or

> He has been employed as an executive of another entity where any of the company's executives serve on that entity's compensation committee.

Audit Committees

Companies that desire to have their shares traded on Nasdaq are required to adopt a formal written charter that specifies the scope of the audit committee's responsibilities and the means by which it carries out those responsibilities. The charter must also specify the audit committee's responsibility to ensure the independence of the outside auditor. Nasdaq now requires that audit committees have a minimum of three members and be comprised of independent directors only. All directors must be able to read and understand fundamental financial statements, including a company's balance sheet, income statement, and cash flow statement. In addition, at least one director must have past employment experience in finance or accounting, requisite professional certification in accounting, or other comparable experience or background, including a current or past position as a chief executive or financial officer or other senior officer with financial oversight responsibilities.

Under exceptional and limited circumstances, however, the new Nasdaq rules allow *one* nonindependent director to serve on the audit committee, provided that the board determines it to be in the best interests of the corporation and its shareholders, and the board discloses the reasons for the determination in the company's next annual proxy statement. Current employees or officers, or their immediate family members, however, are not able to serve on the audit committee under this exception.

Disclosure Obligations of Officers, Directors and Substantial Shareholders

In addition to the obligations imposed on the corporation after an initial public offering, there are also obligations and responsibilities that apply to the individual officers, directors and primary shareholders of publicly traded companies. Counsel for publicly traded companies must ensure that all of the officers, directors and principal shareholders of a newly public company understand that there are numerous regulations applicable to them in their personal capacity. This is particularly true in the case of new media companies because many of those involved will become subject to reporting and filing requirements for the first time. Consequently, it is easy to inadvertently fail to comply with the various rules.

The restrictions applicable to officers, directors and principal shareholders of publicly traded companies can be broken down into two types: (1) substantive restrictions on the purchase and sale of the company's securities by such individuals, including restrictions on insider trading; and (2) reporting and filing requirements relating to the acquisition or disposition of the company's securities by those individuals.

Short-Swing Profits

Corporate insiders are often surprised to learn that any profits earned within six months of a purchase and sale of the company's stock by an officer, director or principal shareholder (a shareholder with a greater than 10% interest) as a result of a purchase and sale of the company's stock within a six-month period are recoverable by the company. This rule, known as the "short-swing profit rule," is contained in Section 16 of the Exchange Act.[27] It applies whether or not they traded on inside information or intended to profit based on such information. The short-swing profit rule is extremely broad, applying to all purchases and sales of securities, as long as both the purchase and the sale occur within six months of each other. It also applies to purchases and sales of derivative securities such as stock options. Officers, directors and shareholders with an interest that is greater than 10% that profitably trade their company's securities within the six-month window are strictly liabl, and there is no need to show any intent to violate the law.

It is incumbent upon a company's counsel, therefore, to ensure that officers, directors and principal shareholders are aware that they should not purchase and sell their company's stock in the open market, or otherwise, within a six-month window. Under the Exchange Act,[28] the definition of "officer" includes a company's president, principal financial officer, principal accounting officer (or, if there is no accounting officer, the controller), any vice-president of the company in charge of a principal business unit, division or function (such as sales, marketing or administration) and any other officer or person who performs similar policy making functions.

Officers, directors and shareholders with an interest that is greater than 10% are also prohibited by Section 16(c) of the Exchange Act from making "short sales" of equity securities of their company.[29] In other words, such persons cannot sell equity securities of the company if they do not already own the securities they intend to sell. This rule, in effect, prohibits officers, directors and shareholders

----

[27] 15 U.S.C. § 78p.

[28] Rule 16a-1(f), 17 C.F.R. § 240.16a-1(f).

[29] 15 U.S.C. § 78p.

with an interest that is greater than 10% from profiting if their company's stock price declines.

Restricted Stock

Counsel for new media companies will often be requested to provide guidance to those shareholders that acquired a company's stock prior to the public offering. Stock issued in a private transaction prior to an initial public offering is known as "restricted stock" because it cannot be freely sold by the owners. Holders of restricted stock should make resales of stock only in accordance with SEC Rule 144,[30] which restricts the amount, manner of sale and timing of such resales. In addition, affiliates of the company, who are defined as people who control or are controlled by the company, will also be subject to the restrictions of Rule 144 when they resell their company's stock. Often, the company's stock transfer agent will require an opinion letter from counsel stating that a particular shareholder's sale of restricted stock is allowable under Rule 144.

Because of the prevalence of stock options among new media companies, the companies and their counsel must also be familiar with SEC Rule 701,[31] which applies to resales of common stock acquired before the public offering upon the exercise of stock options. Rule 701 enables nonaffiliates to resell such shares without having to comply with most of the Rule 144 restrictions. However, sales under Rule 701 can only commence ninety days after the company becomes subject to the reporting requirements of the Exchange Act. Rule 701 allows a company's employees to publicly sell stock that they had acquired in a nonpublic offering.

---

[30] 17 C.F.R. § 230.144.

[31] 17 C.F.R. § 230.701.

The foregoing discussion covered the principal substantive restrictions on the securities trading of officers, directors and principal shareholders of public companies. Next, we turn to the various reporting and filing obligations placed on these individuals.

Reporting Obligations

Section 16(a) of the Exchange Act sets up a comprehensive regulatory scheme whereby officers, directors and principal shareholders must publicly disclose their beneficial ownership of their company's stock and any changes thereto. Each director, officer and principal shareholder of a publicly traded company must file with the SEC an Initial Statement of Beneficial Ownership of Securities on Form 3.[32]

If, at a later time, another person becomes an officer, director or principal shareholder, he must also file a Form 3. If there is a change in the ownership of an officer, director or principal shareholder, that change must be reported on a Form 4,[33] entitled Changes in Beneficial Ownership of Securities, within the first ten days of the month following the sale.

It is important to note that while most changes in beneficial ownership will be the result of purchases and sales of the company's securities, other events might trigger the need to file a Form 4, such as giving shares as a gift. Also, the acquisition or disposition of a derivative security (such as an option) is treated and reported as an acquisition or disposition of the underlying stock. If an officer or director of the company ceases to serve in such capacity, but prior to ceasing such service he executes a transaction, he must file a statement on Form 4 if he executes a

---

[32] A copy of a Form 3 is included as Appendix 8D *infra.*

[33] A copy of a Form 4 is included as Appendix 8E *infra.*

transaction within six months of the transaction executed while he was an officer or director. All transactions must be reported on Form 4, except for small acquisitions not exceeding $10,000 and certain other exempted transactions involving options positions.

A Form 5[34] must be filed within forty-five days after the company's fiscal year end by any officer, director or principal shareholder who, at any time during the fiscal year, engaged in transactions that were not previously reported. The Form 5 will disclose all transactions that constituted small acquisitions or were otherwise exempt from previous reporting.

To help ensure compliance, counsel should advise a publicly traded company to appoint a person to receive and review a copy of each Form 3, 4 and 5 prior to its filing with the SEC. In addition, officers, directors and principal shareholders should be requested to forward to the designated person at the company copies of all Forms 3, 4 and 5 to be filed with the SEC. Any person filing a Form 3, 4 or 5 should retain a copy for his files.

Further Disclosure Obligations

In addition to the requirements of Section 16(a), certain stockholders of the company are subject to disclosure requirements under Section 13 of the Exchange Act, the purpose of which is to alert the public and the company to any significant ownership or trading of the company's securities. Any person who acquires, directly or indirectly, the beneficial ownership of over 5% of a class of publicly traded equity securities must file a Schedule 13D, which requires disclosure of the purpose of the acquisition, the source of the funds for the acquisition of the securities and the level of ownership. Direct or indirect beneficial ownership includes securities

---

[34] A copy of a Form 5 is included as Appendix 8F *infra*.

held through corporations, trusts and partnerships and, usually, stock held by members of the stockholder's immediate family.

The Schedule 13D is filed with the SEC and sent to the issuer within ten days after the acquisition of securities bringing the total amount of share ownership over the 5% threshold. It should be noted that when two or more people act as a group and collectively acquire over 5% of a class of a company's stock, even if no individual member of the group owns over 5%, a Schedule 13D may have to be filed by that group.

As the foregoing discussion illustrates, there are numerous rules and regulations that apply personally to officers, directors and principal shareholders of publicly traded companies. To assist these individuals in complying with these important regulations, counsel to new media companies should consider preparing clearly written guidelines to ensure that the individuals affected understand the various rules that apply to them and the steps that should be taken to comply with those rules.

In addition, many companies have adopted the salutary practice of providing regular written reminders to ensure that the various regulations are not mistakenly overlooked. Through these actions, new media companies, as well as their officers, directors and shareholders, can best ensure that they are in full compliance with the numerous regulations that apply to them.

CHOOSING WHERE TO TRADE AND THE APPLICABLE STANDARDS

Once a company conducts its IPO, its shares will be freely tradable among investors. Post-IPO stock trading among investors is know as "aftermarket trading." Determining where the aftermarket trading of a company's stock will take place is an essential part of IPO planning. Often, technology and new media companies prefer to trade on Nasdaq because it is an electronic and technology-oriented marketplace in keeping with the new media image and experience. However, many large and well-known technology companies, such as IBM, are listed for trading on the New York Stock Exchange, one of the U.S.'s seven national securities exchanges. Many new media companies may not be able to meet the stringent listing requirements of an exchange or Nasdaq and may have to trade in alternative marketplaces. In deciding where a company's stock will trade, company management will be driven primarily by a desire to have the company's stock trade on the most liquid and efficient market, allowing the company's investors to easily purchase and sell shares of the company's stock.

The vast majority of aftermarket trading in the United States takes place in one of the following forums: (1) one of the seven national securities exchanges, such as the New York Stock Exchange or American Stock Exchange; (2) Nasdaq; (3) the Over-the-Counter Bulletin Board ("OTCBB"); or (4) the Pink Sheets. Stock issued by large and relatively well-known companies will usually trade on an exchange or on the Nasdaq system. Stock issued by companies that are smaller regional companies will often be traded on the OTCBB or the Pink Sheets. What follows is a brief description of trading on each of the four marketplaces.

National Securities Exchanges. There are seven national securities exchanges in the United States. The largest is the New York Stock Exchange and the others are the American, Boston, Cincinnati, Chicago, Pacific and Philadelphia Stock Exchanges. All seven exchanges are physical locations where brokers come together to purchase and sell stocks listed and approved for trading on the individual exchanges. Typically, the exchanges assign each stock to a "specialist" who is responsible for maintaining an orderly market in the stock. The specialists at the exchanges conduct an auction market where brokers bid for and sell stocks among themselves and the market price is set by the supply and demand for each stock. Each specialist maintains a post on the exchange floor where brokers gather to purchase and sell the stock. The specialists will only step in to purchase and sell a security when it is necessary to maintain an orderly market. It is important to note that a single stock can be listed—and traded—on more than one exchange. As discussed below, exchanges have strict listing requirements that companies must meet in order to be eligible to have their shares traded on the exchange.

Among the seven exchanges, the New York Stock Exchange ("NYSE") is of particular note because its is the largest equities marketplace in the world. Over 3,000 companies worth more than $17 trillion in global market capitalization are listed with the NYSE. As of year-end 2000, the NYSE had over 313 billion shares listed and available for trading. These shares were valued at approximately $12.3 trillion. Each of the exchanges has strict listing requirements. The NYSE's listing requirements are attached as Appendix 8G.

Securities not traded on an exchange are traded in the over-the-counter ("OTC") market. Companies that do not meet the listing requirements of the major exchanges issue the majority of OTC stocks. OTC stocks are traded on Nasdaq, the OTCBB and the Pink Sheets.

Nasdaq. In contrast to traditional floor-based stock markets, Nasdaq has no single specialist through which transactions pass. Instead, Nasdaq consists of an electronic network of numerous broker-dealers that make a market in particular stocks. Through a highly sophisticated computer system, the securities dealers post the prices at which they are willing to buy a particular stock (the bid price) and sell a particular stock (the ask price). The price at which a particular broker-dealer will sell a stock is always higher than the price at which the broker is willing to buy the stock. The difference between the bid and the ask price is called the spread and the spread represents the dealer's profit for making a market in the particular security.

Nasdaq is comprised of two separate markets—the Nasdaq National Market and the Nasdaq SmallCap. Nasdaq's largest and most actively traded stocks trade on the Nasdaq National Market. Currently, over 4,000 companies have their securities traded on the National Market System. To be listed on the National Market, a company must satisfy certain financial, capitalization, and corporate governance standards.

Nasdaq National Market Initial Listing Requirements and Fees			
Requirements	Alternative 1	Alternative 2	Alternative 3
Net Tangible Assets[35]	$6 million	$18 million	N/A
Market Capitalization	N/A	N/A	$75 million
or			
Total Assets	N/A	N/A	$75 million
or			
Total Revenue	N/A	N/A	$75 million
Pretax Income (latest fiscal year or 2 of last 3 fiscal years)	$1 million	N/A	N/A
Public Float (Shares)[36]	1.1 million	1.1 million	1.1 million

[35] Net tangible assets means total assets (excluding goodwill) minus total liabilities.

[36] Public float is defined as shares that are not held directly or indirectly by any officer or director of the issuer or by any other person who is the beneficial owner of more than 10% of the total shares outstanding.

Requirements	Alternative 1	Alternative 2	Alternative 3
Operating History	N/A	2 years	N/A
Market Value Of Public Float	$8 million	$18 million	$20 million
Minimum Bid Price	$5	$5	$5
Shareholders (100 shares or more)	400	400	400
Market Makers	3	3	4
Corporate Governance	Yes	Yes	Yes

National Market System Listing Fees

There is a $5,000 one-time company initial listing fee for the Nasdaq National Market, which includes a nonrefundable $1,000 application fee. In addition, there is an annual listing fee that ranges from $10,710 to $50,000 depending on the number of shares outstanding.

The Nasdaq SmallCap is the market where emerging growth companies trade. Over 1,000 companies have their stock traded on the SmallCap market. The financial criteria for listing on this market are less stringent than on the Nasdaq National Market and are set out below. However, the corporate governance standards are the same, for both the National Market and the SmallCap. Frequently, as Nasdaq SmallCap companies grow and become more established, they move up to the Nasdaq National Market.

Nasdaq SmallCap Initial and Continuing Listing Requirements and Fees		
Requirements	Initial Listing	Continued Listing
Net Tangible Assets[37]	$4 million	$2 million
or		
Market Capitalization	$50 million	$35 million
or		
Net Income (in latest fiscal year or 2 of the last 3 fiscal years)	$750,000	$500,000
Public Float (shares)[38]	1 million	500,000
Market Value of Public Float	$5 million	$1 million
Minimum Bid Price	$4	$1
Shareholders (100 shares or more)	300	300
Operating History	1 year	N/A
or		
Market Capitalization	$50 million	N/A
Market Makers	3	2
Corporate Governance	Yes	Yes

SmallCap Listing Fees

There is a $5,000 one-time listing fee plus a variable entry fee for each class of security. For a listing of all equity securities the variable entry fee is the greater of $1,000 or $0.001 per share. The maximum entry fees cannot exceed $10,000, including the $5,000 listing fee.

---

[37] Net tangible assets means total assets (excluding goodwill) minus total liabilities.

[38] Public float is defined as shares that are not held directly or indirectly by any officer or director of the issuer and by any other person who is the beneficial owner of more than 10% of the total shares outstanding.

OTCBB. The OTC Bulletin Board ("OTCBB") is a regulated quotation service that displays real-time quotes, last-sale prices, and volume information on OTC securities. Stocks that trade on the OTCBB generally do not meet the listing requirements of the Nasdaq SmallCap. An issuer does not list its stock on the OTCBB. Rather, a broker-dealer that desires to make a market in a particular stock must apply to the OTCBB for permission to do so. OTCBB securities include national, regional and foreign equity issues, among others. Because the OTCBB is not a market or exchange, it does not have any listing requirements. However, to be eligible for quotation on the OTCBB, issuers must remain current in their filings with the SEC or applicable regulatory authority. While Nasdaq runs the OTCBB, the latter should not be confused with either of the two Nasdaq markets, both of which maintain strict listing requirements.

Pink Sheets. The Pink Sheets is an alternative quotation service similar to the OTCBB. The Pink Sheets provides pricing and financial information for the over-the-counter (OTC) securities markets. The Pink Sheets had its start in the early 1900s as a paper-based product containing trading and pricing information for over-the-counter securities. The paper on which this information was printed was a distinctive shade of pink and that was how the Pink Sheets got its name. The pricing and trading information for OTC securities is now available in electronic form from Pink Sheets through Internet-based technology. Most stocks traded on the Pink Sheets do not meet the listing requirements for the Nasdaq SmallCap.

Generally speaking, most publicly traded new media companies desire to trade on either the NYSE or Nasdaq. There is a great deal of prestige associated with being traded on either, and the advanced market structures of each go a long way to make sure that investors will have an orderly and liquid market in which to buy and sell the companies' shares. In addition, the listing requirements of the NYSE and Nasdaq ensure that only companies that have broad investor interest will be permitted to trade on those marketplaces.

When a company applies to have its stock traded on either an exchange or Nasdaq, it agrees to be bound by the corporate governance and disclosure standards that are in place at the exchanges and Nasdaq. A copy of the NYSE's sample listing agreement is attached as Appendix 8H. The exchanges and Nasdaq have promulgated specific substantive requirements that companies listed for trading must follow, including rules relating to the disclosure of material information, shareholder voting and the composition and operation of the board of directors. In contrast, federal securities laws have only a limited role in substantive issues of corporate governance. Such substantive rules can be found in the New York Stock Exchange Listed Company Manual and in the NASD Manual. The New York Stock Exchange Listed Company Manual is a comprehensive rule book that all listed companies must follow. The NYSE and the NASD Manuals also detail the original and continued listing requirements for each marketplace and contain the rules and policies on corporate governance and shareholder communications, as well as other matters.

AUDITOR INDEPENDENCE STANDARDS

The federal securities laws frequently require that the financial and accounting information filed with the SEC by public companies be audited by an independent public accountant. An auditor does not create the original accounting records for the company, which is done by the company's bookkeepers and accountants. It is the auditor's role to double check the work of the company's accountants to ensure that all financial information is presented fairly and in accordance with the Generally Accepted Accounting Principles. The auditing of financial information is designed to provide the investing public with a high level of confidence that the financial information released by publicly traded companies has been independently scrutinized for accuracy. The SEC has stated that "[i]nvestor confidence in the integrity of publicly available financial information is the cornerstone of our securities markets. Capital formation depends on the willingness of investors to invest in the securities of public companies. Investors are more likely to invest, and pricing is more likely to be efficient, the greater the assurance that the financial information disclosed by issuers is reliable. The federal securities laws contemplate that that assurance will flow from knowledge that the financial information has been subjected to rigorous examination by competent and objective auditors."[39]

In November 2000, the SEC adopted Rule 2-10 to ensure that auditors of companies were truly independent, particularly in light of the significant non-audit fees that the auditing firms were earning from their corporate clients. The preliminary note to Rule 2-01 states that "Rule 2-10 is designed to ensure that auditors are qualified and independent of their audit clients both in fact and in appearance. Accordingly, the rule sets forth restrictions on financial, employment, and business relationships between an accountant and an audit client and restrictions on an accountant providing certain non-audit services to an audit client."[40]

Rule 2-01(c)(1) prohibits an auditor from having a direct investment in an audit client, such as acquiring a stock, bond or option of the audit client. This rule is designed to maintain an auditor's independence free from any direct financial ties to the audit client. The SEC also recognized that certain activities were antithetical to

---

[39] SEC Rel. No. 33-7919 (Nov. 21, 2000).
[40] Id.

the auditor's role as an independent "second set of eyes," and bans auditors from engaging in such activities. Towards that end, Rule 201(c)(4) prohibits an auditor from maintaining a client's books or accounting records. Rule 201(c)(4) also prohibits, with limited exceptions, an auditor from providing an audit client with valuation, actuarial services, management services, internal auditing services, human resources services, broker-dealer services and legal services. All of the foregoing activities were deemed to create too great a conflict of interest for auditors. In addition, Rule 201(c)(5) prohibits the auditor from taking on any assignment on a contingency basis for fear that the auditors would have an economic incentive to look the other way in case accounting problems were uncovered in the audit. Finally, public companies are also required to disclose in their annual proxy filings the amount of fees paid to their auditors both for auditing and non-auditing services.

Publicly traded companies can help the audit process go smoothly by having senior management meet with the auditing team prior to the audit. At this meeting, the scope and anticipated progress of the audit should be discussed. It is important for senior management to realize that an audit is a time-consuming process that will require the cooperation of many of the company's employees. The auditors will want to examine numerous accounting records and physically inspect the important assets of the company. The management of the company should alert the company's employees of the need to respond to the auditor's requests for information promptly so that the audit can be completed on time. Typically, an audit will examine all facets of how a company gathers and reports financial data to ensure that the systems that are used are properly structured. An audit will also examine whether the proper internal controls have been established to ensure that a dishonest employee does not have the ability to change the company's accounting data to cover up improper transactions. Internal controls that require more than one person to approve transactions are frequently employed. By taking steps to work closely with the auditor, the company's management can ensure that investors remain confident that the company's financial statements are accurate.

SPECIAL ISSUES PUBLIC COMPANIES FACE IN BAD ECONOMIC TIMES

When economic conditions are bad, publicly traded companies face special issues. Bad economic times often result in declining revenues and smaller profit margins. As a result, the price of a company's stock can decline dramatically. Even if a company has a unique niche and is able to maintain its revenues and profit margins, a decline in the overall stock market can also lead to significantly lower prices for the company's stock. When a company's share price decreases substantially there is a danger that the company's stock will fail to meet the minimum per share price that is required by the stock exchange on which the company trades. If a company fails to meet the minimum listing requirements for the exchange on which it trades, the company's shares will be in danger of being delisted. Delisting can be disastrous for both the shareholders and the company. Shareholders will have an extremely hard time finding a buyer for shares that have been delisted because there will no longer be an organized, liquid and transparent market. For the company, delisting means that it will lose many of the benefits associated with being a publicly traded company, including the ability to raise capital in the public markets.

When a public company's share price drops below the minimum listing requirements, the exchange where it trades will notify the company and provide a period of time—generally between thirty and ninety days—for the company to come back into compliance with the minimum standards. During that time, the company can pursue additional outside financing to shore up its balance sheet. However, outside financing may be difficult to arrange in bad economic times, particularly for a company that may be experiencing business difficulties. As a result, one of the more common methods that companies use to bring their stock price back into compliance with minimum listing standards is a reverse stock split. This has the effect of raising the stock's price immediately. For example in a one-for-ten reverse stock split each holder of ten shares before the stock split will only hold one share after the split. However, the price of shares will generally increase by a factor of ten. Therefore, if a company's stock trades at $0.50 per share prior to the one-for-ten reverse stock split, the stock will trade at $5 per share post-split. As a result of the reverse spilt the number of shares that are issued and outstanding will also decrease by a factor of ten. A company that desires to conduct a reverse stock split must obtain shareholder approval prior to the split. Once the split is complete the company must file a Form 8-K with the SEC.

While a reverse stock split can boost the price of a company's stock immediately, it will only provide temporary relief if the company cannot turn its business around or give the market assurances that better times are ahead for the company. For many companies, a reverse stock split can give additional breathing room. However, if business conditions do not improve the share price will continue to fall and the company will again be in danger of being delisted. Unfortunately, for some companies, a bankruptcy filing is the only way to keep creditors at bay and keep their business operating. In a Chapter 11 bankruptcy, the company can continue operating under the watchful eye of the Bankruptcy Court. While trading in a company's stock is often suspended when the company files for bankruptcy, the shares of a company in Chapter 11 can resume trading shortly after the filing, assuming that the minimum listing requirements are met. If a company does not have a viable way to turn its business around, a Chapter 7 bankruptcy may be the only option. In a Chapter 7 bankruptcy, the company's assets are liquidated and the funds are used to pay back creditors. In either type of bankruptcy, a Form 8-K must be filed with the SEC in order to inform the market that a bankruptcy petition has been filed.

APPENDIX 8A

Form 10-K

SEC 1673 (6-00)   Potential persons who are to respond to the collection of information contained in this form are not required to respond unless the form displays a currently valid OMB control number.

UNITED STATES

SECURITIES AND EXCHANGE COMMISSION

Washington, D.C. 20549

OMB APPROVAL
OMB Number: 3235-0063
Expires: March 31, 2003
Estimated average burden hours per response: 430.00

ANNUAL REPORT PURSUANT TO SECTION 13 OR 15(d) OF THE SECURITIES EXCHANGE ACT OF 1934

GENERAL INSTRUCTIONS

A. Rule as to Use of Form 10-K.

This Form shall be used for annual reports pursuant to Section 13 or 15(d) of the Securities Exchange Act of 1934 (the "Act") for which no other form is prescribed. This form also shall be used for transition reports filed pursuant to Section 13 or 15(d) of the Act. Annual reports on this form shall be filed within 90 days after the end of the fiscal year covered by the report. Transition reports on this form shall be filed in accordance with the requirements set forth in § 240.13a-10 or § 240.15d10 applicable when the registrant changes its fiscal year end. However, all schedules required by Article 12 of Regulation S-X may, at the option of the registrant, be filed as an amendment to the annual report not later than 120 days after the end of the fiscal year covered by the report or, in the case of a transition report, not later than 30 days after the due date of the report.

B. Application of General Rules and Regulations.

    (1) The General Rules and Regulations under the Act (17 CFR 240) contain certain general requirements which are applicable to reports on any form. These general requirements should be carefully read and observed in the preparation and filing of reports on this Form.

    (2) Particular attention is directed to Regulation 12B which contains general requirements regarding matters such as the kind and size of paper to be used, the legibility of the report, the information to be given whenever the title of securities is required to be stated, and the filing of the report. The definitions contained in Rule 12b-2 should be especially noted. See also Regulations 13A and 15D.

C. Preparation of Report.

    (1) This form is not to be used as a blank form to be filled in, but only as a guide in the preparation of the report on paper meeting the requirements of Rule 12b-12. Except as provided in General Instruction G, the answers to the items shall be prepared in the manner specified in Rule 12b-13.

    (2) Except where information is required to be given for the fiscal year or as of a specified date, it shall be given as of the latest practicable date.

    (3) Attention is directed to Rule 12b-20, which states: "In addition to the information expressly required to be included in a statement or report, there shall be added such further material information, if any, as may be necessary to make the required statements, in the light of the circumstances under which they are made, not misleading."

D. Signature and Filing of Report.

    (1) Three complete copies of the report, including financial statements, financial statement schedules, exhibits, and all other papers and documents filed as a part thereof, and five additional copies which need not include exhibits, shall be filed with the Commission. At least one complete copy of the report, including financial statements, financial statement schedules, exhibits, and all other papers and documents filed as a part thereof, shall be filed with each exchange on which any class of securities of the registrant is registered. At least one complete copy of the report filed with the Commission and one such copy filed with each exchange shall be manually signed. Copies not manually signed shall bear typed or printed signatures.

    (2) (a) The report shall be signed by the registrant, and on behalf of the registrant by its principal executive officer or officers, its principal financial officer, its controller or principal accounting officer, and by

at least the majority of the board of directors or persons performing similar functions. Where the registrant is a limited partnership, the report shall be signed by the majority of the board of directors of any corporate general partner who signs the report.

(b) The name of each person who signs the report shall be typed or printed beneath his signature. Any person who occupies more than one of the specified positions shall indicate each capacity in which he signs the report. Attention is directed to Rule 12b-11 (17 CFR 240.12b-11) concerning manual signatures and signatures pursuant to powers of attorney.

(3) Registrants are requested to indicate in a transmittal letter with the Form 10-K whether the financial statements in the report reflect a change from the preceding year in any accounting principles or practices, or in the method of applying any such principles or practices.

E. Disclosure With Respect to Foreign Subsidiaries.

Information required by any item or other requirement of this form with respect to any foreign subsidiary may be omitted to the extent that the required disclosure would be detrimental to the registrant. However, financial statements and financial statement schedules, otherwise required, shall not be omitted pursuant to this Instruction. Where information is omitted pursuant to this Instruction, a statement shall be made that such information has been omitted and the names of the subsidiaries involved shall be separately furnished to the Commission. The Commission may, in its discretion, call for justification that the required disclosure would be detrimental.

F. Information as to Employee Stock Purchase, Savings and Similar Plans.

Attention is directed to Rule 15d-21 which provides that separate annual and other reports need not be filed pursuant to Section 15(d) of the Act with respect to any employee stock purchase, savings or similar plan if the issuer of the stock or other securities offered to employees pursuant to the plan furnishes to the Commission the information and documents specified in the Rule.

G. Information to be Incorporated by Reference.

(1) Attention is directed to Rule 12b-23 which provides for the incorporation by reference of information contained in certain documents in answer or partial answer to any item of a report.

(2) The information called for by Parts I and II of this form (Items I through 9 or any portion thereof) may, at the registrant's option, be incorporated by reference from the registrant's annual report to security holders furnished to the Commission pursuant to Rule 14a-3(b) or Rule 14c-3(a) or from the registrant's annual report to security holders, even if not furnished to the

Commission pursuant to Rule 14a-3(b) or Rule 14c-3(a), provided such annual report contains the information required by Rule 14a-3.

Note 1. In order to fulfill the requirements of Part I of Form 10-K, the incorporated portion of the annual report to security holders must contain the information required by Items 1-3 of Form 10-K; to the extent applicable.

Note 2. If any information required by Part I or Part II is incorporated by reference into an electronic format document from the annual report to security holders as provided in General Instruction G, any portion of the annual report to security holders incorporated by reference shall be filed as an exhibit in electronic format, as required by Item 601(b)(13) of Regulation S-K.

(3) The information required by Part III (Items 10, 11, 12 and 13) may be incorporated by reference from the registrant's definitive proxy statement (filed or required to be filed pursuant to Regulation 14A) or definitive information statement (filed or to be filed pursuant to Regulation 14C) which involves the election of directors, if such definitive proxy statement or information statement is filed with the Commission not later than 120 days after the end of the fiscal year covered by the Form 10-K. However, if such definitive proxy statement or information statement is not filed with the Commission in the l20day period or is not required to be filed with the Commission by virtue of Rule 3a12-3(b) under the Exchange Act, the Items comprising the Part III information must be filed as part of the Form 10-K, or as an amendment to the Form l0-K, not later than the end of the 120-day period. It should be noted that the information regarding executive officers required by Item 401 of Regulation S-K (§ 229.401 of this chapter) may be included in Part I of Form 10-K under an appropriate caption. See Instruction 3 to Item 401(b) of Regulation S-K (§ 229.401(b) of this chapter).

(4) No item numbers of captions of items need be contained in the material incorporated by reference into the report. However, the registrant's attention is directed to Rule 12b-23(e) (17 CFR 240.12b(e)) regarding the specific disclosure required in the report concerning information incorporated by reference. When the registrant combines all of the information in Parts I and II of this Form (Items 1 through 9) by incorporation by reference from the registrant's annual report to security holders and all of the information in Part III of this Form (Items 10 through 13) by incorporating by reference from a definitive proxy statement or information statement involving the election of directors, then, notwithstanding General Instruction C(1), this Form shall consist of the facing or cover page, those sections incorporated from the annual report to security holders, the proxy or information statement, and the

information, if any, required by Part IV of this Form, signatures, and a cross-reference sheet setting forth the item numbers and captions in Parts I, II and III of this Form and the page and/or pages in the referenced materials where the corresponding information appears.

H. Integrated Reports to Security Holders.

Annual reports to security holders may be combined with the required information of Form 10-K and will be suitable for filing with the Commission if the following conditions are satisfied:

(1) The combined report contains full and complete answers to all items required by Form 10-K. When responses to a certain item of required disclosure are separated within the combined report, an appropriate cross-reference should be made. If the information required by Part III of Form 10-K is omitted by virtue of General Instruction G, a definitive proxy or information statement shall be filed.

(2) The cover page and the required signatures are included. As appropriate, a cross-reference sheet should be filed indicating the location of information required by the items of the Form.

(3) If an electronic filer files any portion of an annual report to security holders in combination with the required information of Form 10-K, as provided in this instruction, only such portions filed in satisfaction of the Form 10-K requirements shall be filed in electronic format.

I. Omission of Information by Certain Wholly-Owned Subsidiaries.

If, on the date of the filing of its report on Form 10-K, the registrant meets the conditions specified in paragraph (1) below, then such registrant may furnish the abbreviated narrative disclosure specified in paragraph (2) below.

(1) Conditions for availability of the relief specified in paragraph (2) below.

(a) All of the registrant's equity securities are owned, either directly or indirectly, by a single person which is a reporting company under the Act and which has filed all the material required to be filed pursuant to section 13, 14, or 15(d) thereof, as applicable, and which is named in conjunction with the registrant's description of its business;

(b) During the preceding thirty-six calendar months and any subsequent period of days, there has not been any material default in the payment of principal, interest, a sinking or purchase fund installment, or any other material default not cured within thirty days, with respect to any indebtedness of the registrant or its subsidiaries, and there has not been any material default in the payment of rentals under material long-term leases; and

(c) There is prominently set forth, on the cover page of the Form 10-K, a statement that the registrant meets the conditions set forth in General Instruction (I)(1)(a) and (b) of Form 10-K and is therefore filing this Form with the reduced disclosure format.

(2) Registrants meeting the conditions specified in paragraph (1) above are entitled to the following relief:

(a) Such registrants may omit the information called for by Item 6, Selected Financial Data, and Item 7, Management's Discussion and Analysis of Financial Condition and Results of Operations provided that the registrant includes in the Form 10-K a management's narrative analysis of the results of operations explaining the reasons for material changes in the amount of revenue and expense items between the most recent fiscal year presented and the fiscal year immediately preceding it. Explanations of material changes should include, but not be limited to, changes in the various elements which determine revenue and expense levels such as unit sales volume, prices charged and paid, production levels, production cost variances, labor costs and discretionary spending programs. In addition, the analysis should include an explanation of the effect of any changes in accounting principles and practices or method of application that have a material effect on net income as reported.

(b) Such registrants may omit the list of subsidiaries exhibit required by Item 601 of Regulation S-K (§ 229.601 of this chapter).

(c) Such registrants may omit the information called for by the following otherwise required Items: Item 4, Submission of Matters to a Vote of Security Holders; Item 10, Directors and Executive Officers of the Registrant; Item 11, Executive Compensation; Item 12, Security Ownership of Certain Beneficial Owners and Management; and Item 13, Certain Relationships and Related Transactions.

(d) In response to Item I, Business, such registrant only need furnish a brief description of the business done by the registrant and its subsidiaries during the most recent fiscal year which will, in the opinion of management, indicate the general nature and scope of the business of the registrant and its subsidiaries, and in response to Item 2, Properties, such registrant only need furnish a brief description of the material properties of the registrant and its subsidiaries to the extent, in the opinion of the management, necessary to an understanding of the business done by the registrant and its subsidiaries.

UNITED STATES

SECURITIES AND EXCHANGE COMMISSION

Washington, D.C. 20549

OMB APPROVAL
OMB Number: 3235-0063
Expires: March 31, 2003
Estimated average burden hours per response: 430.00

FORM 10-K

(Mark One)

❏ ANNUAL REPORT PURSUANT TO SECTION 13 OR 15(d) OF THE SECURITIES EXCHANGE ACT OF 1934

For the fiscal year ended _____

or

❏ TRANSITION REPORT PURSUANT TO SECTION 13 OR 15(d) OF THE SECURITIES EXCHANGE ACT OF 1934

For the transition period from _____ to

_____

Commission file number _____

_____

(Exact name of registrant as specified in its charter)

_____	_____
(State or other jurisdiction of incorporation or organization)	(I.R.S. Employer Identification No.)

_____

(Address of principal executive offices)   (Zip Code)

Registrant's telephone number, including area code _____

Securities registered pursuant to Section 12(b) of the Act:

Title of each class	Name of each exchange on which registered
_____	_____
_____	_____

Securities registered pursuant to section 12(g) of the Act:

_____

(Title of class)

_____

(Title of class)

Indicate by check mark whether the registrant (1) has filed all reports required to be filed by Section 13 or 15(d) of the Securities Exchange Act of 1934 during the preceding 12 months (or for such shorter period that the registrant was required to file such reports), and (2) has been subject to such filing requirements for the past 90 days.

❑ Yes   ❑ No

Indicate by check mark if disclosure of delinquent filers pursuant to Item 405 of Regulation S-K (§ 229.405 of this chapter) is not contained herein, and will not be contained, to the best of registrant's knowledge, in definitive proxy or information statements incorporated by reference in Part III of this Form 10-K or any amendment to this Form 10-K.   ❑

State the aggregate market value of the voting and non-voting common equity held by non-affiliates of the registrant. The aggregate market value shall be computed by reference to the price at which the common equity was sold, or the average bid and asked prices of such common equity, as of a specified date within 60 days prior to the date of filing. (See definition of affiliate in Rule 405, 17 CFR 230.405.)

Note.—If a determination as to whether a particular person or entity is an affiliate cannot be made without involving unreasonable effort and expense, the aggregate market value of the common stock held by non-affiliates may be calculated on the basis of assumptions reasonable under the circumstances, provided that the assumptions are set forth in this Form.

APPLICABLE ONLY TO REGISTRANTS INVOLVED IN BANKRUPTCY PROCEEDINGS DURING THE PRECEDING FIVE YEARS:

Indicate by check mark whether the registrant has filed all documents and reports required to be filed by Section 12, 13 or 15(d) of the Securities Exchange Act of 1934 subsequent to the distribution of securities under a plan confirmed by a court.

❑ Yes   ❑ No

(APPLICABLE ONLY TO CORPORATE REGISTRANTS)

Indicate the number of shares outstanding of each of the registrant's classes of common stock, as of the latest practicable date.

DOCUMENTS INCORPORATED BY REFERENCE

List hereunder the following documents if incorporated by reference and the Part of the Form 10-K (e.g., Part I, Part II, etc.) into which the document is incorporated: (1) Any annual report to security holders; (2) Any proxy or information statement; and (3) Any prospectus filed pursuant to Rule 424(b) or (c) under the Securities Act of 1933. The listed documents should be clearly described for identification purposes (e.g., annual report to security holders for fiscal year ended December 24, 1980).

PART I

[See General Instruction G(2)]

Item 1. Business.

Furnish the information required by Item 101 of Regulation S-K (§ 229.101 of this chapter) except that the discussion of the development of the registrant's business need only include developments since the beginning of the fiscal year for which this report is filed.

Item 2. Properties.

Furnish the information required by Item 102 of Regulation S-K (§ 229.102 of this chapter).

Item 3. Legal Proceedings.

(a) Furnish the information required by Item 103 of Regulation S-K (§ 229.103 of this chapter).

(b) As to any proceeding that was terminated during the fourth quarter of the fiscal year covered by this report, furnish information similar to that required by Item 103 of Regulation S-K (§ 229.103 of this chapter), including the date of termination and a description of the disposition thereof with respect to the registrant and its subsidiaries.

Item 4. Submission of Matters to a Vote of Security Holders.

If any matter was submitted during the fourth quarter of the fiscal year covered by this report to a vote of security holders, through the solicitation of proxies or otherwise, furnish the following information:

(a) The date of the meeting and whether it was an annual or special meeting.

(b) If the meeting involved the election of directors, the name of each director elected at the meeting and the name of each other director whose term of office as a director continued after the meeting.

(c)   A brief description of each other matter voted upon at the meeting and state the number of votes cast for, against or withheld, as well as the number of abstentions and broker non-votes as to each such matter, including a separate tabulation with respect to each nominee for office.

(d)   A description of the terms of any settlement between the registrant and any other participant (as defined in Rule 14a-11 (17 CFR 240.14a-11) of Regulation 14A under the Act) terminating any solicitation subject to Rule 14a-11, including the cost or anticipated cost to the registrant.

Instructions:

1.   If any matter has been submitted to a vote of security holders otherwise than at a meeting of such security holders, corresponding information with respect to such submission shall be furnished. The solicitation of any authorization or consent (other than a proxy to vote at a stockholders' meeting) with respect to any matter shall be deemed a submission of such matter to a vote of security holders within the meaning of this item.

2.   Paragraph (a) need be answered only if paragraph (b) or (c) is required to be answered.

3.   Paragraph (b) need not be answered if (i) proxies for the meeting were solicited pursuant to Regulation 14A under the Act, (ii) there was no solicitation in opposition to the management's nominees as listed in the proxy statement, and (iii) all of such nominees were elected. If the registrant did not solicit proxies and the board of directors as previously reported to the Commission was re-elected in its entirety, a statement to that effect in answer to paragraph (b) will suffice as an answer thereto.

4.   Paragraph (c) must be answered for all matters voted upon at the meeting, including both contested and uncontested elections of directors.

5.   If the registrant has furnished to its security holders proxy soliciting material containing the information called for by paragraph (d), the paragraph may be answered by reference to the information contained in such material.

6.   If the registrant has published a report containing all the information called for by this item, the item may be answered by a reference to the information contained in such report.

PART II

[(See General Instruction G(2)]

Item 5. Market for Registrant's Common Equity and Related Stockholder Matters.

(a)   Furnish the information required by Item 201 of Regulation S-K (§229.201 of this chapter) and Item 701 of Regulation S-K (§229.701 of this chapter) as to all equity securities of the registrant sold by the registrant during the period covered by the report that were not registered under the Securities Act. If the Item 701 information previously has been included in a Quarterly Report on Form 10-Q or 10-QSB (§249.308a or 249.308b of this chapter) it need not be furnished.

(b) If required pursuant to Rule 463 (17 CFR 230.463) of the Securities Act of 1933, furnish the information required by Item 701(f) of Regulation S-K (§229.701(f) of this chapter).

Item 6. Selected Financial Data.

Furnish the information required by Item 301 of Regulation S-K (§ 229.301 of this chapter).

Item 7. Management's Discussion and Analysis of Financial Condition and Results of Operation.

Furnish the information required by Item 303 of Regulation S-K (§ 229.303 of this chapter).

Item 7A. Quantitative and Qualitative Disclosures About Market Risk.

Furnish the information required by Item 305 of RegulationS-K (§ 229.305 of this chapter).

Item 8. Financial Statements and Supplementary Data.

Furnish financial statements meeting the requirements of Regulation S-X (§ 210 of this chapter), except § 210.3-05 and Article 11 thereof, and the supplementary financial information required by Item 302 of Regulation S-K (§ 229.302 of this chapter). Financial statements of the registrant and its subsidiaries consolidated (as required by Rule 14a-3(b)) shall be filed under this item. Other financial statements and schedules required under Regulation S-X may be filed as "Financial Statement Schedules" pursuant to Item 13, Exhibits, Financial Statement Schedules, and Reports on Form 8-K, of this form.

Notwithstanding the above, if the issuer is subject to the reporting provisions of Section 15(d) and such obligation results solely from the issuer having filed a registration statement on Form S-18 which became effective under the Securities Act of 1933 during the last fiscal year, or such obligation applies as to the first or second fiscal year after the registration statement on Form S-18 became effective solely because the issuer had on the first day of the pertinent fiscal year 300 or more record holders of any of its securities to which the Form S-18 related, audited financial statements for the issuer, or for the issuer and its predecessors, may be presented as provided below. The report of the independent accountant shall in all events comply with the requirements of Article 2 of Regulation S-X.

(a) A Form 10-K filed for the fiscal year during which the registrant had a registration statement on Form S-18 become effective may include the following financial statements prepared in accordance with generally accepted accounting principles:

    (I) A balance sheet as of the end of each of the two most recent fiscal years; and

    (2) Consolidated statements of income, statements of cash flows, and statements of other stockholders' equity for each of the two fiscal years preceding the date of the most recent audited balance sheet being filed.

(b) A Form 10-K filed for the first fiscal year after the registrant had a registration statement on Form S-18 become effective may include financial statements prepared as follows:

    (I) Financial statements for the most recent fiscal year prepared in accordance with Regulation S-X, Form and Content of and Requirements for Financial Statements; and

    (2) Financial statements previously disclosed in accordance with paragraph (a) for the prior year. These statements do not need to include the compliance items and schedules of Regulation S-X, but should be recast to show the same line items as are set forth for the most recent fiscal year.

(c) A Form 10-K filed for the second fiscal year after the registrant had a registration statement on Form S-18 become effective may include financial statements for the two most recent fiscal years prepared in accordance with Regulation S-X (17 CFR 210).

Item 9. Changes in and Disagreements With Accountants on Accounting and Financial Disclosure.

Furnish the information required by Item 304 of Regulation S-K (§ 229.304 of this chapter).

PART III
[See General Instruction G(3)]

Item 10. Directors and Executive Officers of the Registrant.

Furnish the information required by Items 401 and 405 of Regulation S-K (§ 229.401 and § 229.405 of this chapter).

Instruction

Checking the box provided on the cover page of this Form to indicate that Item 405 disclosure of delinquent Form 3, 4, or 5 filers is not contained herein is intended to facilitate Form processing and review. Failure to provide such indication will not create liability for violation of the federal securities laws. The space should be checked only if there is no disclosure in this Form of reporting person delinquencies in response to Item 405 and the registrant, at the time of filing the Form 10-K, has reviewed the information necessary to ascertain, and has determined that, Item 405 disclosure is not expected to be contained in Part III of the Form 10-K or incorporated by reference.

Item 11. Executive Compensation.

Furnish the information required by Item 402 of Regulation S-K (§ 229.402 of this chapter).

Item 12. Security Ownership of Certain Beneficial Owners and Management.

Furnish the information required by Item 403 of Regulation S-K (§ 229.403 of this chapter).

Item 13. Certain Relationships and Related Transactions.

Furnish the information required by Item 404 of Regulation S-K (§ 229.404 of this chapter).

PART IV

Item 14. Exhibits, Financial Statement Schedules, and Reports on Form 8-K.

(a) List the following documents filed as a part of the report:

(1) All financial statements.

(2) Those financial statement schedules required to be filed by Item 8 of this form, and by paragraph (d) below.

(3) Those exhibits required by Item 601 of Regulation S-K (§ 229.601 of this chapter) and by paragraph (c) below. Identify in the list each management contract or compensatory plan or arrangement required to be filed as an exhibit to this form pursuant to Item 14(c) of this report.

(b) Reports on Form 8-K. State whether any reports on Form 8-K have been filed during the last quarter of the period covered by this report, listing the items reported, any financial statements filed and the dates of any such reports.

(c) Registrants shall file, as exhibits to this form, the exhibits required by Item 601 of Regulation S-K (§ 229.601 of this chapter).

(d) Registrants shall file, as financial statement schedules to this form, the financial statements required by Regulation S-X (17 CFR 210) which are excluded from the annual report to shareholders by Rule 14a-3(b) including (1) separate financial statements of subsidiaries not consolidated and fifty percent or less owned persons; (2) separate financial statements of affiliates whose securities are pledged as collateral; and (3) schedules.

SIGNATURES

[See General Instruction D]

Pursuant to the requirements of Section 13 or 15(d) of the Securities Exchange Act of 1934, the registrant has duly caused this report to be signed on its behalf by the undersigned, thereunto duly authorized.

(Registrant) _____

By (Signature and Title)* _____

Date _____

Pursuant to the requirements of the Securities Exchange Act of 1934, this report has been signed below by the following persons on behalf of the registrant and in the capacities and on the dates indicated.

By (Signature and Title)* _____

Date _____

By (Signature and Title)* _____

Date _____

Supplemental Information to be Furnished
With Reports Filed Pursuant to Section 15(d) of the Act
by Registrants Which Have Not Registered Securities Pursuant
to Section 12 of the Act

(a) Except to the extent that the materials enumerated in (1) and/or (2) below are specifically incorporated into this Form by reference (in which case see Rule 12b-23(d)), every registrant which files an annual report on this Form pursuant to Section 15(d) of the Act shall furnish to the Commission for its information, at the time of filing its report on this Form, four copies of the following:

(1) Any annual report to security holders covering the registrant's last fiscal year; and

---

* Print the name and title of each signing officer under his signature.

(2)   Every proxy statement, form of proxy or other proxy soliciting material sent to more than ten of the registrant's security holders with respect to any annual or other meeting of security holders.

(b)   The foregoing material shall not be deemed to be "filed" with the Commission or otherwise subject to the liabilities of Section 18 of the Act, except to the extent that the registrant specifically incorporates it in its annual report on this Form by reference.

(c)   If no such annual report or proxy material has been sent to security holders, a statement to that effect shall be included under this caption. If such report or proxy material is to be furnished to security holders subsequent to the filing of the annual report of this Form, the registrant shall so state under this caption and shall furnish copies of such material to the Commission when it is sent to security holders.

http://www.sec.gov/divisions/corpfin/forms/10k.htm

Last update: 06/27/2000

APPENDIX 8B

Form 10-Q

SEC 1296 (6-00)   Potential persons who are to respond to the collection of information contained in this form are not required to respond unless the form displays a currently valid OMB control number.

UNITED STATES
SECURITIES AND EXCHANGE COMMISSION
Washington, D.C. 20549

OMB APPROVAL
OMB Number: 3235-0070
Expires: April 30, 2003
Estimated average burden hours per response . . . 34.00

GENERAL INSTRUCTIONS

A. Rule as to Use of Form 10-Q.

1. Form 10-Q shall be used for quarterly reports under Section 13 or 15(d) of the Securities Exchange Act of 1934, filed pursuant to Rule 13a-13 (17 CFR 240.13a-13) or Rule 15d-13 (17 CFR 240.15d-13). A quarterly report on this form pursuant to Rule 13a-13 or Rule 15d-13 shall be filed within 45 days after the end of each of the first three fiscal quarters of each fiscal year. No report need be filed for the fourth quarter of any fiscal year.

2. Form 10-Q also shall be used for transition and quarterly reports under Section 13 or 15(d) of the Securities Exchange Act of 1934, filed pursuant to Rule 13a-10 (17 CFR 240.13a-10) or Rule 15d-10 (17 CFR 240.15d-10). Such transition or quarterly reports shall be filed in accordance with the requirements set forth in Rule 13a-10 or Rule 15d-10 applicable when the registrant changes its fiscal year end.

B. Application of General Rules and Regulations.

1. The General Rules and Regulations under the Act contain certain general requirements which are applicable to reports on any form. These general requirements should be carefully read and observed in the preparation and filing of reports on this form.

2. Particular attention is directed to Regulation 12B which contains general requirements regarding matters such as the kind and size of paper to be used, the legibility of the report, the information to be given whenever the title of securities is required to be stated, and the filing of the report. The definitions contained in Rule 12b-2 (17 CFR 240. 12b-2) should be especially noted. See also Regulations 13A and 15D.

C. Preparation of Report.

1. This is not a blank form to be filled in. It is a guide copy to be used in preparing the report in accordance with Rules 12b11 (17 CFR 240.12b-11) and 12b-12 (17 CFR 240.12b-12). The Commission does not furnish blank copies of this form to be filled in for filing.

2. These general instructions are not to be filed with the report. The instructions to the various captions of the form are also to be omitted from the report as filed.

D. Incorporation by Reference.

1. If the registrant makes available to its stockholders or otherwise publishes, within the period prescribed for filing the report, a document or statement containing information meeting some or all of the requirements of Part I of this form, the information called for may be incorporated by reference from such published document or statement, in answer or partial answer to any item or items of Part I of this form, provided copies thereof are filed as an exhibit to Part I of the report on this form.

2. Other information may be incorporated by reference in answer or partial answer to any item or items of Part II of this form in accordance with the provisions of Rule 12b-23 (17 CFR 240.12b-23).

3. If any information required by Part I or Part II is incorporated by reference into an electronic format document from the quarterly report to security holders as provided in General Instruction D, any portion of the quarterly report to security holders incorporated by reference shall be filed as an exhibit in electronic format, as required by Item 601(b)(13) of Regulation S-K.

E. Integrated Reports to Security Holders.

Quarterly reports to security holders may be combined with the required information of Form 10-Q and will be suitable for filing with the Commission if the following conditions are satisfied:

1. The combined report contains full and complete answers to all items required by Part I of this form. When responses to a certain item of required disclosure are separated within the combined report, an appropriate cross-reference should be made.

2. If not included in the combined report, the cover page, appropriate responses to Part II, and the required signatures shall be included in the Form 10-Q. Additionally, as appropriate, a cross-reference sheet should be filed indicating the location of information required by the items of the form.

3. If an electronic filer files any portion of a quarterly report to security holders in combination with the required information of Form 10-Q, as provided in this instruction, only such portions filed in satisfaction of the Form 10-Q requirements shall be filed in electronic format.

F. Filed Status of Information Presented.

1. Pursuant to Rule 13a-13(d) and Rule 15d-13(d), the information presented in satisfaction of the requirements of Items 1, 2 and 3 of Part I of this form, whether included directly in a report on this form, incorporated therein by reference from a report, document or statement filed as an exhibit to Part I of this form pursuant to Instruction D(1) above, included in an integrated report pursuant to Instruction E above, or contained in a statement regarding computation of per share earnings or a letter regarding a change in accounting principles filed as an exhibit to Part I pursuant to Item 601 of Regulation S-K (§ 229.601 of this chapter), except as provided by Instruction F(2) below, shall not be deemed filed for the purpose of Section 18 of the Act or otherwise subject to the liabilities of that section of the Act but shall be subject to the other provisions of the Act.

2. Information presented in satisfaction of the requirements of this form other than those of Items 1, 2 and 3 of Part I shall be deemed filed for the purpose of Section 18 of the Act; except that, where information presented in response to Item 1 or 2 of Part I (or as an exhibit thereto) is also used to satisfy Part II requirements through incorporation by reference, only that portion of Part I (or exhibit thereto) consisting of the information required by Part II shall be deemed so filed.

G. Signature and Filing of Report.

Three complete copies of the report, including any financial statements, exhibits or other papers or documents filed as a part thereof, and five additional copies which need not include exhibits shall be filed with the Commission. At least one complete copy of the report, including any financial statements, exhibits or other papers or documents filed as a part thereof, shall be filed with each exchange on which any class of securities of the registrant is registered. At least one complete copy of the report filed with the Commission and one such copy filed with each exchange shall be manually signed on the registrant's behalf by a duly authorized officer of the registrant and by the principal financial or chief accounting officer of the registrant. Copies not manually signed shall bear typed or printed signatures. In the case where the principal financial officer or chief accounting officer is also duly authorized to sign on behalf of the registrant, one signature is acceptable provided that the registrant clearly indicates the dual responsibilities of the signatory.

H. Omission of Information by Certain Wholly-Owned Subsidiaries.

If on the date of the filing of its report on Form 10-Q, the registrant meets the conditions specified in paragraph (1) below, then such registrant may omit the information called for in the items specified in paragraph (2) below.

1. Conditions for availability of the relief specified in paragraph (2) below:

    a. All of the registrant's equity securities are owned, either directly or indirectly, by a single person which is a reporting company under the Act and which has filed all the material required to be filed pursuant to Section 13, 14 or 15(d) thereof, as applicable;

    b. During the preceding thirty-six calendar months and any subsequent period of days, there has not been any material default in the payment of principal, interest, a sinking or purchase fund installment, or any other material default not cured within thirty days, with respect to any indebtedness of the registrant or its subsidiaries, and there has not been any material default in the payment of rentals under material long-term leases; and

    c. There is prominently set forth, on the cover page of the Form 10-Q, a statement that the registrant meets the conditions set forth in General Instruction H(1)(a) and (b) of Form 10-Q and is therefore filing this form with the reduced disclosure format.

2. Registrants meeting the conditions specified in paragraph (1) above are entitled to the following relief:

    a. Such registrants may omit the information called for by Item 2 of Part I, Management's Discussion and Analysis of Financial Condition and Results of Operations, provided that the registrant includes in the Form 10-Q a management's narrative analysis of the results of operations explaining the reasons for material changes in the amount of revenue and expense items between the most recent fiscal year-to-date period presented and the corresponding year-to-date period in the preceding fiscal year. Explanations of material changes should include, but not be limited to, changes in the various elements which determine revenue and expense levels such as unit sales volume, prices charged and paid, production levels, production cost variances, labor costs and discretionary spending programs. In addition, the analysis should include an explanation of the effect of any changes in accounting principles and practices or method of application that have a material effect on net income as reported.

b. Such registrants may omit the information called for in the following Part II Items: Item 2, Changes in Securities; Item 3, Defaults Upon Senior Securities; and Item 4, Submission of Matters to a Vote of Security Holders.

c. Such registrants may omit the information called for by Item 3 of Part I, Quantitative and Qualitative Disclosures About Market Risk.

UNITED STATES

SECURITIES AND EXCHANGE COMMISSION

Washington, D.C. 20549

OMB APPROVAL
OMB Number: 3235-0070
Expires: April 30, 2003
Estimated average burden hours per response . . . 34.00

FORM 10-Q

(Mark One)

❑ QUARTERLY REPORT PURSUANT TO SECTION 13 OR 15(d) OF THE SECURITIES EXCHANGE ACT OF 1934

For the quarterly period ended _____

or

❑ TRANSITION REPORT PURSUANT TO SECTION 13 OR 15(d) OF THE SECURITIES EXCHANGE ACT OF 1934

For the transition period from _____ to _____

Commission File Number: _____

_____
(Exact name of registrant as specified in its charter)

_____
(State or other jurisdiction of incorporation or organization)   (I.R.S. Employer Identification No.)

_____
(Address of principal executive offices)   (Zip Code)

_____
(Registrant's telephone number, including area code)

_____
(Former name, former address and former fiscal year, if changed since last report)

Indicate by check mark whether the registrant (1) has filed all reports required to be filed by Section 13 or 15(d) of the Securities Exchange Act of 1934 during the preceding 12 months (or for such shorter period that the registrant was required to file such reports), and (2) has been subject to such filing requirements for the past 90 days.

        ❑ Yes   ❑ No

APPLICABLE ONLY TO ISSUERS INVOLVED IN BANKRUPTCY
PROCEEDINGS DURING THE PRECEDING FIVE YEARS:

Indicate by check mark whether the registrant has filed all documents and reports required to be filed by Sections 12, 13 or 15(d) of the Securities Exchange Act of 1934 subsequent to the distribution of securities under a plan confirmed by a court.

❏ Yes   ❏ No

APPLICABLE ONLY TO CORPORATE ISSUERS:

Indicate the number of shares outstanding of each of the issuer's classes of common stock, as of the latest practicable date.

PART I—FINANCIAL INFORMATION

Item 1. Financial Statements.

Provide the information required by Rule 10-01 of Regulation S-X (17 CFR Part 210).

Item 2. Management's Discussion and Analysis of Financial Condition and Results of Operations.

Furnish the information required by Item 303 of Regulation S-K (§ 229.303 of this chapter).

Item 3. Quantitative and Qualitative Disclosures About Market Risk.

Furnish the information required by Item 305 of Regulation S-K (§ 229.305 of this chapter).

PART II—OTHER INFORMATION

Instruction. The report shall contain the item numbers and captions of all applicable items of Part II, but the text of such items may be omitted provided the responses clearly indicate the coverage of the item. Any item which is inapplicable or to which the answer is negative may be omitted and no reference thereto need be made in the report. If substantially the same information has been previously reported by the registrant, an additional report of the information on this form need not be made. The term "previously reported" is defined in Rule 12b-2 (17 CFR 240. 12b-2). A separate response need not be presented in Part II where information called for is already disclosed in the financial information provided in Part I and is incorporated by reference into Part II of the report by means of a statement to that effect in Part II which specifically identifies the incorporated information.

Item 1. Legal Proceedings.

Furnish the information required by Item 103 of Regulation S-K (§ 229.103 of this chapter). As to such proceedings which have been terminated during the period covered by the report, provide similar information, including the date of termination and a description of the disposition thereof with respect to the registrant and its subsidiaries.

Instruction. A legal proceeding need only be reported in the 10-Q filed for the quarter in which it first became a reportable event and in subsequent quarters in which there have been material developments. Subsequent Form 10-Q filings in the same fiscal year in which a legal proceeding or a material development is reported should reference any previous reports in that year.

Item 2. Changes in Securities and Use of Proceeds.

(a) If the constituent instruments defining the rights of the holders of any class of registered securities have been materially modified, give the title of the class of securities involved and state briefly the general effect of such modification upon the rights of holders of such securities.

(b) If the rights evidenced by any class of registered securities have been materially limited or qualified by the issuance or modification of any other class of securities, state briefly the general effect of the issuance or modification of such other class of securities upon the rights of the holders of the registered securities.

(c) Furnish the information required by Item 701 of Regulation S-K (§ 229.701 of this chapter) as to all equity securities of the registrant sold by the registrant during the period covered by the report that were not registered under the Securities Act.

(d) If required pursuant to Rule 463 (17 CFR 230.463) of the Securities Act of 1933, furnish the information required by Item 701(f) of Regulation S-K (§ 229.701(f) of this chapter).

Instruction. Working capital restrictions and other limitations upon the payment of dividends are to be reported hereunder.

Item 3. Defaults Upon Senior Securities.

(a) If there has been any material default in the payment of principal, interest, a sinking or purchase fund installment, or any other material default not cured within 30 days, with respect to any indebtedness of the registrant or any of its significant subsidiaries exceeding 5 percent of the total assets of the registrant and its consolidated subsidiaries, identify the indebtedness and state the nature of the default. In the case of such a default in the payment of principal, interest, or a sinking or purchase fund installment, state the amount of the default and the total arrearage on the date of filing this report.

Instruction. This paragraph refers only to events which have become defaults under the governing instruments, i.e., after the expiration of any period of grace and compliance with any notice requirements.

(b) If any material arrearage in the payment of dividends has occurred or if there has been any other material delinquency not cured within 30 days, with respect to any class of preferred stock of the registrant which is registered or which ranks prior to any class of registered securities, or with respect to any class of preferred stock of any significant subsidiary of the registrant, give the title of the class and state the nature of the arrearage or delinquency. In the case of an arrearage in the payment of dividends, state the amount and the total arrearage on the date of filing this report.

Instruction. Item 3 need not be answered as to any default or arrearage with respect to any class of securities all of which is held by, or for the account of, the registrant or its totally held subsidiaries.

Item 4. Submission of Matters to a Vote of Security Holders.

If any matter has been submitted to a vote of security holders during the period covered by this report, through the solicitation of proxies or otherwise, furnish the following information:

(a) The date of the meeting and whether it was an annual or special meeting.

(b) If the meeting involved the election of directors, the name of each director elected at the meeting and the name of each other director whose term of office as a director continued after the meeting.

(c) A brief description of each matter voted upon at the meeting and state the number of votes cast for, against or witheld, as well as the number of abstentions and broker non-votes, as to each such matter, including a separate tabulation with respect to each nominee for office.

(d) A description of the terms of any settlement between the registrant and any other participant (as defined in Rule 14a-11 (17 CFR 240.14a-11) of Regulation 14A under the Act) terminating any solicitation subject to Rule 14a-11, including the cost or anticipated cost to the registrant.

Instructions:

1. If any matter has been submitted to a vote of security holders otherwise than at a meeting of such security holders, corresponding information with respect to such submission shall be furnished. The solicitation of any authorization or consent (other than a proxy to vote at a stockholders' meeting) with respect to any matter shall be deemed a

submission of such matter to a vote of security holders within the meaning of this item.

2. Paragraph (a) need be answered only if paragraph (b) or (c) is required to be answered.

3. Paragraph (b) need not be answered if (i) proxies for the meeting were solicited pursuant to Regulation 14 under the Act, (ii) there was no solicitation in opposition to the management's nominees as listed in the proxy statement, and (iii) all of such nominees were elected. If the registrant did not solicit proxies and the board of directors as previously reported to the Commission was re-elected in its entirety, a statement to that effect in answer to paragraph (b) will suffice as an answer thereto.

4. Paragraph (c) must be answered for all matters voted upon at the meeting, including both contested and uncontested elections of directors.

5. If the registrant has furnished to its security holders proxy soliciting material containing the information called for by paragraph (d), the paragraph may be answered by reference to the information contained in such material.

6. If the registrant has published a report containing all of the information called for by this item, the item may be answered by a reference to the information contained in such report.

Item 5. Other Information.

The registrant may, at its option, report under this item any information, not previously reported in a report on Form 8-K, with respect to which information is not otherwise called for by this form. If disclosure of such information is made under this item, it need not be repeated in a report on Form 8-K which would otherwise be required to be filed with respect to such information or in a subsequent report on Form 10-Q.

Item 6. Exhibits and Reports on Form 8-K (§ 249.308 of this chapter).

(a) Furnish the exhibits required by Item 601 of Regulation S-K (§ 229.601 of this chapter).

(b) Reports on Form 8-K. State whether any reports on Form 8-K have been filed during the quarter for which this report is filed, listing the items reported, any financial statements filed, and the dates of any such reports.

SIGNATURES*

Pursuant to the requirements of the Securities Exchange Act of 1934, the registrant has duly caused this report to be signed on its behalf by the undersigned thereunto duly authorized.

_____
(Registrant)

_____   _____
Date   (Signature)**

_____   _____
Date   (Signature)**

http://www.sec.gov/divisions/corpfin/forms/10q.htm
Last update: 06/20/2000

---

* See General Instruction E.

** Print name and title of the signing officer under his signature.

APPENDIX 8C

Form 8-K

SEC 873 (10/2000)   Potential persons who are to respond to the collection of information contained in this form are not required to respond unless the form displays a currently valid OMB control number.

UNITED STATES

SECURITIES AND EXCHANGE COMMISSION

Washington, D.C. 20549

OMB APPROVAL
OMB Number: 3235-0060
Expires: March 31, 2003
Estimated average burden hours per response. . . . 1.25

CURRENT REPORT
Pursuant to Section 13 OR 15(d) of the Securities Exchange Act of 1934

Date of Report (Date of earliest reported) _____

_____
(Exact name of registrant as specified in its chapter)

_____

(State or other jurisdiction of incorporation	(Commission File Number)	(IRS Employer Identification No.)

_____

(Address of principal executive offices)   (Zip Code)

Registrant's telephone number, including area code _____

_____
(Former name or former address, if changed since last report.)

GENERAL INSTRUCTIONS

A. Rule as to Use of Form 8-K.

Form 8-K shall be used for current reports under Section 13 or 15(d) of the Securities Exchange Act of 1934, filed pursuant to Rule 13a-11 or Rule 15d-11 and for reports of nonpublic information required to be disclosed by Regulation FD (17 CFR 243.100 and 243.101).

B. Events to be Reported and Time for Filing of Reports.

1. A report on this form is required to be filed upon the occurrence of any one or more of the events specified in Items 1-4 and 6 of this form. A report of an event specified in Items 1-3 is to be filed within 15 calendar days after the occurrence of the event. A report of an event specified in Item 4 or 6 is to be filed within 5 business days after the occurrence of the event; if the event occurs on a Saturday, Sunday, or holiday on which the Commission is not open for business then the 5 business day period shall begin to run on and include the first business day thereafter. A report on this form pursuant to Item 8 is required to be filed within 15 calendar days after the date on which the registrant makes the determination to use a fiscal year end different from that used in its most recent filing with the Commission. A registrant either furnishing a report on this form under Item 9 or electing to file a report on this form under Item 5 solely to satisfy its obligations under Regulation FD (17 CFR 243.100 and 243.101) must furnish such report or make such filing in accordance with the requirements of Rule 100(a) of Regulation FD (17 CFR 243.100(a)).

2. The information in a report furnished pursuant to Item 9 shall not be deemed to be "filed" for the purposes of Section 18 of the Exchange Act or otherwise subject to the liabilities of that section, except if the registrant specifically states that the information is to be considered "filed" under the Exchange Act or incorporates it by reference into a filing under the Securities Act or the Exchange Act.

3. If substantially the same information as that required by this form has been previously reported by the registrant, an additional report of the information on this form need not be made. The term "previously reported" is defined in Rule 12b-2 (17 CFR 240.12b-2).

4. When considering current reporting on this form, particularly of other events of material importance pursuant to Item 5 and of information pursuant to Item 9, registrants should have due regard for the accuracy, completeness and currency of the information in registration statements filed under the Securities Act of 1933 which incorporate by reference

information in reports filed pursuant to the Securities Exchange Act of 1934, including reports on this form.

5. A registrant's report under Item 5 or Item 9 will not be deemed an admission as to the materiality of any information in the report that is required to be disclosed solely by Regulation FD.

C. Application of General Rules and Regulations.

1. The General Rules and Regulations under the Act (17 CFR Part 240) contain certain general requirements which are applicable to reports on any form. These general requirements should be carefully read and observed in the preparation and filing of reports on this form.

2. Particular attention is directed to Regulation 12B (17 CFR 240.12b-1 et seq.) which contains general requirements regarding matters such as the kind and size of paper to be used, the legibility of the report, the information to be given whenever the title of securities is required to be stated, and the filing of the report. The definitions contained in Rule 12b2 should be especially noted. See also Regulations 13A (17 CFR 240.13a-1 et seq.) and 15D(17 CFR 240.15d-1 et seq.).

3. A "small business issuer," defined under Rule 12b-2 of the Exchange Act (§240.12b-2 of this chapter), shall refer to the disclosure items in Regulation S-B (17 CFR 228.10 et seq.) and not Regulation S-K. If there is no comparable disclosure item in Regulation S-B, a small business issuer need not provide the information requested. A small business issuer shall provide the information required by Item 310 (c) and (d) of Regulation S-B in lieu of the financial information required by Item 7 of this Form.

D. Preparation of Report.

This form is not to be used as a blank form to be filled in, but only as a guide in the preparation of the report on paper meeting the requirements of Rule 12b-12 (17 CFR 240.12b-12). The report shall contain the numbers and captions of all applicable items, but the text of such items may be omitted, provided the answers thereto are prepared in the manner specified in Rule 12b-13 (17 CFR 240.12b13). All items that are not required to be answered in a particular report may be omitted and no reference thereto need be made in the report. All instructions should also be omitted.

E. Signature and Filing of Report.

Three complete copies of the report, including any financial statements, exhibits or other papers or documents filed as a part thereof, and five additional copies which need not include exhibits, shall be filed with the Commission. At least one complete copy of the report, including any financial statements, exhibits or other papers or documents filed as a part thereof, shall be filed, with each exchange on which any class of securities of the registrant is registered. At least one complete copy of the report filed with the Commission and one such copy filed with each exchange shall be manually signed. Copies not manually signed shall bear typed or printed signatures.

F. Incorporation by Reference.

If the registrant makes available to its stockholders or otherwise publishes, within the period prescribed for filing the report, a press release or other document or statement containing information meeting some or all of the requirements of this form, the information called for may be incorporated by reference to such published document or statement, in answer or partial answer to any item or items of this form, provided copies thereof are filed as an exhibit to the report on this form.

INFORMATION TO BE INCLUDED IN THE REPORT

Item 1. Changes in Control of Registrant.

(a) If, to the knowledge of management, a change in control of the registrant has occurred, state the name of the person(s) who acquired such control; the amount and the source of the consideration used by such person(s); the basis of the control; the date and a description of the transaction(s) which resulted in the change in control; the percentage of voting securities of the registrant now beneficially owned directly or indirectly by the person(s) who acquired control; and the identity of the person(s) from whom control was assumed. If the source of all or any part of the consideration used is a loan made in the ordinary course of business by a bank as defined by Section 3(a)(6) of the Act, the identity of such bank shall be omitted provided a request for confidentiality has been made pursuant to Section 13(d)(1)(B) of the Act by the person(s) who acquired control. In lieu thereof, the material shall indicate that disclosure of the identity of the bank has been so omitted and filed separately with the Commission.

Instructions.

1. State the terms of any loans or pledges obtained by the new control group for the purpose of acquiring control, and the names of the lenders or pledgees.

2. Any arrangements or understandings among members of both the former and new control groups and their associates with respect to election of directors or other matters should be described.

(b) Furnish the information required by Item 403(c) of Regulation S-K (§ 229.403(c) of this chapter).

Item 2. Acquisition or Disposition of Assets.

If the registrant or any of its majority-owned subsidiaries has acquired or disposed of a significant amount of assets, otherwise than in the ordinary course of business, furnish the following information:

(a) The date and manner of the acquisition or disposition and a brief description of the assets involved, the nature and amount of consideration given or received therefor, the principle followed in determining the amount of such consideration, the identity of the person(s) from whom the assets were acquired or to whom they were sold and the nature of any material relationship between such person(s) and the registrant or any of its affiliates, any director or officer of the registrant, or any associate of any such director or officer. If the transaction being reported is an acquisition, identify the source(s) of the funds used unless all or any part of the consideration used is a loan made in the ordinary course of business by a bank as defined by Section 3(a)(6) of the Act in which case the identity of such bank shall be omitted provided a request for confidentiality has been made pursuant to Section 13(d)(1)(B) of the Act. In lieu thereof, the material shall indicate that the identity of the bank has been so omitted and filed separately with the Commission.

(b) If any assets so acquired by the registrant or its subsidiaries constituted plant, equipment or other physical property, state the nature of the business in which the assets were used by the persons from whom acquired and whether the registrant intends to continue such use or intends to devote the assets to other purposes, indicating such other purposes.

Instructions.

1. No information need be given as to (i) any transaction between any person and any wholly-owned subsidiary of such person; (ii) any transaction between two or more wholly-owned subsidiaries of any person; or (iii) the redemption or other acquisition of securities from the public, or the sale or other disposition of securities to the public, by the issuer of such securities.

2. The term "acquisition" includes every purchase, acquisition by lease, exchange, merger, consolidation, succession or other acquisition; provided that such term does not include the construction or development of property by or for the registrant or its subsidiaries or the acquisition of materials for such purpose. The term "disposition" includes every sale, disposition by lease,

exchange, merger, consolidation, mortgage, assignment, or hypothecation of assets, whether for the benefit of creditors or otherwise, abandonment, destruction, or other disposition.

3. The information called for by this item is to be given as to each transaction or series of related transactions of the size indicated. The acquisition or disposition of securities shall be deemed the indirect acquisition or disposition of the assets represented by such securities if it results in the acquisition or disposition of control of such assets.

4. An acquisition or disposition shall be deemed to involve a significant amount of assets (i) if the registrant's and its other subsidiaries' equity in the net book value of such assets or the amount paid or received therefor upon such acquisition or disposition exceeded 10 percent of the total assets of the registrant and its consolidated subsidiaries, or (ii) if it involved a business (see §210.11-01(d)) which is significant (see §210.11.01(b)). Acquisitions of individually insignificant businesses are not required to be reported pursuant to this item unless they are related businesses (see §210.3-05(a)(3)) and are, in the aggregate, significant.

5. Where assets are acquired or disposed of through the acquisition or disposition of control of a person, the person from whom such control was acquired or to whom it was disposed of shall be deemed the person from whom the assets were acquired or to whom they were disposed of, for the purposes of this item. Where such control was acquired from or disposed of to not more than five persons, their names shall be given; otherwise it will suffice to identify in an appropriate manner the class of such persons.

6. Attention is directed to the requirements in Item 7 of the form with respect to the filing of (i) financial statements for businesses acquired, (ii) pro forma financial information, and (iii) copies of the plans of acquisition or disposition as exhibits to the report.

Item 3. Bankruptcy or Receivership.

(a) If a receiver, fiscal agent or similar officer has been appointed for a registrant or its parent, in a proceeding under the Bankruptcy Act or in any other proceeding under State or Federal law in which a court or governmental agency has assumed jurisdiction over substantially all of the assets or business of the registrant or its parent, or if such jurisdiction has been assumed by leaving the existing directors and officers in possession but subject to the supervision and orders of a court or governmental body, identify the proceeding, the court or governmental body, the date jurisdiction was assumed, the identity of the receiver, fiscal agent or similar officer and the date of his appointment.

(b) If an order confirming a plan of reorganization, arrangement or liquidation has been entered by a court or governmental authority having supervision or jurisdiction over substantially all of the assets or business of the registrant or its parent, furnish the following:

(1) the identity of the court or governmental authority;

(2) the date the order confirming the plan was entered by the court or governmental authority;

(3) a fair summarization of the material features of the plan and, pursuant to Item 6 of this form relating to exhibits, a copy of the plan as confirmed;

(4) the number of shares or other units of the registrant or its parent issued and outstanding, the number reserved for future issuance in respect of claims and interests filed and allowed under the plan, and the aggregate total of such numbers; and

(5) information as to the assets and liabilities of the registrant or its parent as of the date the order confirming the plan was entered, or a date as close thereto as practicable. Such information may be presented in the form in which it was furnished to the court or governmental authority.

Item 4. Changes in Registrant's Certifying Accountant.

(a) If an independent accountant who was previously engaged as the principal accountant to audit the registrant's financial statements, or an independent accountant upon whom the principal accountant expressed reliance in its report regarding a significant subsidiary, resigns (or indicates it declines to stand for re-election after the completion of the current audit) or is dismissed, then provide the information required by Item 304(a)(1), including compliance with Item 304(a)(3) of Regulation S-K, § 229.304(a)(1) and (a)(3) of this chapter, and the related instructions to Item 304.

(b) If a new independent accountant has been engaged as either the principal accountant to audit the registrant's financial statements or as an independent accountant on whom the principal accountant has expressed, or is expected to express, reliance in its report regarding a significant subsidiary, then provide the information required by Item 304(a)(2) of Regulation S-K, § 229.304(a)(2) of this chapter.

Instruction.

The resignation or dismissal of an independent accountant, or its declination to stand for re-election, is a reportable event separate from the engagement of a new independent accountant. On some occasions two reports on Form 8-K will be required for a single change in accountants, the first on the resignation (or declination to stand for re-election) or dismissal of the former accountant and the second when the new accountant is engaged. Information required in the second Form 8-K in such situations need not be provided to the extent it has been previously reported in the first such Form 8-K.

Item 5. Other Events and Regulation FD Disclosure.

The registrant may, at its option, report under this item any events, with respect to which information is not otherwise called for by this form, that the registrant deems of importance to security holders. The registrant may, at its option, file a report under this item disclosing the nonpublic information required to be disclosed by Regulation FD (17 CFR 243.100-243.103).

Item 6. Resignations of Registrant's Directors.

(a) If a director has resigned or declined to stand for re-election to the board of directors since the date of the last annual meeting of shareholders because of a disagreement with the registrant on any matter relating to the registrant's operations, policies or practices, and if the director has furnished the registrant with a letter describing such disagreement and requesting that the matter be disclosed, the registrant shall state the date of such resignation or declination to stand for re-election and summarize the director's description of the disagreement.

(b) If the registrant believes that the description provided by the director is incorrect or incomplete, it may include a brief statement presenting its views of the disagreement.

(c) The registrant shall file a copy of the director's letter as an exhibit with all copies of the Form 8-K required to be filed pursuant to General Instruction E.

Item 7. Financial Statements and Exhibits.

List below the financial statements, pro forma financial information and exhibits, if any, filed as a part of this report.

(a) Financial statements of businesses acquired.

(1) For any business acquisition required to be described in answer to Item 2 above, financial statements of the business acquired shall be filed for the periods specified in 210.3-05(b).

(2) The financial statements shall be prepared pursuant to Regulation S-X except that supporting schedules need not be filed. A manually signed accountants' report should be provided pursuant to Rule 2-02 of Regulation S-X [17 CFR 210.2-02].

(3) With regard to the acquisition of one or more real estate properties, the financial statements and any additional information specified by Rule 3-14 of Regulation S-X shall be filed.

(4) Financial statements required by this item may be filed with the initial report, or by amendment not later than 60 days after the date that the initial report on Form 8-K must be filed. If the financial statements are not included in the initial report, the registrant should so indicate in the Form 8-K report and state when the required financial statements will be filed. The registrant may, at its option, include unaudited financial statements in the initial report on Form 8-K.

(b) Pro forma financial information.

(1) For any transaction required to be described in answer to Item 2 above, furnish any pro form a financial information that would be required pursuant to Article 11 of Regulation S-X.

(2) The provisions of (a)(4) above shall also apply to pro forma financial information relative to the acquired business.

(c) Exhibits. The exhibits shall be furnished in accordance with the provisions of Item 601 of Regulation S-K (§ 229.601 of this chapter).

Instructions.

1. During the period after a registrant has reported a business combination pursuant to Item 2 above until the date on which the financial statements specified by Item 7 above must be filed, the registrant will be deemed current for purposes of its reporting obligations under Section 13(a) or 15(d) of the Securities Exchange Act of 1934. With respect to filings under the Securities Act of 1933, however, registration statements will not be declared effective and post-effective amendments to registrations statements will not be declared effective unless financial statements meeting the requirements of Rule 3-05 of Regulation S-X (§ 210.3-05 of this chapter) are provided. In addition, offerings should not be made pursuant to effective registrations statements or pursuant to Rules 505 and 506 of Regulation D (§§ 230.501 through 506 of this chapter), where any purchasers are not accredited investors under Rule 501(a) of that Regulation, until the audited financial statements required by Rule 3-05 of Regulation S-X (§ 210.3-05 of this chapter) are filed. Provided, however, that the following offerings or sales of securities may proceed notwithstanding that financial statements of the acquired business have not be filed:

(a) offerings or sales of securities upon the conversion of outstanding convertible securities or upon the exercise of outstanding warrants or rights;

(b) dividend or interest reinvestment plans;

(c) employee benefit plans;

(d) transactions involving secondary offerings; or

(e) sales of securities pursuant to Rule 144 (§230.144 of this chapter).

Item 8. Change in Fiscal Year.

If the registrant determines to change the fiscal year from that used in its most recent filing with the Commission, state the date of such determination, the date of the new fiscal year end, and the form (e.g., Form 10-K or Form 10-Q) on which the report covering the transition period will be filed.

Item 9. Regulation FD Disclosure.

Unless filed under Item 5, report under this item only information the registrant elects to disclose through Form 8-K pursuant to Regulation FD (17 CFR 243.100-243.103).

SIGNATURES

Pursuant to the requirements of the Securities Exchange Act of 1934, the registrant has duly caused this report to be signed on its behalf by the undersigned hereunto duly authorized.

_____

(Registrant)

_____   _____

Date   (Signature)*

http://www.sec.gov/divisions/corpfin/forms/8-k.htm

Last update: 06/27/2001

---

* Print name and title of the signing officer under his signature.

APPENDIX 8D

Form 3

SEC 1472 (7-97) Potential persons who are to respond to the collection of information contained in this form are not required to respond unless the form displays a currently valid OMB control number.

UNITED STATES

SECURITIES AND EXCHANGE COMMISSION

Washington, D.C. 20549

OMB APPROVAL
OMB Number: 3235-0104
Expires: December 31, 2001
Estimated average burden hours per response. . . . 0.5

INITIAL STATEMENT OF BENEFICIAL OWNERSHIP OF SECURITIES

The Commission is authorized to solicit the information required by this Form pursuant to Sections 16(a) and 23(a) of the Securities Exchange Act of 1934, Sections 17(a) and 20(a) of the Public Utility Holding Company Act of 1935, and Sections 30(f) and 38 of the Investment Company Act of 1940, and the rules and regulations thereunder.

Disclosure of information specified on this form is mandatory, except for disclosure of the I.R.S. identification number of the reporting person if such person is an entity, which is voluntary. If such numbers are furnished, they will assist the Commission in distinguishing reporting persons with similar names and will facilitate the prompt processing of the form. The information will be used for the primary purpose of disclosing the holdings of directors, officers, and beneficial owners of registered companies. Information disclosed will be a matter of public record and available for inspection by members of the public. The Commission can use

345

it in investigations or litigation involving the federal securities laws or other civil, criminal, or regulatory statutes or provisions, as well as for referral to other governmental authorities and self-regulatory organizations. Failure to disclose required information may result in civil or criminal action against persons involved for violations of the federal securities laws and rules.

GENERAL INSTRUCTIONS

1. Who Must File

(a) This Form must be filed by the following persons ("reporting person"):

  (i) any director or officer of an issuer with a class of equity securities registered pursuant to Section 12 of the Securities Exchange Act of 1934 ("Exchange Act"); (Note: Title is not determinative for purposes of determining "officer" status. See Rule 16a-1(f) for the definition of "officer");

  (ii) any beneficial owner of greater than 10% of a class of equity securities registered under Section 12 of the Exchange Act, as determined by voting or investment control over the securities pursuant to Rule 16a-1(a)(l) ("ten percent holder");

  (iii) any officer or director of a registered holding company pursuant to Section 17 of the Public Utility Holding Company Act of 1935;

  (iv) any officer, director, member of an advisory board, investment adviser, affiliated person of an investment adviser or beneficial owner of more than 10% of any class of outstanding securities (other than short-term paper) of a registered closed-end investment company, under Section 30(f) of the Investment Company Act of 1940; and

  (v) any trust, trustee, beneficiary or settlor required to report pursuant to Rule 16a-8.

(b) If a reporting person is not an officer, director, or ten percent holder, the person should check "other" in Item 5 (Relationship of Reporting Person to Issuer) and describe the reason for reporting status in the space provided.

(c) If a person described above does not beneficially own any securities required to be reported (See Rule 16a-1 and Instruction 5), the person is required to file this Form and state that no securities are beneficially owned.

2. When Form Must be Filed

(a) This Form must be filed within 10 days after the event by which the person becomes a reporting person (i.e., officer, director, ten percent holder or other person). This Form and any amendment is deemed filed with the Commission or the Exchange on the date it is received by the Commission or the Exchange, respectively. See, however, Rule 16a-3(h) regarding delivery to a third party business that guarantees delivery of the filing no later than the specified due date.

(b) A reporting person of an issuer that is registering securities for the first time under Section 12 of the Exchange Act must file this Form no later than the effective date of the registration statement.

(c) A separate Form shall be filed to reflect beneficial ownership of securities of each issuer, except that a single statement shall be filed with respect to the securities of a registered public utility holding company and all of its subsidiary companies.

3. Where Form Must be Filed

(a) File three copies of this Form or any amendment, at least one of which is manually signed, with the Securities and Exchange Commission, 450 5th Street, N.W., Washington, D.C. 20549. (Note: Acknowledgment of receipt by the Commission may be obtained by enclosing a self-addressed stamped postcard identifying the Form or amendment filed.) Alternatively, this Form is permitted to be submitted to the Commission in electronic format at the option of the reporting person pursuant to §232.101(b)(4) of this chapter.

(b) At the time this Form or any amendment is filed with the Commission, file one copy with each Exchange on which any class of securities of the issuer is registered. If the issuer has designated a single Exchange to receive Section 16 filings, the copy shall be filed with that Exchange only.

(c) Any person required to file this Form or amendment shall, not later than the time the Form or amendment is transmitted for filing with the Commission, send or deliver a copy to the person designated by the issuer to receive the copy or, if no person is so designated, the issuer's corporate secretary (or person performing similar functions) in accordance with Rule 16a-3(e).

4. Class of Securities Reported

(a) (i) Persons reporting pursuant to Section 16(a) of the Exchange Act shall include information as to their beneficial ownership of any class of equity securities of the issuer, even though one or more of such classes may not be registered pursuant to Section 12 of the Act.

(ii) Persons reporting pursuant to Section 17(a) of the Public Utility Holding Company Act of 1935 shall include information as to their beneficial ownership of any class of securities (equity or debt) of the registered holding company and all of its subsidiary companies and specify the name of the parent or subsidiary issuing the securities.

(iii) Persons reporting pursuant to Section 30(f) of the Investment Company Act of 1940 shall include information as to their beneficial ownership of any class of securities (equity or debt) of the registered closed-end investment company (other than "short-term paper" as defined in Section 2(a)(38) of the Investment Company Act).

(b) The title of the security should clearly identify the class, even if the issuer has only one class of securities outstanding; for example, "Common Stock," "Class A Common Stock," "Class B Convertible Preferred Stock," etc.

(c) The amount of securities beneficially owned should state the face amount of debt securities (U.S. Dollars) or the number of equity securities, whichever is appropriate.

5. Holdings Required to be Reported

(a) General Requirements. Report holdings of each class of securities of the issuer beneficially owned as of the date of the event requiring the filing of this Form. See Instruction 4 as to securities required to be reported.

(b) Beneficial Ownership Reported (Pecuniary Interest).

(i) Although for purposes of determining status as a ten percent holder, a person is deemed to beneficially own securities over which that person has voting or investment control (see Rule 16a-1(a)(1)), for reporting purposes, a person is deemed to be the beneficial owner of securities if that person has or shares the opportunity, directly or indirectly, to profit or share in any profit derived from a transaction in the securities ("pecuniary interest"). See Rule 16a-1(a)(2). See also Rule 16a-8 for the application of the beneficial ownership definition to trust holdings and transactions.

(ii) Both direct and indirect beneficial ownership of securities shall be reported. Securities beneficially owned directly are those held in the reporting person's name or in the name of a bank, broker or nominee for the account of the reporting person. In addition, securities held as joint tenants, tenants in common, tenants by the entirety, or as community property are to be reported as held directly. If a person has a pecuniary interest, by reason of any contract, understanding or relationship (including a family relationship or arrangement) in securities held in the name of another person, that person is an indirect beneficial owner of those securities. See Rule 16a-1(a)(2)(ii) for certain indirect beneficial ownerships.

(iii) Report securities beneficially owned directly on a separate line from those beneficially owned indirectly. Report different forms of indirect ownership on separate lines. The nature of indirect ownership shall be stated as specifically as possible; for example, "By Self as Trustee for X," "By Spouse," "By X Trust," "By Y Corporation," etc.

(iv) In stating the amount of securities owned indirectly through a partnership, corporation, trust, or other entity, report the number of securities representing the reporting person's proportionate interest in securities beneficially owned by that entity. Alternatively, at the option of the reporting person, the entire amount of the entity's interest may be reported. See Rule 16a-1(a)(2)(ii)(B) and Rule 16a-1(a)(2)(iii).

(v) Where more than one person beneficially owns the same equity securities, such owners may file Form 3 individually or jointly. Joint and group filings may be made by any designated beneficial owner. Holdings of securities owned separately by any joint or group filer are permitted to be included in the joint filing. Indicate only the name and address of the designated filer in Item 1 of Form 3 and attach a listing of the names and IRS or social security numbers (or addresses in lieu thereof) of each other reporting person. Joint and group filings must include all required information for each beneficial owner, and such filings must be signed by each beneficial owner, or on behalf of such owner by an authorized person. If the space provided for signatures is insufficient, attach a signature page. Submit any attached listing of names or signatures on another Form 3, copy of Form 3 or separate page of 8 1/2 by 11 inch white paper, indicate the number of pages comprising the report (Form plus attachments) at the bottom of each report page (e.g., 1 of 3, 2 of 3, 3 of 3), and include the name of the designated filer and information required by Items 2 and 4 of the Form on the attachment.

(c) Non-Derivative and Derivative Securities.

(i) Report non-derivative securities beneficially owned in Table I and derivative securities (e.g., puts, calls, options, warrants, convertible securities, or other rights or obligations to buy or sell securities) beneficially owned in Table II. Derivative securities beneficially owned that are both equity securities and convertible or exchangeable for other equity securities (e.g., convertible preferred securities) should be reported only on Table II.

(ii) The title of a derivative security and the title of the equity security underlying the derivative security should be shown separately in the appropriate columns in Table II. The "puts" and "calls" reported in Table II include, in addition to separate puts and calls, any combination of the two, such as spreads and straddles. In reporting an option in Table II, state whether it represents a right to buy, a right to sell, an obligation to buy, or an obligation to sell the equity securities subject to the option.

(iii) Describe in the appropriate columns in Table II characteristics of derivative securities, including title, exercise or conversion price, date exercisable, expiration date, and the title and amount of securities underlying the derivative security.

(iv) Securities constituting components of a unit shall be reported separately on the applicable table (e.g., if a unit has a non-derivative security component and a derivative security component, the non-derivative security component shall be reported in Table I and the derivative security component shall be reported in Table II). The relationship between individual securities comprising the unit shall be indicated in the space provided for explanation of responses.

6. Additional Information

If the space provided in the line items of this Form or space provided for additional comments is insufficient, attach another Form 3, copy of Form 3 or separate page of 8 1/2 by 11 inch white paper to Form 3, completed as appropriate to include the additional comments. Each attached page must include information required in Items 1, 2 and 4 of the Form. The number of pages comprising the report (Form plus attachments) shall be indicated at the bottom of each report page (e.g., 1 of 3, 2 of 3, 3 of 3). If additional information is not reported in this manner, it will be assumed that no additional information was provided.

7. Signature

(a) If the Form is filed for an individual, it shall be signed by that person or specifically on behalf of the individual by a person authorized to sign for the individual. If signed on behalf of the individual by another person, the authority of such person to sign the Form shall be confirmed to the Commission in writing in an attachment to the Form or as soon as practicable in an amendment by the individual for whom the Form is filed, unless such a confirmation still in effect is on file with the Commission. The confirming statement need only indicate that the reporting person authorizes and designates the named person or persons to file the Form on the reporting person's behalf, and state the duration of the authorization.

(b) If the Form is filed for a corporation, partnership, trust, or other entity, the capacity in which the individual signed shall be set forth (e.g., John Smith, Secretary, on behalf of X Corporation).

SEC 1473 (7-97)   Potential persons who are to respond to the collection of information contained in this form are not required to respond unless the form displays a currently valid OMB control number.

FORM 3	OMB APPROVAL
	OMB Number: 3235-0104
	Expires: December 31, 2001
	Estimated average burden hours per response. . . . 0.5

UNITED STATES SECURITIES AND EXCHANGE COMMISSION
Washington, D.C. 20549

INITIAL STATEMENT OF BENEFICIAL OWNERSHIP OF SECURITIES

Filed pursuant to Section 16(a) of the Securities Exchange Act of 1934, Section 17(a) of the Public Utility Holding Company Act of 1935 or Section 30(f) of the Investment Company Act of 1940

(Print or Type Responses)

1. Name and Address of Reporting Person*	2. Date of Event Requiring Statement (Month/Day/Year)	4. Issuer Name and Ticker or Trading Symbol
(Last) (First) (Middle)	3. I.R.S. Identification Number of Reporting Person, if an entity (voluntary)	5. Relationship of Reporting Person(s) to Issuer (Check all applicable) ❑ Director ❑ 10% Owner ❑ Officer (give ❑ Other (specify below) title below) _____
(Street)		
(City) (State) (Zip)		

6. If Amendment, Date of Original (Month/Day/Year)
7. Individual or Joint/ Group Filing (Check Applicable Line) ❑ Form filed by One Reporting Person ❑ Form filed by More than One Reporting Person

Reminder: Report on a separate line for each class of securities beneficially owned directly or indirectly.

* If the form is filed by more than one reporting person, see Instruction 5(b)(v).

Table I — Non-Derivative Securities Beneficially Owned

1. Title of Security (Instr. 4)	2. Amount of Securities Beneficially Owned (Instr. 4)	3. Ownership Form: Direct (D) or Indirect (I) (Instr. 5)	4. Nature of Indirect Beneficial Ownership (Instr. 5)

Table II — Derivative Securities Beneficially Owned (e.g., puts, calls, warrants, options, convertible securities)

1. Title of Derivative Security (Instr. 4)	2. Date Exercisable and Expiration Date (Month/Day/Year)		3. Title and Amount of Securities Underlying Derivative Security (Instr. 4)		4. Conversion or Exercise Price of Derivative Security	5. Ownership Form of Derivative Securities: Direct (D) or Indirect (I) (Instr. 5)	6. Nature of Indirect Beneficial Ownership (Instr. 5)
	Date Exercisable	Expiration Date	Title	Amount or Number of Shares			

Explanation of Responses:

_____

_____   _____
**Signature of Reporting Person   Date

** Intentional misstatements or omissions of facts constitute Federal Criminal Violations. See 18 U.S.C. 1001 and 15 U.S.C. 78ff(a).

Note: File three copies of this Form, one of which must be manually signed. If space is insufficient, See Instruction 6 for procedure.

http://www.sec.gov/divisions/corpfin/forms/form3.htm
Last update: 08/23/1999

APPENDIX 8E

Form 4

UNITED STATES

SECURITIES AND EXCHANGE COMMISSION

Washington, D.C. 20549

OMB APPROVAL
OMB Number: 3235-0287
Expires: December 31, 2001
Estimated average burden hours per response. . . . 0.5

STATEMENT OF CHANGES OF
BENEFICIAL OWNERSHIP OF SECURITIES

The Commission is authorized to solicit the information required by this Form pursuant to Sections 16(a) and 23(a) of the Securities Exchange Act of 1934, Sections 17(a) and 20(a) of the Public Utility Holding Company Act of 1935, and Sections 30(f) and 38 of the Investment Company Act of 1940, and the rules and regulations thereunder.

Disclosure of information specified on this Form is mandatory, except for disclosure of the I.R.S. identification number of the reporting person if such person is an entity, which is voluntary. If such numbers are furnished, they will assist the Commission in distinguishing reporting persons with similar names and will facilitate the prompt processing of the Form. The information will be used for the primary purpose of disclosing the transactions and holdings of directors, officers, and beneficial owners of registered companies. Information disclosed will be a matter of public record and available for inspection by members of the public. The Commission can use it in investigations or litigation involving the federal securities laws or other civil, criminal, or regulatory statutes or provisions, as well as for referral to other governmental authorities and self-regulatory organizations. Failure to disclose required information may result in civil or criminal action against persons involved for violations of the Federal securities laws and rules.

GENERAL INSTRUCTIONS

1. When Form Must Be Filed

(a) This Form must be filed on or before the tenth day after the end of the month in which a change in beneficial ownership has occurred (the term "beneficial owner" is defined in Rule 16a-1(a)(2) and discussed in Instruction 4). This Form and any amendment is deemed filed with the Commission or the Exchange on the date it is received by the Commission or Exchange, respectively. See, however, Rule 16a-3(h) regarding delivery to a third party business that guarantees delivery of the filing no later than the specified due date.

(b) A reporting person no longer subject to Section 16 of the Securities Exchange Act of 1934 ("Exchange Act") must check the exit box appearing on this Form. However, Form 4 and 5 obligations may continue to be applicable. See Rule 16a-3(f); see also Rule 16a-2(b) (transactions after termination of insider status). Form 5 transactions to date may be included on this Form and subsequent Form 5 transactions may be reported on a later Form 4 or Form 5, provided all transactions are reported by the required date.

(c) A separate Form shall be filed to reflect beneficial ownership of securities of each issuer, except that a single statement shall be filed with respect to the securities of a registered public utility holding company and all of its subsidiary companies.

(d) If a reporting person is not an officer, director, or ten percent holder, the person should check "other" in Item 6 (Relationship of Reporting Person to Issuer) and describe the reason for reporting status in the space provided.

2. Where Form Must be Filed

(a) File three copies of this Form or any amendment, at least one of which is manually signed, with the Securities and Exchange Commission, 450 5th Street, N.W., Washington, D.C. 20549. (Note: Acknowledgment of receipt by the Commission may be obtained by enclosing a self-addressed stamped postcard identifying the Form or amendment filed.) Alternatively, this Form is permitted to be submitted to the Commission in electronic format at the option of the reporting person pursuant to § 232.101(b)(4) of this chapter.

(b) At the time this Form or any amendment is filed with the Commission, file one copy with each Exchange on which any class of securities of the issuer is registered. If the issuer has designated a single Exchange to receive Section 16 filings, the copy shall be filed with that Exchange only.

(c) Any person required to file this Form or amendment shall, not later than the time the Form or amendment is transmitted for filing with the Commission, send or deliver a copy to the person designated by the issuer to receive the copy or, if no person is so designated, the issuer's corporate secretary (or person performing similar functions) in accordance with Rule 16a-3(e).

3. **Class of Securities Reported**

(a) (i) Persons reporting pursuant to Section 16(a) of the Exchange Act shall report each transaction resulting in a change in beneficial ownership of any class of equity securities of the issuer and the beneficial ownership at the end of the month of that class of equity securities, even though one or more of such classes may not be registered pursuant to Section 12 of the Exchange Act.

(ii) Persons reporting pursuant to Section 17(a) of the Public Utility Holding Company Act of 1935 shall report each transaction resulting in a change in beneficial ownership of any class of securities (equity or debt) of the registered holding company and all of its subsidiary companies and the beneficial ownership at the end of the month of that class of securities. Specify the name of the parent or subsidiary issuing the securities.

(iii) Persons reporting pursuant to Section 30(f) of the Investment Company Act of 1940 shall report each transaction resulting in a change in beneficial ownership of any class of securities (equity or debt) of the registered closed-end investment company (other than "short-term paper" as defined in Section 2(a)(38) of the Investment Company Act) and the beneficial ownership at the end of the month of that class of securities.

(b) The title of the security should clearly identify the class, even if the issuer has only one class of securities outstanding; for example, "Common Stock," "Class A Common Stock," "Class B Convertible Preferred Stock," etc.

(c) The amount of securities beneficially owned should state the face amount of debt securities (U.S. Dollars) or the number of equity securities, whichever is appropriate.

357

4. Transactions and Holdings Required To Be Reported

(a) *General Requirements*

(i) Report, in accordance with Rule 16a-3(g), all transactions not exempt from Section 16(b) of the Act and all exercises and conversions of derivative securities, regardless of whether exempt from Section 16(b) of the Act, resulting in a change of beneficial ownership in the issuer's securities. Every transaction shall be reported even though acquisitions and dispositions during the month are equal. Report total beneficial ownership as of the end of the month for each class of securities in which a transaction was reported.

Note: The amount of securities beneficially owned at the end of the month specified in Column 5 of Table I and Column 9 of Table II should reflect those holdings reported or required to be reported by the date of the Form. Transactions and holdings eligible for deferred reporting on Form 5 need not be reflected in the month end total unless the transactions were reported earlier or are included on this Form.

(ii) Each transaction should be reported on a separate line. Transaction codes specified in Item 8 should be used to identify the nature of the transaction resulting in an acquisition or disposition of a security.

Note: Transactions reportable on Form 5 may, at the option of the reporting person, be reported on a Form 4 filed before the due date of the Form 5. (See Instruction 8 for the code for voluntarily reported transactions.)

(b) *Beneficial Ownership Reported (Pecuniary Interest)*

(i) Although for purposes of determining status as a ten percent holder, a person is deemed to beneficially own securities over which that person exercises voting or investment control (see Rule 16a-1(a)(1)), for reporting transactions and holdings, a person is deemed to be the beneficial owner of securities if that person has the opportunity, directly or indirectly, to profit or share in any profit derived from a transaction in the securities ("pecuniary interest"). See Rule 16a1(a)(2). See also Rule 16a-8 for the application of the beneficial ownership definition to trust holdings and transactions.

(ii) Both direct and indirect beneficial ownership of securities shall be reported. Securities beneficially owned directly are those held in the reporting person's name or in the name of a bank, broker or nominee for the account of the reporting person. In addition, securities held as joint tenants, tenants in common, tenants by the entirety, or as community property are to be reported as held directly. If a person has a pecuniary interest, by reason of any contract, understanding or relationship (including a family relationship or arrangement), in securities held in the name of another person, that person is an indirect beneficial owner of the securities. See Rule 16a-1(a)(2)(ii) for certain indirect beneficial ownerships.

(iii) Report transactions in securities beneficially owned directly on a separate line from those beneficially owned indirectly. Report different forms of indirect ownership on separate lines. The nature of indirect ownership shall be stated as specifically as possible; for example, "By Self as Trustee for X," "By Spouse," "By X Trust," "By Y Corporation," etc.

(iv) In stating the amount of securities acquired, disposed of, or beneficially owned indirectly through a partnership, corporation, trust, or other entity, report the number of securities representing the reporting person's proportionate interest in transactions conducted by that entity or holdings of that entity. Alternatively, at the option of the reporting person, the entire amount of the entity's interest may be reported. See Rule 16a-1(a)(2)(ii)(B) and Rule 16a1(a)(2)(iii).

(v) Where more than one beneficial owner of the same equity securities must report transactions on Form 4, such owners may file Form 4 individually or jointly. Joint and group filings may be made by any designated beneficial owner. Transactions with respect to securities owned separately by any joint or group filer are permitted to be included in the joint filing. Indicate only the name and address of the designated filer in Item 1 of Form 4 and attach a listing of the names and IRS or social security numbers (or addresses in lieu thereof) of each other reporting person. Joint and group filings must include all required information for each beneficial owner, and such filings must be signed by each beneficial owner, or on behalf of such owner by an authorized person. If the space provided for signatures is insufficient, attach a signature page. Submit any attached listing of names or signatures on another Form 4, copy of Form 4 or separate page of 8 1/2 by 11 inch white paper, indicate the number of pages comprising the report (Form plus attachments) at the bottom of each report page (e.g., 1 of 3, 2 of 3, 3 of 3), and include the name of the designated filer and information required by Items 2 and 4 of the Form on the attachment.

(c) *Non-Derivative and Derivative Securities*

(i) Report acquisitions or dispositions and holdings of non-derivative securities in Table I. Report acquisitions or dispositions and holdings of derivative securities (e.g., puts, calls, options, warrants, convertible securities, or other rights or obligations to buy or sell securities) in Table II. Report the exercise or conversion of a derivative security in Table II (as a disposition of the derivative security) and report in Table I the holdings of the underlying security. Report acquisitions or dispositions and holdings of derivative securities that are both equity securities and convertible or exchangeable for other equity securities (e.g., convertible preferred securities) only in Table II.

(ii) The title of a derivative security and the title of the equity security underlying the derivative security should be shown separately in the appropriate columns in Table II. The "puts" and "calls" reported in Table II include, in addition to separate puts and calls, any combination of the two, such as spreads and straddles. In reporting an option in Table II, state whether it represents a right to buy, a right to sell, an obligation to buy, or an obligation to sell the equity securities subject to the option.

(iii) Describe in the appropriate columns in Table II characteristics of derivative securities, including title, exercise or conversion price, date exercisable, expiration date, and the title and amount of securities underlying the derivative security. If the transaction reported is a purchase or a sale of a derivative security, the purchase or sale price of that derivative security shall be reported in column 8. If the transaction is the exercise or conversion of a derivative security, leave column 8 blank and report the exercise or conversion price of the derivative security in column 2.

(iv) Securities constituting components of a unit shall be reported separately on the applicable table (e.g., if a unit has a non-derivative security component and a derivative security component, the non-derivative security component shall be reported in Table I and the derivative security component shall be reported in Table II). The relationship between individual securities comprising the unit shall be indicated in the space provided for explanation of responses. When securities are purchased or sold as a unit, state the purchase or sale price per unit and other required information regarding the unit securities.

5. Price of Securities

(a) Prices of securities shall be reported in U.S. dollars on a per share basis, not an aggregate basis, except that the aggregate price of debt shall be stated. Amounts reported shall exclude brokerage commissions and other costs of execution.

(b) If consideration other than cash was paid for the security, describe the consideration, including the value of the consideration, in the space provided for explanation of responses.

6. Additional Information

If the space provided in the line items of this Form or space provided for additional comments is insufficient, attach another Form 4, copy of Form 4 or separate page of 8 1/2 by 11 inch white paper to Form 4, completed as appropriate to include the additional comments. Each attached page must include information required in Items 1, 2 and 4 of the Form. The number of pages comprising the report (Form plus attachments) shall be indicated at the bottom of each report page (e.g., 1 of 3, 2 of 3, 3 of 3). If additional information is not reported in this manner, it will be assumed that no additional information was provided.

7. Signature

(a) If the Form is filed for an individual, it shall be signed by that person or specifically on behalf of the individual by a person authorized to sign for the individual. If signed on behalf of the individual by another person, the authority of such person to sign the Form shall be confirmed to the Commission in writing in an attachment to the Form or as soon as practicable in an amendment by the individual for whom the Form is filed, unless such a confirmation still in effect is on file with the Commission. The confirming statement need only indicate that the reporting person authorizes and designates the named person or persons to file the Form on the reporting person's behalf, and state the duration of the authorization.

(b) If the Form is filed for a corporation, partnership, trust, or other entity, the capacity in which the individual signed shall be set forth (e.g., John Smith, Secretary, on behalf of X Corporation).

8. Transaction Codes

Use the codes listed below to indicate in Table I, Column 3 and Table II, Column 4 the character of the transaction reported. Use the code that most appropriately describes the transaction. If the transaction is not specifically listed, use transaction Code "J" and describe the nature of the transaction in the space for explanation of responses. If a transaction is voluntarily reported earlier than required, place "V" in the appropriate column to so indicate; otherwise, the column should be left blank. If a transaction involves an equity swap or instrument with similar characteristics, use transaction code "K" in addition to the code(s) that most appropriately describes the transaction, e.g., "S/K" or "P/K."

General Transaction Codes

P — Open market or private purchase of non-derivative or derivative security

S — Open market or private sale of non-derivative or derivative security

V — Transaction voluntarily reported earlier than required

Rule 16b-3 Transaction Codes

A — Grant, award or other acquisition pursuant to Rule 16b-3(d)

D — Disposition to the issuer of issuer equity securities pursuant to Rule 16b-3(e)

F — Payment of exercise price or tax liability by delivering or withholding securities incident to the receipt, exercise or vesting of a security issued in accordance with Rule 16b-3

I — Discretionary transaction in accordance with Rule 16b-3(f) resulting in acquisition or disposition of issuer securities

M — Exercise or conversion of derivative security exempted pursuant to Rule 16b-3

Derivative Securities Codes (Except for transactions exempted pursuant to Rule 16b-3)

C — Conversion of derivative security

E — Expiration of short derivative position

H — Expiration (or cancellation) of long derivative position with value received

O — Exercise of out-of-the-money derivative security

X — Exercise of in-the-money or at-the-money derivative security

Other Section 16(b) Exempt Transaction and Small Acquisition Codes (except for Rule 16b-3 codes above)

G — Bona fide gift

L — Small acquisition under Rule 16a-6

W — Acquisition or disposition by will or the laws of descent and distribution

Z — Deposit into or withdrawal from voting trust

Other Transaction Codes

J — Other acquisition or disposition (describe transaction)

K — Transaction in equity swap or instrument with similar characteristics

U — Disposition pursuant to a tender of shares in a change of control transaction

FORM 4

❏ Check this box if no longer subject to Section 16. Form 4 or Form 5 obligations may continue. See Instruction 1(b).

OMB APPROVAL
OMB Number: 3235-0287
Expires: December 31, 2001
Estimated average burden hours per response. . . . 0.5

UNITED STATES SECURITIES AND EXCHANGE COMMISSION
Washington, D.C. 20549

STATEMENT OF CHANGES IN BENEFICIAL OWNERSHIP

Filed pursuant to Section 16(a) of the Securities Exchange Act of 1934, Section 17(a) of the Public Utility Holding Company Act of 1935 or Section 30(f) of the Investment Company Act of 1940

(Print or Type Responses)

1. Name and Address of Reporting Person*	2. Issuer Name and Ticker or Trading Symbol	6. Relationship of Reporting Person(s) to Issuer (Check all applicable)
(Last) (First) (Middle)	3. I.R.S. Identification Number of Reporting Person, if an entity (voluntary)	❏ Director ❏ 10% Owner ❏ Officer (give title below) ❏ Other (specify below)
(Street)	4. Statement for Month/Year	7. Individual or Joint/Group Filing (Check Applicable Line)
(City) (State) (Zip)	5. If Amendment, Date of Original (Month/Year)	❏ Form filed by One Reporting Person ❏ Form filed by More than One Reporting Person

Reminder: Report on a separate line for each class of securities beneficially owned directly or indirectly.

* If the form is filed by more than one reporting person, see Instruction 5(b)(v).

Table I — Non-Derivative Securities Acquired, Disposed of, or Beneficially Owned

1. Title of Security (Instr. 3)	2. Transaction Date (Month/Day/Year)	3. Transaction Code (Instr. 8)		4. Securities Acquired (A) or Disposed of (D) (Instr. 3, 4 and 5)			5. Amount of Securities Beneficially Owned at End of Month (Instr. 3 and 4)	6. Ownership Form: Direct (D) or Indirect (I) (Instr. 4)	7. Nature of Indirect Beneficial Ownership (Instr. 4)
		Code	V	Amount	(A) or (D)	Price			

Table II—Derivative Securities Acquired, Disposed of, or Beneficially Owned (e.g., puts, calls, warrants, options, convertible securities)

1. Title of Derivative Security (Instr. 3)	2. Conversion or Exercise Price of Derivative Security	3. Transaction Date (Month/Day/Year)	4. Transaction Code (Instr. 8)		5. Number of Derivative Securities Acquired (A) or Disposed of (D) (Instr. 3, 4 and 5)		6. Date Exerciseable and Expiration Date (Month/Day/Year)		7. Title and Amount of Underlying Securities (Instr. 3 and 4)		8. Price of Derivative Security (Instr. 5)	9. Number of Derivative Securities Beneficially Owned at End of Month (Instr. 4)	10. Ownership Form of Derivative Security Direct (D) or Indirect (I) (Instr. 4)	11. Nature of Indirect Beneficial Ownership (Instr. 4)
			Code	V	(A)	(D)	Date Exercisable	Expiration Date	Title	Amount or Number of Shares				

Explanation of Responses:

_____   _____
                            **Signature of Reporting Person   Date

** Intentional misstatements or omissions of facts constitute Federal Criminal Violations. See 18 U.S.C. 1001 and 15 U.S.C. 78ff(a).

Note: File three copies of this Form, one of which must be manually signed. If space is insufficient, *see* Instruction 6 for procedure.

http://www.sec.gov/divisions/corpfin/forms/form3.htm
Last update: 11/05/1999

APPENDIX 8F

Form 5

SEC 2270 (3-99)   Potential persons who are to respond to the collection of information contained in this form are not required to respond unless the form displays a currently valid OMB control number.

UNITED STATES

SECURITIES AND EXCHANGE COMMISSION

Washington, D.C. 20549

OMB APPROVAL
OMB Number: 3235-0362
Expires: December 31, 2001
Estimated average burden hours per response. . . . 1.0

ANNUAL STATEMENT OF BENEFICIAL
OWNERSHIP OF SECURITIES

The Commission is authorized to solicit the information required by this Form pursuant to Sections 16(a) and 23(a) of the Securities Exchange Act of 1934, Sections 17(a) and 20(a) of the Public Utility Holding Company Act of 1935, and Sections 30(f) and 38 of the Investment Company Act of 1940, and the rules and regulations thereunder.

Disclosure of information specified on this Form is mandatory, except for disclosure of the I.R.S. identification number of the reporting person if such person is an entity, which is voluntary. If such numbers are furnished, they will assist the Commission in distinguishing reporting persons with similar names and will facilitate the prompt processing of the Form. The information will be used for the primary purpose of disclosing the transactions and holdings of directors, officers, and beneficial owners of registered companies. Information disclosed will be a matter of public record and available for inspection by members of the public. The Commission can use it in investigations or litigation involving the federal securities laws or other civil, criminal, or regulatory statutes or provisions, as well as for referral to other governmental authorities and self-regulatory organizations. Failure to disclose required information may result in civil or criminal action against persons involved for violations of the Federal securities laws and rules.

GENERAL INSTRUCTIONS

1. When Form Must Be Filed

(a) This Form must be filed on or before the 45th day after the end of the issuer's fiscal year in accordance with Rule 16a-3(f). This Form and any amendment is deemed filed with the Commission or the Exchange on the date it is received by the Commission or Exchange, respectively. See, however, Rule 16a-3(h) regarding delivery to a third party business that guarantees delivery of the filing no later than the specified due date.

(b) A reporting person no longer subject to Section 16 of the Securities Exchange Act of 1934 ("Exchange Act") must check the exit box appearing on this Form. Transactions and holdings previously reported are not required to be included on this Form. Form 4 or Form 5 obligations may continue to be applicable. See Rule 16a-3(f); see also Rule 16a2(b) (transactions after termination of insider status).

(c) A separate Form shall be filed to reflect beneficial ownership of securities of each issuer, except that a single statement shall be filed with respect to the securities of a registered public utility holding company and all of its subsidiary companies.

(d) If a reporting person is not an officer, director, or ten percent holder, the person should check "other" in Item 6 (Relationship of Reporting Person to Issuer) and describe the reason for reporting status in the space provided.

2. Where Form Must be Filed

(a) File three copies of this Form or any amendment, at least one of which is manually signed, with the Securities and Exchange Commission, 450 5th Street, N.W., Washington, D.C. 20549. (Note: Acknowledgment of receipt by the Commission may be obtained by enclosing a self-addressed stamped postcard identifying the Form or amendment filed.) Alternatively, this Form is permitted to be submitted to the Commission in electronic format at the option of the reporting person pursuant to § 232.101(b)(4) of this chapter.

(b) At the time this Form or any amendment is filed with the Commission, file one copy with each Exchange on which any class of securities of the issuer is registered. If the issuer has designated a single Exchange to receive Section 16 filings, the copy shall be filed with that Exchange only.

(c) Any person required to file this Form or amendment shall, not later than the time the Form or amendment is transmitted for filing with the Commission, send or deliver a copy to the person designated by the issuer to receive the copy or, if no person is so designated, the issuer's corporate secretary (or person performing similar functions) in accordance with Rule 16a-3(e).

3. Class of Securities Reported

(a) (i) Persons reporting pursuant to Section 16(a) of the Exchange Act shall include information as to transactions and holdings required to be reported in any class of equity securities of the issuer and the beneficial ownership at the end of the year of that class of equity securities, even though one or more of such classes may not be registered pursuant to Section 12 of the Exchange Act.

(ii) Persons reporting pursuant to Section 17(a) of the Public Utility Holding Company Act of 1935 shall include transactions and holdings required to be reported in any class of securities (equity or debt) of the registered holding company and any of its subsidiary companies and the beneficial ownership at the end of the issuer's fiscal year of that class of securities. Specify the name of the parent or subsidiary issuing the securities.

(iii) Persons reporting pursuant to Section 30(f) of the Investment Company Act of 1940 shall include transactions and holdings required to be reported in any class of securities (equity or debt) of the registered closed-end investment company (other than "short-term paper as defined in Section 2(a)(38) of the Investment Company Act) and the beneficial ownership at the end of the year of that class of securities.

(b) The title of the security should clearly identify the class, even if the issuer has only one class of securities outstanding; for example, "Common Stock," "Class A Common Stock," "Class B Convertible Preferred Stock," etc.

(c) The amount of securities beneficially owned should state the face amount of debt securities (U.S. Dollars) or the number of equity securities, whichever is appropriate.

4. Transactions and Holdings Required to be Reported

(a) *General Requirements*

    (i) Pursuant to Rule 16a-3(f), if not previously reported, the following transactions, and total beneficial ownership as of the end of the issuer's fiscal year (or an earlier date applicable to a person ceasing to be an insider during the fiscal year) for any class of securities in which a transaction is reported, shall be reported:

        (A) any transaction during the issuer's most recent fiscal year that was exempt from Section 16(b) of the Act, except: (1) any exercise or conversion of derivative securities exempt under either §240.16b-3 or §240.16b-6(b) (these are required to be reported on Form 4); (2) any transaction exempt from Section 16(b) of the Act pursuant to Rule 16b3(c) of this section, which is exempt from Section 16(a) of the Act; and (3) any transaction exempt from Section 16 of the Act pursuant to another Section 16(a) rule;

        (B) any small acquisition or series of acquisitions in a six month period during the issuer's fiscal year not exceeding $10,000 in market value (see Rule 16a-6);

        (C) any transactions or holdings that should have been reported during the issuer's fiscal year on a Form 3 or Form 4, but were not reported. The first Form 5 filing obligation shall include all holdings and transactions that should have been reported in each of the issuer's last two fiscal years but were not. See Instruction 8 for the code to identify delinquent Form 3 holdings or Form 4 transactions reported on this Form 5.

Note: A required Form 3 or Form 4 must be filed within the time specified by this Form. Form 3 holdings or Form 4 transactions reported on Form 5 represent delinquent Form 3 and Form 4 filings.

    (ii) Each transaction should be reported on a separate line. Transaction codes specified in Item 8 should be used to identify the nature of the transactions resulting in an acquisition or disposition of a security.

    (iii) Every transaction shall be reported even though acquisitions and dispositions with respect to a class of securities are equal. Report total beneficial ownership as of the end of the issuer's fiscal year for all classes of securities in which a transaction was reported.

(b) *Beneficial Ownership Reported (Pecuniary Interest)*

    (i) Although for purposes of determining status as a ten percent holder, a person is deemed to beneficially own securities over which that person exercises voting or investment control (see Rule 16a-1(a)(1)), for reporting transactions and holdings, a person is deemed to be the beneficial owner of securities if that person has or shares the opportunity, directly or indirectly, to profit or share in any profit derived from a transaction in the securities ("pecuniary interest"). See Rule 16a-1(a)(2). See also Rule 16a-8 for the application of the beneficial ownership definition to trust holdings and transactions.

(ii) Both direct and indirect beneficial ownership of securities shall be reported. Securities beneficially owned directly are those held in the reporting person's name or in the name of a bank, broker or nominee for the account of the reporting person. In addition, securities held as joint tenants, tenants in common, tenants by the entirety, or as community property are to be reported as held directly. If a person has a pecuniary interest, by reason of any contract, understanding or relationship (including a family relationship or arrangement) in securities held in the name of another person, that person is an indirect beneficial owner of the securities. See Rule 16a-1(a)(2)(ii) for certain indirect beneficial ownerships.

(iii) Report transactions in securities beneficially owned directly on a separate line from those beneficially owned indirectly. Report different forms of indirect ownership on separate lines. The nature of indirect ownership shall be stated as specifically as possible; for example, "By Self as Trustee for X," "By Spouse," "By X Trust," "By Y Corporation," etc.

(iv) In stating the amount of securities acquired, disposed of, or beneficially owned indirectly through a partnership, corporation, trust, or other entity, report the number of securities representing the reporting person's proportionate interest in transactions conducted by that entity or holdings of that entity. Alternatively, at the option of the reporting person, the entire amount of the entity's interest may be reported. See Rule 16a-1(a)(2)(ii)(B) and Rule 16a1(a)(2)(iii).

(v) Where more than one beneficial owner of the same equity securities must report on Form 5, such owners may file Form 5 individually or jointly. Joint and group filings may be made by any designated beneficial owner. Transactions and holdings with respect to securities owned separately by any joint or group filer are permitted to be included in the joint filing. Indicate only the name and address of the designated filer in Item 1 of Form 5 and attach a listing of the names and IRS or social security numbers (or addresses in lieu thereof) of each other reporting person. Joint and group filings must include all required information for each beneficial owner, and such filings must be signed by each beneficial owner, or on behalf of such owner by an authorized person. If the space provided for signatures is insufficient, attach a signature page. Submit any attached listing of names or signatures on another Form 5, copy of Form 5 or separate page of 8 1/2 by 11 inch white paper, indicate the number of pages comprising the report (Form plus attachments) at the bottom of each report page (e.g., 1 of 3, 2 of 3, 3 of 3), and include the name of the designated filer and information required by Items 2 and 4 of the Form on the attachment.

(c) *Non-Derivative and Derivative Securities*

   (i) Report acquisitions or dispositions and holdings of non-derivative securities in Table I. Report acquisitions or dispositions and holdings of derivative securities (e.g., puts, calls, options, warrants, convertible securities, or other rights or obligations to buy or sell securities) in Table II. Report the exercise or conversion of a derivative security in Table II (as a disposition of the derivative security) and report in Table I the holdings of the underlying security. Report acquisitions or dispositions and holdings of derivative securities that are both equity securities and convertible or exchangeable for other equity securities (e.g., convertible preferred securities) only in Table II.

   (ii) The title of a derivative security and the title of the equity security underlying the derivative security should be shown separately in the appropriate columns in Table II. The "puts" and "calls" reported in Table II include, in addition to separate puts and calls, any combination of the two, such as spreads and straddles. In reporting an option in Table II, state whether it represents a right to buy, a right to sell, an obligation to buy, or an obligation to sell the equity securities subject to the option.

   (iii) Describe in the appropriate columns in Table II characteristics of derivative securities, including title, exercise or conversion price, date exercisable, expiration date, and the title and amount of securities underlying the derivative security. If the transaction reported is a purchase or a sale of a derivative security, the purchase or sale price of that derivative security shall be reported in column 8. If the transaction is the exercise or conversion of a derivative security, leave column 8 blank and report the exercise or conversion price of the derivative security in column 2.

   (iv) Securities constituting components of a unit shall be reported separately on the applicable table (e.g., if a unit has a non-derivative security component and a derivative security component, the non-derivative security component shall be reported in Table I and the derivative security component shall be reported in Table II). The relationship between individual securities comprising the unit shall be indicated in the space provided for explanation of responses. When securities are purchased or sold as a unit, state the purchase or sale price per unit and other required information regarding the unit securities.

5. Price of Securities

(a) Prices of securities shall be reported in U.S. dollars on a per share basis, not an aggregate basis, except that the aggregate price of debt shall be stated. Amounts reported shall exclude brokerage commissions and other costs of execution.

(b) If consideration other than cash was paid for the security, describe the consideration, including the value of the consideration, in the space provided for explanation of responses.

6. Additional Information

If the space provided in the line items of this Form or space provided for additional comments is insufficient, attach another Form 5, copy of Form 5 or separate page of 8 1/2 by 11 inch white paper to Form 5, completed as appropriate to include the additional comments. Each attached page must include information required in Items 1, 2 and 4 of the Form. The number of pages comprising the report (Form plus attachments) shall be indicated at the bottom of each report page (e.g., 1 of 3, 2 of 3, 3 of 3). If additional information is not reported in this manner, it will be assumed that no additional information was provided.

7. Signature

(a) If the Form is filed for an individual, it shall be signed by that person or specifically on behalf of the individual by a person authorized to sign for the individual. If signed on behalf of the individual by another person, the authority of such person to sign the Form shall be confirmed to the Commission in writing in an attachment to the Form or as soon as practicable in an amendment by the individual for whom the Form is filed, unless such a confirmation still in effect is on file with the Commission. The confirming statement need only indicate that the reporting person authorizes and designates the named person or persons to file the Form on the reporting person's behalf, and state the duration of the authorization.

(b) If the Form is filed for a corporation, partnership, trust, or other entity, the capacity in which the individual signed shall be set forth (e.g., John Smith, Secretary, on behalf of X Corporation).

8. Transaction Codes

Use the codes listed below to indicate in Table I, Column 3 and Table II, Column 4 the character of the transaction reported. Use the code that most appropriately describes the transaction. If the transaction is not specifically listed, use transaction code "J" and describe the nature of the transaction in the space for explanation of responses. If a transaction involves an equity swap or instrument with similar characteristics, use transaction Code "K" in addition to the code(s) that most appropriately describes the transaction, e.g., "S/K" or "P/K."

General Transaction Codes

P — Open market or private purchase of non-derivative or derivative security

S — Open market or private sale of non-derivative or derivative security

Rule 16b-3 Transaction Codes

A — Grant, award or other acquisition pursuant to Rule 16b-3(d)

D — Disposition to the issuer of issuer equity securities pursuant to Rule 16b-3(e)

F — Payment of exercise price or tax liability by delivering or withholding securities incident to the receipt, exercise or vesting of a security issued in accordance with Rule 16b-3

I — Discretionary transaction in accordance with Rule 16b-3(f) resulting in acquisition or disposition of issuer securities

M— Exercise or conversion of derivative security exempted pursuant to Rule 16b-3

Derivative Securities Codes (Except for transactions exempted pursuant to Rule 16b-3)

C — Conversion of derivative security

E — Expiration of short derivative position

H — Expiration (or cancellation) of long derivative position with value received

O — Exercise of out-of-the-money derivative security

X — Exercise of in-the-money or at-the-money derivative security

Other Section 16(b) Exempt Transaction and Small Acquisition Codes (except for Rule 16b-3 codes above)

G — Bona fide gift

L — Small acquisition under Rule 16a-6

W— Acquisition or disposition by will or the laws of descent and distribution

Z — Deposit into or withdrawal from voting trust

Other Transaction Codes

J — Other acquisition or disposition (describe transaction)

K — Transaction in equity swap or instrument with similar characteristics

U — Disposition pursuant to a tender of shares in a change of control transaction

Form 3, 4 or 5 Holdings or Transactions Not Previously Reported

To indicate that a holding should have been reported previously on Form 3, place a "3" in Table I, column 3 or Table II, column 4, as appropriate. Indicate in the space provided for explanation of responses the event triggering the Form 3 filing obligation. To indicate that a transaction should have been reported previously on Form 4, place a "4" next to the transaction code reported in Table I, column 3 or Table II, column 4 (e.g., an open market purchase of a non-derivative security that should have been reported previously on Form 4 should be designated as "P4"). To indicate that a transaction should have been reported on a previous Form 5, place a "5" in Table I, column 3 or Table II, column 4, as appropriate. In addition, the appropriate box on the front page of the Form should be checked.

FORM 5

☐ Check this box if no longer subject to Section 16. Form 4 or Form 5 obligations may continue. See Instruction 1(b).
☐ Form 3 Holdings Repored
☐ Form 4 Transactions Repored

UNITED STATES SECURITIES AND EXCHANGE COMMISSION
Washington, D.C. 20549

ANNUAL STATEMENT OF CHANGES IN BENEFICIAL OWNERSHIP

Filed pursuant to Section 16(a) of the Securities Exchange Act of 1934, Section 17(a) of the Public Utility Holding Company Act of 1935 or Section 30(f) of the Investment Company Act of 1940

(Print or Type Responses)

OMB APPROVAL
OMB Number: 3235-0287
Expires: December 31, 2001
Estimated average burden hours per response. . . . 0.5

1. Name and Address of Reporting Person*	2. Issuer Name and Ticker or Trading Symbol	6. Relationship of Reporting Person(s) to Issuer (Check all applicable)
(Last) (First) (Middle)		☐ Director ☐ 10% Owner
	3. I.R.S. Identification Number of Reporting Person, if an entity (voluntary)	☐ Officer (give title below) ☐ Other (specify below)
(Street)	4. Statement for Month/Year	7. Individual or Joint/Group Filing (Check Applicable Line)
(City) (State) (Zip)	5. If Amendment, Date of Original (Month/Year)	☐ Form filed by One Reporting Person ☐ Form filed by More than One Reporting Person

* If the form is filed by more than one reporting person, see Instruction 5(b)(v).

375

Table I — Non-Derivative Securities Acquired, Disposed of, or Beneficially Owned

1. Title of Security (Instr. 3)	2. Transaction Date (Month/Day/Year)	3. Transaction Code (Instr. 8)	4. Securities Acquired (A) or Disposed of (D) (Instr. 3, 4 and 5)			5. Amount of Securities Beneficially Owned at End of Issuer's Fiscal Year (Instr. 3 and 4)	6. Ownership Form: Direct (D) or Indirect (I) (Instr. 4)	7. Nature of Indirect Beneficial Ownership (Instr. 4)
			Amount	(A) or (D)	Price			

Table II—Derivative Securities Acquired, Disposed of, or Beneficially Owned (e.g., puts, calls, warrants, options, convertible securities)

1. Title of Derivative Security (Instr.3)	2. Conversion or Exercise Price of Derivative Security	3. Transaction Date (Month/Day/Year)	4. Transaction Code (Instr. 8)	5. Number of Derivative Securities Acquired (A) or Disposed of (D) (Instr. 3, 4 and 5)		6. Date Exerciseable and Expiration Date (Month/Day/Year)		7. Title and Amount of Underlying Securities (Instr. 3 and 4)		8. Price of Derivative Security (Instr. 5)	9. Number of Derivative Securities Beneficially Owned at End of Year (Instr. 4)	10. Ownership of Derivative Security: Direct (D) or Indirect (I) (Instr. 4)	11. Nature of Indirect Beneficial Ownership (Instr. 4)
				(A)	(D)	Date Exercisable	Expiration Date	Title	Amount or Number of Shares				

Explanation of Responses:

_____   _____
**Signature of Reporting Person   Date

** Intentional misstatements or omissions of facts constitute Federal Criminal Violations. See 18 U.S.C. 1001 and 15 U.S.C. 78ff(a).

Note: File three copies of this Form, one of which must be manually signed. If space is insufficient, *see Instruction 6 for procedure.*

http://www.sec.gov/divisions/corpfin/forms/form3.htm
Last update: 08/23/1999

APPENDIX 8G

NYSE Listing Requirements[41]

Domestic listing requirements call for minimum distribution of a company's shares within the United States. Distribution of shares can be attained through U.S. public offerings, acquisitions made in the U.S., or by other similar means. Note that there are alternatives to the round lot-holder and pretax earnings standards.

Minimum Quantitative Standards: Distribution and Size Criteria	
Round-lot Holders (A) (number of holders of a unit of trading—generally 100 shares)	2,000 U.S.
or:	
Total Shareholders	2,200
. . . together with:	
Average Monthly Trading Volume (for the most recent 6 months)	100,000 shares
or:	
Total Shareholders	500
. . . together with:	
Average Monthly Trading Volume (for the most recent 12 months)	1,000,000 shares
Public Shares (B)	1,100,000 outstanding

---

[41] *New York Stock Exchange Listed Company Manual* § 9.

Market Value of Public Shares (B, C):	
Public Companies	$100,000,000
IPOs, Spin-Offs, Carve-Outs	$60,000,000

Minimum Quantitative Standards: Financial Criteria Earnings

Aggregate pretax earnings (D) over the last three years of $6,500,000 achievable as:

Most Recent Year	$2,500,000
Each of Two Preceding Years	$2,000,000

or:

Most Recent Year (All three years must be profitable)	$4,500,000

or:

Operating Cash Flow

For companies with not less than $500 million in global market capitalization and $200 million in revenues in the last 12 months:

Aggregate for the Three Years Operating Cash Flow (E) (each year must report a positive amount)	$25,000,000

or:

Global Market Capitalization

Revenues for the Last Fiscal Year	$100,000,000
Average Global Market Capitalization (F)	$1,000,000,000
REITs (less than 3 years operating history) (B) Stockholders' equity	$60,000,000
Funds (less than 3 years operating history) (B) Net assets	$60,000,000

(A) The number of beneficial holders of stock held in "street name" will be considered in addition to the holders of record. The Exchange will make any necessary check of such holdings that are in the name of Exchange member organizations.

(B) In connection with initial public offerings, the NYSE will accept an undertaking from the company's underwriter to ensure that the offering will meet or exceed the NYSE's standards.

(C) If a company either has a significant concentration of stock or changing market forces have adversely impacted the public market value of a company that otherwise would qualify for an Exchange listing, such that its public market value is no more than 10% below the minimum, the Exchange will consider stockholders' equity of $60 million or $100 million, as applicable, as an alternate measure of size.

(D) Pretax income is adjusted for various items as defined in the NYSE Listed Company Manual.

(E) Represents net cash provided by operating activities excluding the changes in working capital or in operating assets and liabilities, as adjusted for various items as defined in the NYSE Listed Company Manual.

(F) Average global market capitalization for already existing public companies is represented by the most recent six months of trading history. For IPOs, spin-offs and carve-outs, it is represented by the valuation of the company as represented by, in the case of a spin-off, the distribution ratio as priced, or, in the case of an IPO/carve-out, the as-priced offering in relation to the total company's capitalization.

Additional Considerations

In addition to meeting the minimum numerical standards listed above, there are other factors which must necessarily be considered. The company must be a going concern or be the successor to a going concern.

The Exchange has broad discretion regarding the listing of a company. The Exchange is committed to list only those companies that are suited for auction market trading and that have attained the status of being eligible for trading on the Exchange. Thus, the Exchange may deny listing or apply additional or more stringent criteria based on any event, condition, or circumstance that makes the listing of the company inadvisable or unwarranted in the opinion of the Exchange. Such determination can be made even if the company meets the standards set forth above.

NOTE: Other factors are also taken into consideration. The Company must be a going concern or be the successor to a going concern. Although the amount of assets and earnings and the aggregate market value are considerations, greater emphasis is placed on such questions as the degree of national interest in the company, the character of the market for its products, its relative stability and position in its industry, and whether or not it is engaged in an expanding industry with prospects for maintaining its position. The Exchange is also concerned with such matters as voting rights of shareholders, voting arrangements and pyramiding of control, and related party transactions. When there is an indication of a lack of public interest in the securities of a company evidenced, for example, by low trading volume on another exchange, lack of dealer interest in the over-the-counter market, unusual geographic concentration of holders of shares, slow growth in the number of shareholders, low rate of transfers, etc., higher distribution standards may apply. In this connection, particular attention will be directed to the number of holders of from 100 to 1,000 shares and the total number of shares in this category.

APPENDIX 8H

NYSE Listing Agreement for Domestic Companies

Nothing in the following Agreement shall be so construed as to require the Issuer to do any acts in contravention of law or in violation of any rule or regulation of any public authority exercising jurisdiction over the Issuer.

_____ (hereinafter called the "Corporation"), in consideration of the listing of the securities covered by this application, hereby agrees with the New York Stock Exchange (hereinafter called the "Exchange"), as follows:

I
_____

1. The Corporation will promptly notify the Exchange of any change in the general character or nature of its business.

2. The Corporation will promptly notify the Exchange of any changes of officers or directors.

3. The Corporation will promptly notify the Exchange in the event that it or any company controlled by it shall dispose of any property or of any stock interest in any of its subsidiary or controlled companies, if such disposal will materially affect the financial position of the Corporation or the nature or extent of its operations.

4. The Corporation will promptly notify the Exchange of any change in, or removal of, collateral deposited under any mortgage or trust indenture, under which securities of the Corporation listed on the Exchange have been issued.

5. The Corporation will:

   a. File with the Exchange four copies of all material mailed by the Corporation to its stockholders with respect to any amendment or proposed amendment to its Certificate of Incorporation.

   b. File with the Exchange a copy of any amendment to its Certificate of Incorporation, or resolution of Directors in the nature of an amendment, certified by the Secretary of State for the state of incorporation, as soon as such amendment or resolution shall have been filed in the appropriate state office.

   c. File with the Exchange a copy of any amendment to its Bylaws, certified by a duly authorized officer of the Corporation, as soon as such amendment becomes effective.

6. The Corporation will disclose in its annual report to shareholders, for the year covered by the report: (i) the number of shares of its stock issuable under outstanding options at the beginning of the year; separate totals of changes in the number of shares of its stock under option resulting from issuance, exercise, expiration or cancellation of options; and the number of shares issuable under outstanding options at the close of the year, (ii) the number of unoptioned shares available at the beginning and at the close of the year for the granting of options under an option plan, and (iii) any changes in the exercise price of outstanding options, through cancellation and reissuance or otherwise, except price changes resulting from the normal operation of anti-dilution provisions of the options.

7. The Corporation will report to the Exchange, within ten days after the close of a fiscal quarter, in the event any previously issued shares of any stock of the Corporation listed on the Exchange have been reacquired or disposed of, directly or indirectly, for the account of the Corporation during such fiscal quarter, such report showing separate totals for acquisitions and dispositions and the number of shares of such stock so held by it at the end of such quarter.

8. The Corporation will promptly notify the Exchange of all facts relating to the purchase, direct or indirect, of any of its securities listed on the Exchange at a price in excess of the market price of such security prevailing on the Exchange at the time of such purchase.

9. The Corporation will not select any of its securities listed on the Exchange for redemption otherwise than by lot or pro rata, and will not set a redemption date earlier than fifteen days after the date corporate action is taken to authorize the redemption.

10. The Corporation will promptly notify the Exchange of any corporate action which will result in the redemption, cancellation or retirement, in whole or in part, of any of its securities listed on the Exchange, and will notify the Exchange as soon as the Corporation has notice of any other action which will result in any such redemption, cancellation or retirement.

11. The Corporation will promptly notify the Exchange of action taken to fix a stockholders' record date, or to close the transfer books, for any purpose, and will take such action at such time as will permit giving the Exchange at least ten days' notice in advance of such record date or closing of the books.

12. In case the securities to be listed are in temporary form, the Corporation agrees to order permanent engraved securities within thirty days after the date of listing.

13. The Corporation will furnish to the Exchange on demand such information concerning the Corporation as the Exchange may reasonably require.

14. The Corporation will not make any change in the form or nature of any of its securities listed on the Exchange, nor in the rights or privileges of the holders thereof, without having given twenty days' prior notice to the Exchange of the proposed change, and having made application for the listing of the securities as changed if the Exchange shall so require.

15. The Corporation will make available to the Exchange, upon request, the names of member firms of the Exchange which are registered owners of stock of the Corporation listed on the Exchange if at any time the need for such stock for loaning purposes on the Exchange should develop and, in addition, if found necessary, will use its best efforts with any known large holders to make reasonable amounts of such stock available for such purposes in accordance with the rules of the Exchange.

16. The Corporation will promptly notify the Exchange of any diminution in the supply of stock available for the market occasioned by deposit of stock under voting trust agreements or other deposit agreements, if knowledge of any such actual or proposed deposits should come to the official attention of the officers or directors of the Corporation.

17. The Corporation will make application to the Exchange for the listing of additional amounts of securities listed on the

Exchange sufficiently prior to the issuance thereof to permit action in due course upon such application.

II

1. The Corporation will publish at least once a year and submit to its stockholders at least fifteen days in advance of the annual meeting of such stockholders and not later than three months after the close of the last preceding fiscal year of the Corporation a balance sheet as of the end of such fiscal year, and a surplus and income statement for such fiscal year of the Corporation as a separate corporate entity and of each corporation in which it holds directly or indirectly a majority of the equity stock; or, in lieu thereof, eliminating all intercompany transactions, a consolidated balance sheet of the Corporation and its subsidiaries as of the end of its last previous fiscal year, and a consolidated surplus statement and a consolidated income statement of the Corporation and its subsidiaries for such fiscal year. If any such consolidated statement shall exclude corporations a majority of whose equity stock is owned directly or indirectly by the Corporation:

    a. the caption of, or a note to, such statement will show the degree of consolidation;

    b. the consolidated income account will reflect, either in a footnote or otherwise, the parent company's proportion of the sum of, or difference between, current earnings or losses and the dividends of such unconsolidated subsidiaries for the period of the report; and

    c. the consolidated balance sheet will reflect, either in a footnote or otherwise, the extent to which the equity of the parent company in such subsidiaries has been increased or diminished since the date of acquisition as a result of profits, losses and distributions.

Appropriate reserves, in accordance with good accounting practice, will be made against profits arising out of all transactions with unconsolidated subsidiaries in either parent company statements or consolidated statements.

Such statements will reflect the existence of any default in interest, cumulative dividend requirements, sinking fund or redemption fund requirements of the Corporation and of any controlled corporation, whether consolidated or unconsolidated.

2. All financial statements contained in annual reports of the Corporation to its stockholders will be audited by independent public accountants qualified under the laws of some state or country, and will be accompanied by a copy of the certificate made by them with respect to their audit of such statements showing the scope of such audit and the qualifications, if any, with respect thereto.

    The Corporation will promptly notify the Exchange if it changes its independent public accountants regularly auditing the books and accounts of the Corporation.

3. All financial statements contained in annual reports of the Corporation to its stockholders shall be in the same form as the corresponding statements contained in the listing application in connection with which this Listing Agreement is made, and shall disclose any substantial items of unusual or nonrecurrent nature.

4. The Corporation will publish quarterly statements of earnings on the basis of the same degree of consolidation as in the annual report. Such statements will disclose any substantial items of unusual or nonrecurrent nature and will show either net income before and after federal income taxes or net income and the amount of federal income taxes.

5. The Corporation will not make, nor will it permit any subsidiary directly or indirectly controlled by it to make, any substantial charges against capital surplus, without notifying the Exchange. If so requested by the Exchange, the Corporation will submit such charges to stockholders for approval or ratification.

6. The Corporation will not make any substantial change, nor will it permit any subsidiary directly or indirectly controlled by it to make any substantial change, in accounting methods, in policies as to depreciation and depletion or in bases of valuation of inventories or other assets, without notifying the Exchange and disclosing the effect of any such change in its next succeeding interim and annual report to its stockholders.

7. The Corporation will maintain an audit committee in conformity with Exchange requirements (effective June 30, 1978).

III

1. The Corporation will maintain in the Borough of Manhattan, City of New York, in accordance with the requirements of the Exchange:

   a. An office or agency where the principal of and interest on all bonds of the Corporation listed on the Exchange shall be payable and where any such bonds which are registerable as to principal or interest may be registered.

   b. An office or agency where:

      i. All stock of the Corporation listed on the Exchange shall be transferable.

      ii. Checks for dividends and other payments with respect to stock listed on the Exchange may be presented for immediate payment.

iii. A security listed on the Exchange which is convertible will be accepted for conversion.

If at any time the transfer office or agency for a security listed on the Exchange shall be located north of Chambers Street, the Corporation will arrange, at its own cost and expense, that its registrar's office, or some other suitable office satisfactory to the Exchange and south of Chambers Street, will receive and redeliver all securities there tendered for the purpose of transfer.

If the transfer books for a security of the Corporation listed on the Exchange should be closed permanently, the Corporation will continue to split up certificates for such security into certificates of smaller denominations in the same name so long as such security continues to be dealt in on the Exchange.

If checks for dividends or other payments with respect to stock listed on the Exchange are drawn on a bank located outside the City of New York, the Corporation will also make arrangements for payment of such checks at a bank, trust company or other agency located in the Borough of Manhattan, City of New York.

c. A registrar where stock of the Corporation listed on the Exchange shall be registerable. Such registrar shall be a bank or trust company not acting as transfer agent for the same security.

2. The Corporation will not appoint a transfer agent, registrar or fiscal agent of, nor a trustee under a mortgage or other instrument relating to, any security of the Corporation listed on the Exchange without prior notice to the Exchange, and the Corporation will not appoint a registrar for its stock listed on the Exchange unless such registrar, at the time of its appointment becoming effective, is qualified with the Exchange as a registrar for securities listed on the Exchange, nor will the Corporation select an officer or director of the Corporation as a trustee under a mortgage or other instrument

relating to a security of the Corporation listed on the Exchange.

3. The Corporation will have on hand at all times a sufficient supply of certificates to meet the demands for transfer. If at any time the stock certificates of the Corporation do not recite the preferences of all classes of its stock, it will furnish to its stockholders, upon request and without charge, a printed copy of preferences of all classes of such stock.

4. The Corporation will publish immediately to the holders of any of its securities listed on the Exchange any action taken by the Corporation with respect to dividends or to the allotment of rights to subscribe or to any rights or benefits pertaining to the ownership of its securities listed on the Exchange; will give prompt notice to the Exchange of any such action; will afford the holders of its securities listed on the Exchange a proper period within which to record their interests and to exercise their rights; and will issue all such rights or benefits in form approved by the Exchange and will make the same transferable, exercisable, payable and deliverable in the Borough of Manhattan in the City of New York.

5. The Corporation will solicit proxies for all meetings of stockholders.

6. The Corporation will issue new certificates for securities listed on the Exchange replacing lost ones forthwith upon notification of loss and receipt of proper indemnity. If any duplicate bond is issued to replace a bond which has been alleged to be lost, stolen or destroyed and the original bond subsequently appears in the hands of an innocent bondholder, either the original or the duplicate bond will be taken up and cancelled and the Corporation will deliver to such holder another bond theretofore issued and outstanding.

7. The Corporation will pay when due any applicable Listing Fees established from time to time by the Exchange.

By _____

Date _____

Alternative Methods of Going Public— Direct Public Offerings and Reverse Mergers

W hen the overall stock market is weak, companies will face greater challenges in locating an underwriter for an IPO. The window of opportunity for an IPO can be closed quickly and an underwriter's willingness to go forward with a particular IPO depends heavily on current stock market conditions. Difficulties finding underwriters in a weak market often force companies to seek alternative methods of going public. Two of the most common alternatives are a direct public offering ("DPO") over the Internet and a reverse merger. These two alternative methods of going public are particularly useful in challenging economic times because they do not require the participation of an underwriter. Companies can therefore take the initiative and go public through their own efforts. However, a company that is contemplating either alternative must be aware of the advantages and disadvantages of each option and what steps must be taken to ensure compliance with all appropriate regulatory rules.

DIRECT PUBLIC OFFERINGS OVER THE INTERNET

The Internet allows communication with millions of people in an extremely cost-effective manner. As a result, company executives are thinking about how to use Internet technologies to help raise capital. In recent years, more and more companies have been using the Internet to offer their securities directly to investors without the use of an underwriter. This type of an IPO—known as a direct public offering or DPO—provides companies with an opportunity to go public even when market forces or other factors make a traditional IPO inadvisable.

One of the key factors that led to the increased interest in DPOs was an SEC Release that allowed companies, with the consent of the investor, to provide the required offering documents in electronic, rather than paper, format.[1] As a result, companies could significantly reduce the costs associated with a public offering because they no longer had to prepare and mail huge numbers of offering documents to investors. In its Release, entitled Use of Electronic Media for Delivery Purposes, the SEC recognized the widespread use and availability of computer technology. It stated that:

> "Advances in computers and electronic media technology are enabling companies to disseminate information to more people at a faster and more cost-effective rate than traditional distribution methods, which have been largely paper-based. The Commission appreciates the promise of electronic distribution of information in enhancing investors' ability to access, research, and analyze information, and in facilitating the provision of information by issuers and others. The Commission believes that, given the numerous benefits of electronic distribution of information and the fact that in many respects it may be more useful to investors than paper, its use should not be disfavored."[2]

In order to conduct a DPO over the Internet, a company must make one of several filings with the SEC. A company may make a Regulation A filing with the SEC for an offering of up to $5 million. Alternatively, it may file a Form SB-1, for an offering of up to $10

---

[1] Use of Electronic Media for Delivery Purposes, SEC Rel. No. 33-7233 (Oct. 1995).

[2] *Id.*

million, or a Form SB-2, which, in practice, is limited to offerings of up to $25 million. The choice of which filing to use depends primarily on the amount of capital that the company wants to raise. By making one of these filings with the SEC, and by complying with any relevant state securities laws, the company is permitted to conduct a public offering of its own securities. Because general solicitations are permitted in a DPO, a company can use Internet banner ads, e-mail and other technologies to assist in marketing and promoting the offering. In addition, the Internet also allows the company to make the prospectus for the offering available electronically to prospective investors. By conducting the offering itself, without the assistance of an underwriter, the company saves on the underwriting discount and commissions that it would otherwise have to pay to its underwriters and brokers.

In general, Internet DPOs work best for companies that already have a large customer base that would have a natural interest in investing in the company. Companies that have a large customer base, a well-known brand or a special connection with their customers are often good candidates for Internet DPOs because their customers are likely to be very familiar with the company and its business. Many technology and new media companies are also good candidates for an Internet DPO because their customers are comfortable with the Internet and other related technologies. In addition, new media and technology company executives are often highly skilled at marketing and promoting Web sites, and such skills can be put to great use when selling securities over the Internet. Because an underwriter is not involved in the DPO, the success or failure of the offering is entirely dependent on the efforts and skill of the company in selling its own securities.

A DPO can be used in circumstances where poor economic conditions make finding an underwriter for an offering of securities impractical. A company can go public in bad economic times through a DPO; however, the company must be sure to begin planning well in advance of the actual offering. Appropriate planning will include consulting with a securities attorney in order to make sure that all applicable regulatory steps are taken to ensure that the offering qualifies as a DPO. In addition, the company must also identify who will be most likely to invest in its securities so that a marketing and sales plan can be developed that will reach that target audience of potential investors. The company also should retain a stock transfer agent who can keep track of the new investors and the shares that each one owns. Stock transfer agents can provide valuable assistance to newly public companies and help reduce the record keeping hassles that are normally associated with stockholder mailings, stock splits and other similar events.

While proper advance planning can increase a company's chances of successfully conducting a DPO, company executives should not underestimate the difficulties of raising capital without the help of an established underwriter. First, the company's employees will have to devote substantial amounts of time to locating investors and selling the company's securities. In addition, the company and its executives will have to perform a host of other functions that would normally fall to the underwriter, such as properly valuing the company, structuring the offering and properly pricing the securities. If the company does not properly structure or price the offering it can make it extremely difficult to sell its securities to investors. Investors may already have heightened concerns about investing in a DPO because it will be unlikely for the company's stock to trade on an exchange or on the Nasdaq. As a result, investors would have a hard time selling any stock they acquired in a DPO. If a new media company does not have a fairly large base of customers it can be very difficult for it to raise large amounts of capital through the sale of stock without the assistance of an underwriter.

THE REVERSE MERGER

In addition to the DPO over the Internet, a significant number of companies have gone public through reverse mergers in recent years. In a typical reverse merger, a privately operating company locates a dormant publicly trading company and the two companies agree to merge. As part of the merger transaction, the shareholders of the privately held company receive freely trading shares of the public company's stock. Once the merger is completed, the business operations of the privately held company are carried out through the public corporation. In most cases, the name of the publicly traded company is changed to reflect its new business focus. In addition, the new management of the publicly traded company will attempt to arrange for a market maker to publicly quote the shares on the over-the-counter Bulletin Board or, if the company qualifies, on the Nasdaq SmallCap market. The Bulletin Board is a regulated quotation service that is operated by the National Association of Securities Dealers while the Nasdaq is an electronic stock market with defined listing standards that must be met before an issuer's stock can be quoted on the market. If a company succeeds in having its stock quoted on either the Bulletin Board or the Nasdaq, a liquid market for the stock can develop.

Companies that go public through a reverse merger rather than a traditional IPO do so for a number of reasons. But the most common reason is that the company may simply be unable to find an underwriter for its stock. This could be due to a company's size, its business plan or other reasons. During 1998 and 1999, when underwriters were primarily interested in handling IPOs for companies in the Internet and e-commerce industries, companies that were in other more traditional industries found it difficult to find underwriters to bring them public. By going public through a reverse merger, a private company can gain many of the advantages of being a publicly traded company, including the ability to use the company's publicly traded stock to acquire other companies and the possibility that a liquid market for the company's shares could develop.

A reverse merger can also be successfully employed when economic conditions are tough. Like a DPO, an underwriter is not required for a reverse merger. Therefore, the decision on whether or not to go public rests solely with the company and its management. If a suitable public shell can be located, a company can go public regardless of the current economic conditions. A reverse merger has several benefits that a DPO does not have. First, a company that goes public through a reverse merger does not have to locate large numbers of investors for its securities as is required in a DPO. Therefore, a company that does not have a large customer base that is familiar with its products may be better off using a reverse merger than a DPO. Second, a company that lacks marketing and sales expertise may have a difficult time locating purchasers for its stock. In such situations a reverse merger, rather than a DPO, is probably more appropriate. Finally, companies that choose to pursue a reverse merger will also work closely with outside financial advisers, particularly when locating a publicly traded shell. Such advisors are particularly helpful to a company that is going public for the first time as they can assist the company in preparing for its new legal and financial responsibilities. The company's financial advisors can also assist with evaluating the publicly traded shell company as a suitable merger partner. They can also work with a broker-dealer to have the company's securities resume active trading on an exchange or on Nasdaq.

The main drawback of a reverse merger is that new capital is not raised by the company as part of the transaction. Instead, the company hopes to develop a relationship with a market maker and other broker-dealers so that capital can be more easily raised at a later date through the sale of the company's stock. The lack of an immediate inflow of new capital to the company is a significant disadvantage of a reverse merger when compared to a traditional IPO or to a DPO.

Counsel Must Be Involved Early in Reverse Mergers

Counsel for private companies must become involved with a proposed reverse merger transaction at the earliest stage possible. Regulators such as the Securities and Exchange Commission give heightened scrutiny to such transactions. In the 1980s, the stock of a number of companies that went public through reverse mergers became the target of various manipulation schemes. However, in recent years, there have been a number of relatively large and reputable companies that have gone public through reverse mergers. For example, Alford Refrigerated Warehouses, Inc., which is the largest public refrigerated warehousing operation in the southwest United States, went public through a reverse merger in 1998. Its stock currently trades on the Nasdaq SmallCap market.

Due Diligence Is Extremely Important

Attorneys who represent private companies considering a reverse merger must be cautious. One of the most important responsibilities that counsel has is to ensure that all of the necessary due diligence has been performed. First, counsel must make certain that the proposed merger candidate is indeed a publicly reporting company under the Securities and Exchange Act of 1934.[3] Further, counsel must ensure that the merger candidate is current in all of its filings with the Securities and Exchange Commission. Next, counsel must ascertain the public company's operating history. Towards this end, counsel must determine whether the public company was formed solely to seek out a private company for a merger or whether it was once an operating

---

[3] 15 U.S.C. §§ 78a *et seq.*

company that now no longer conducts any active business. One of the most important issues that counsel must address during the due diligence review is whether the publicly traded company has any existing or contingent liabilities. If the publicly traded company was formed in anticipation of completing a merger, it is likely to have little or no operating history, and its existing and contingent liabilities can be determined relatively easily. In the case of a publicly traded company that was formerly an operating company, a significant amount of time will have to be spent performing due diligence. Often such companies have complex histories and it is not uncommon to find that the company has previously filed for bankruptcy. While the bankruptcy filing may give counsel a certain amount of comfort if the company's liabilities were discharged, the filings in bankruptcy court must be carefully reviewed to make sure that this is the case.

Prior to the consummation of a reverse merger, counsel for the private company should review a list of the shareholders of the publicly traded company. The transaction documents must clearly state what the capital structure of the entity will be post-merger and who the shareholders will be. In several unfortunate cases, shareholders in the post-merger company have been surprised to find previous shareholders of the publicly traded company asserting themselves in the new business or selling their stock in the open market once the merger is completed. Selling by previous shareholders can exert downward pressure on the price of the company's stock.

Typically, the actual legal documents that consummate the merger are prepared by the attorney for the public company. Counsel for the private company must carefully review the documents to ensure that they accurately reflect the terms of the deal and the parties' intent. Counsel should also ensure that the publicly traded company has a current set of audited financial statements. A full set of disclosure documents must be filed with the SEC and counsel must be sure to advise the client that all SEC filings must be cleared by the SEC prior to the start of market trading in the company's securities. In a reverse merger, the public company typically files a Form 8-K with the SEC in which detailed disclosures are made about the transaction.

Listing the Issuer's Stock for Trading

Counsel for the private company involved in a reverse merger should also be looking ahead to ensure that everything possible is done to obtain a market maker for the company's stock and that the stock is quoted either on the Nasdaq SmallCap market or the over-the-counter Bulletin Board once the reverse merger is completed. These steps will help increase the likelihood that a liquid market will develop which, in turn, can help the company obtain future financing and provide a way in which the shareholders of the company can sell their shares if they so choose. To be eligible to have its stock price quoted on the Bulletin Board, a company must be current in all of its SEC filings and must find a market maker willing to list price quotes for the company's stock.[4] Often, the individuals associated with the public shell company can assist the private company in locating a suitable market maker. By taking the foregoing steps, executives can enhance their company's chances of successfully going public through a reverse merger.

---

[4] The requirement that all companies listed on the Bulletin Board be current in their SEC filings was approved by the SEC in SEC Rel. No. 34-40878 (Jan. 4, 1999).

ROBERT HEIM is a partner at Meyers & Heim LLP, a law firm in Manhattan that specializes in corporate and securities law. Mr. Heim has represented and worked with publicly traded companies in many different industries as well as private companies that are on the road to becoming public. He is a former Assistant Regional Director of the U.S. Securities and Exchange Commission in New York City.

Mr. Heim frequently speaks about the capital formation process and has appeared at several forums at prominent universities, including the Wharton School of Business, the Yale School of Management and New York University's Stern School of Business. He also writes a regular column for the New York Law Journal and often appears as an expert witness addressing securities law and regulation issues.

ALSO FROM **ALM PUBLISHING:**

Game, Set, Match: Winning the Negotiations Game
by Henry S. Kramer

Biz Dev 3.0: Changing Business As We Know It
by Brad Keywell

The Essential Guide to the Best (and Worst) Legal Sites on the Web
by Robert J. Ambrogi, Esq.

Full Disclosure: The New Lawyer's Must-Read Career Guide
by Christen Civiletto Carey, Esq.

On Trial: Lessons from a lifetime in the courtroom
by Henry G. Miller, Esq.

Inside/Outside: How Businesses Buy Legal Services
by Larry Smith

Other Publications Available from AMERICAN LAWYER MEDIA:

LAW JOURNAL PRESS professional legal treatises—over 100 titles available

Legal Newspapers and Magazines—over 20 national and regional titles available, including:

The American Lawyer
The National Law Journal
New York Law Journal

Legal newsletters—over 25 titles available

Visit us at our websites:
www.lawcatalog.com
and
www.americanlawyermedia.com